Advance Praise for
CRAFTING CRITICAL STORIES

"*Crafting Critical Stories* brings together interdisciplinary scholarship that highlights both the exciting possibilities and the challenges that are present when we incorporate personal, familial, or communal stories to teach, learn, and transform our sociopolitical world. Indeed, this volume demonstrates that critical storytelling comes in many forms and is an essential pedagogical and methodological tool across numerous informal and formal educational contexts. Collectively, the authors demonstrate the ways in which stories can allow us to draw upon knowledge that is often marginalized while simultaneously disrupting normative ways of thinking, teaching, and being. Thank you, Judith Flores Carmona and Kristen V. Luschen, for putting together an amazing must-read book that makes a significant contribution to how we understand the methods and practice of storytelling for social justice!"

Dolores Delgado Bernal, Professor of Education and Ethnic Studies, University of Utah

"*Crafting Critical Stories: Toward Pedagogies and Methodologies of Collaboration, Inclusion, and Voice*, edited by Judith Flores Carmona and Kristen V. Luschen, is a powerful story itself of how the art of storymaking, storytelling, and story-listening is critical to education and educational research and policy. Together, the chapters take readers into many different communities and spaces where critical stories are crafted in the practices of teaching, learning, and research. We hear powerful voices in diverse K–12 and university classrooms, in research sites, in oral histories, digital stories, and *testimonios*. We hear stories of race, class, gender, language, sexuality, citizenship, ethnicity, and place. We learn about diverse ways of knowing and being. This edited collection brilliantly demonstrates how stories are simultaneously method and pedagogy, theory and praxis. Educators and researchers who pick up this book will no doubt be touched by the depth and breadth of its critical stories and their necessity for creating a more just world. I could not put this book down as each chapter drew me into the power of story as the foundation of education."

Sofia Villenas, Associate Professor of Anthropology and Education, Cornell University

CRAFTING CRITICAL STORIES

Studies in the
Postmodern Theory of Education

Shirley R. Steinberg
General Editor

Vol. 449

The Counterpoints series is part of the Peter Lang Education list.
Every volume is peer reviewed and meets
the highest quality standards for content and production.

PETER LANG
New York • Washington, D.C./Baltimore • Bern
Frankfurt • Berlin • Brussels • Vienna • Oxford

CRAFTING CRITICAL STORIES

Toward Pedagogies and Methodologies
of Collaboration, Inclusion, and Voice

Edited by Judith Flores Carmona and Kristen V. Luschen

PETER LANG
New York • Washington, D.C./Baltimore • Bern
Frankfurt • Berlin • Brussels • Vienna • Oxford

Library of Congress Cataloging-in-Publication Data

Crafting critical stories: toward pedagogies and methodologies of collaboration, inclusion, and voice / edited by Judith Flores Carmona, Kristen V. Luschen.
p. cm. — (Counterpoints: studies in the postmodern theory of education; vol. 449)
Includes bibliographical references and index.
1. Critical pedagogy—United States. 2. Storytelling in education. 3. United States—Ethnic relations. I. Carmona, Judith Flores. II. Luschen, Kristen V.
LC196.5.U6C73   370.11'5—dc23   2012038666
ISBN 978-1-4331-2160-9 (hardcover)
ISBN 978-1-4331-2159-3 (paperback)
ISBN 978-1-4539-1017-7 (e-book)
ISSN 1058-1634

Bibliographic information published by **Die Deutsche Nationalbibliothek**.
Die Deutsche Nationalbibliothek lists this publication in the "Deutsche Nationalbibliografie"; detailed bibliographic data is available on the Internet at http://dnb.d-nb.de/.

Grateful acknowledgment is made to the copyright holder for permission to reproduce the following: "Nikki Rosa" from BLACK FEELING, BLACK TALK, BLACK JUDGEMENT by NIKKI GIOVANNI. COPYRIGHT © 1968, 1970 BY NIKKI GIOVANNI. Reprinted by permission of HarperCollins Publishers.

© 2014 Peter Lang Publishing, Inc., New York
29 Broadway, 18th floor, New York, NY 10006
www.peterlang.com

All rights reserved.
Reprint or reproduction, even partially, in all forms such as microfilm, xerography, microfiche, microcard, and offset strictly prohibited.

CONTENTS

Foreword   vii
   Rina Benmayor

Acknowledgments   xi

Introduction: Weaving Together Pedagogies and Methodologies
   of Collaboration, Inclusion, and Voice   1
   Judith Flores Carmona and Kristen V. Luschen

Part I: Striving for Critical Consciousness: Excavating (Hi)stories of Privilege and Oppression

1. Inheriting Footholds and Cushions: Family Legacies
and Institutional Racism   11
Christine Sleeter

2. "I Knew When You Said Your Name in Spanish!": On Being
a White Puerto Rican in the Classroom   27
Ellen Correa

3. Mediated Stories of Educational Mobility: Digital Stories
in Teacher Education   41
Jane Van Galen

4. Here I Stand: College Students' Critical Education Narratives   57
Barbara Kessel and Kim Hackford-Peer

5. A Student-Teacher Testimonio: Reflexivity, Empathy,
and Pedagogy   75
Judith Flores Carmona and Aymee Malena Luciano

Part II: Bridging Diverse Community Knowledges Through Critical Storytelling

6. Engaging Co-Reflexive Critical Dialogues When Entering and Leaving the "Field": Toward Informing Collaborative Research Methods at the Color Line and Beyond 95
Sherick Hughes and Kate Willink

7. The Rose Creek Oral History Project: Elementary Cross-Grade Social Studies Curriculum in Review 115
DeeDee Mower

8. Exploring (Dis)Connections Through Digital Storytelling: Toward Pedagogies of Critical Co-Learning 131
Kristen V. Luschen

Part III: Knowledge(s) of Resistance

9. Critical Storying: Power Through Survivance and Rhetorical Sovereignty 153
Sundy Watanabe

10. The Politics and Poetics of Oral History in Qualitative Research: This One's for Nikki Giovanni 171
Hilton Kelly

11. "Some of Us Got Heard More Than Others": Studying Brown Through Oral History and Critical Race Theory 189
James H. Adams and Natalie G. Adams

12. Mojarra Linguistic Syndrome, Evading Capture by the Tongue: Heritage Speakers of Spanish and Their Stigma 203
J. Luis Loya-García

Index 221

FOREWORD

Teaching through storytelling is a transformative practice, particularly in multicultural classrooms. Story can situate us as tellers of our own truths, as witnesses to the experiences of others, and as compassionate allies to each other. Time after time, I have had the privilege of witnessing this alchemy in the life storytelling classroom. Students of diverse backgrounds and experiences open their ears and their hearts to others' histories in new ways. Every personal story contains larger communal, social, and political meanings, often challenging preconceived stereotypes and prejudices. To repeat the oft-cited phrase from Chicana writer Cherríe Moraga, telling one's story enables a "theorizing from the flesh," transforming emotional memory into situated knowledge. Story has the potential, then, to enable everyone to become teachers and learners, of and from each other. The storytelling act itself creates a safe space for disclosure. As students read and listen to each other's accounts, they recognize their own experiences in them and begin to share. The "I can really relate to that because something similar happened to me" phrase begins the process of telling, affirming, and reflecting. Story begins to work its magic.

If story has huge power to move the listener and/or witness to new realizations, it is also huge for the teller, in what our own storytelling can reveal to our selves about our selves. While telling stories clarifies different realities for others, they are self-clarifying and self-empowering. Not only in the therapeutic act of telling, but also in our ability to see our own experience in a new light, socially and culturally contextualized. This is the dual action of "theorizing from the flesh." When classrooms become safe spaces for sharing, disclosure, and analysis, they also become empowering spaces for each storyteller.

The transforming force of life stories and their centrality to critical pedagogy is at the core of this volume. Anchored in Freirian thought and practice, these essays speak to the power and importance of critical hi/storytelling in an era marked by standardized curricula, significant shifts in national demographics, growing economic disparity across the social strata, increasingly fragile life chances of students from marginalized communities, and renewed nativism and xenophobia. This volume is a vibrant response to the stranglehold that performance-based educational policies have had on the standardized K–12 curriculum in recent decades, endangering, if not completely erasing, experiential pedagogies from the curricular map. In today's classrooms, there seems to be little space for hi/storytelling, despite its extraordinary capacity to empower students, foster engaged pedagogies, and bring schools, teachers, parents, and cultural communities together in common purpose. Building on a rich literature in liberatory education, the essays in this volume offer diverse pedagogical strategies of storytelling—life stories, oral histories, family histories, testimonies, and other forms of narrative—grounded in personal, family, community, and cultural knowledge. Their purpose is to place story at the pedagogical center, to explore new ways to bring marginalized, erased, suppressed voices and histories into focus, and to recenter knowledge construction to benefit all students, teachers, and communities.

In contrast to public schooling, higher education has been trending toward storytelling. Scholars in a wide range of academic disciplines and fields validate personal narratives as a way to gain deeper insight into the lived realities of peoples and communities in the 21st century. In addition to the fields in which story is central—literature, creative writing, theater, history, anthropology, and clinical psychology—storytelling also has commanded the attention of scholars in education, ethnic and cultural studies, legal studies, and even environmental studies. As a result, today we see an explosion of genres, modalities, and practices of storytelling with specialized names—narrative, biography, autobiography, oral history, life story, family history, fiction, creative nonfiction, *testimonio*, eyewitness accounts, counterstory, pedagogies of home, critical story, and so on. I have often thought that universities should offer an interdisciplinary major simply called "Storytelling," where students can explore the centrality and power of this age-old practice across many fields. Academic interest suggests that narratives of lived experience are recognized for their potential to ground scholarly theory and practice, offering new ideas for research, teaching, and learning. Thus, young teachers often come out of their training with some knowledge of experiential pedagogies, and creative teaching and learning strategies. For those who have not, this volume offers a rich range of ideas and practices for classroom exploration.

One of these practices is digital storytelling. Digital multimedia technologies offer a unique opportunity in today's multicultural classroom. Multimedia storytelling can be tremendously empowering, as students of all ages learn how to narrate, craft, share, and explore the power of their own stories and knowledge assets. Students not only tell their stories verbally, but make them as well. In this way, they become "authors" of stories, not just listeners. Making stories engages multiple creative skills in writing, performance, visual imagery, and sound. Today, even the youngest students can make digital stories. My college students make stories that they hope will move their audiences. If sharing stories in the classroom breaks down social and cultural barriers, seeing stories on the big screen multiplies their power tenfold. These intensely personal stories, narrated in the first person voice, bring historical and emotional depth to learning. Each member of the classroom begins to acquire fuller dimension, as an individual situated in a family, a cultural community, and a larger history. Digital technologies are not simply tools; they can be strategies for building communication and understanding.

All communities value storytelling in some fashion, but for marginalized communities storytelling can be a necessity, a strategy for emotional, historical, and cultural survival. Story becomes an integral part of family and community life, a didactic tool for navigating through hostile environments, and a form of cultural affirmation. However, the separation between home culture and school is often stark. Students from vibrant storytelling cultures fall silent at school, as school is identified with the hegemonic culture. However, when school becomes a place where home cultures, strategies, hi/stories, and assets are embraced, everyone wins. This volume offers a rich array of possibilities for integrating and creating new forms of knowledge in the classroom. The authors make a vital contribution to our understanding of the power of critical storytelling as a central feature of liberatory teaching and learning. As the coeditors of this volume argue, critical storytelling is an imperative, a fundamental pedagogy for a more just and humane future.

      Rina Benmayor
      California State University Monterey Bay
      September 16, 2012

ACKNOWLEDGMENTS

We would like to thank Christine Sleeter for suggesting that we work on an edited book that merged our scholarship. We are grateful to Ellen Correa, who has been instrumental and beyond helpful in organizing this book. Thank you for being a third set of eyes, a great colleague, and amazing friend. Similarly, Falguni Sheth has been a constant source of friendship and wise advice. Professor Rina Benmayor graciously agreed to write the foreword, and we are immensely appreciative of her mentorship, scholarship, and support. We thank the students in our Spring 2012 course for reading the first drafts of chapters, and for their insights on content and relevancy. We are indebted to the contributors in this volume for their patience and hard work on this project. Your chapters are powerful and your pedagogy critical in these shifting moments in education. We thank our families—Rodrigo, Glenn, Ethan and Will—as well as our colleagues and friends for their unconditional support. Gracias. Thank you.

We dedicate this book to Gabi Do Amaral, a brilliant student and beautiful human being, gone too soon. Judith dedicates this book to her grandmother, Carmen Romero Pérez, one of her first teachers—a wise storyteller.

INTRODUCTION

Weaving Together Pedagogies and Methodologies of Collaboration, Inclusion, and Voice

Judith Flores Carmona and Kristen V. Luschen

> For many of us who would describe ourselves as teaching for social change, storytelling has been at the heart of our pedagogy. In the context of social change storytelling refers to an opposition to established knowledge, to Foucault's suppressed knowledge, to the experience of the world that is not admitted into dominant knowledge paradigms. Storytelling is central to strategies for social change…(in) education. (Razack, 1998, p. 36)

As critical pedagogues teaching for social change, we believe in the power of stories to engage, transform, and catalyze social action. As teachers and qualitative researchers, we are immersed in stories—our own and those of others—and the productive interplay between the two. As pedagogues whose work focuses on addressing sociological issues in education, we believe that our work in the classroom and in the community is to engage students in critical reflection on their own (hi)stories in order to gain richer, more complex perspectives on the inequities in educational opportunities for historically marginalized populations. Similarly, as qualitative researchers, we experience the ethical tensions and artistry involved in re-presenting the lives of individuals and communities in ways that are authentic and acknowledge the situated nature in which stories are imparted.

This book spans the borders between teaching and research, to explore a practice common to both within social justice education, crafting *critical* stories. Critical stories are those stories that speak to the constitution of experiences within a sociopolitical context (Barone, 1992); that acknowledge their development within historically situated conditions; and that recognize the gaps and silences in dominant ways of knowing, and seek to illuminate counternarratives. Stories remind us that we cannot depend on statistical data to illuminate experience and compel change, but rather, it is also in the crafting of narratives and sharing stories that social transformation happens.

In his book, *The Politics of Storytelling*, Michael Jackson (2002) drew on Arendt to argue that

> storytelling is a strategy for transforming private into public meanings...; the second is existential, seeing storytelling as a human strategy for sustaining a sense of agency in the face of disempowering circumstances. To reconstitute those events in a story is no longer to live those events in passivity, but to actively rework them, both in dialogue with others and within one's own imagination. (p. 15)

In this way, storytelling is an empowering and transformative process. As collective counterstories emerge through dialogue and discussion, as the chapters in this book suggest, they prompt critical transformations in the knowledges of our students, ourselves, and our disciplines.

This book emerged from our powerful experience of imagining and co-teaching the course, *Family and Oral History Pedagogies*. The course drew on various forms of critical (hi)storytelling and methodologies to illuminate knowledges that have been rendered invisible or have been suppressed in schools, communities, and in academia. We also asked students to engage in critical family history (Sleeter, 2008); to explore and excavate family knowledges; to understand in embodied ways how historical narratives are constituted through crucial absences and silences that privilege some and marginalize others. The course meaningfully compelled participants, teachers, and students to reimagine our personal and collective histories and our positionality within relations of oppression and privilege. However, when we prepared the syllabus, while there were many superb resources with which to construct the course, we found that none bridged the projects of teaching and research, or incorporated knowledges developed across disciplines. We found none that probed the intersections between traditions of orality and new digital mediums, engaging both as tools for social change, while concerned with experiences of teachers from all grade levels.

There is a wealth of scholarship on storytelling in the arts, but less so in the social sciences. In his book, *Transforming Tales: How Stories Can Change People*, Rob Parkinson (2009) argued that in education, stories are often considered within the context of language development. They inspire imagination and support creative thinking. This is to say, little work on storytelling in education links to the production of stories as personal and constructed narratives. Personal story sharing is an important aspect of culturally relevant pedagogy and social justice education. Dyson and

Genishi's (1994), *The Need for Story*, addressed how stories are rooted in our experiences as cultural beings (p. 4), and their collection of essays broadly spoke to how connecting with and across children's culturally diverse, personal stories can support building and navigating classroom communities.

Lee Anne Bell's (2010) book, *Storytelling for Social Justice*, offered an excellent framework for the power of stories to facilitate critical teaching and learning about the social and political world. The book centered on how to examine the stories of race that we tell ourselves and each other from a social justice and arts-based approach. She also engaged with the idea of counterstorytelling as a resistant and critical practice to disrupt oppressive constructions of race. The book explored the "Storytelling Project Model" she initiated, and each chapter addressed a different type of story (e.g., stock, concealed, resistance), and offered examples of how various artistic mediums help to document, explore, and analyze these stories in the interest of antiracist pedagogy.

Solinger, Fox, and Irani (2008) offered an engaging contribution to the scholarship on storytelling and social change. While not rooted in educational practice like Bell's (2010) and Dyson and Genishi's (1994) texts, *Telling Stories to Change the World* is a collection of essays about projects and organizations employing stories and storytelling to make social justice claims. The beauty of this book—similar to *Telling to Live: Latina Feminist Testimonios* (The Latina Feminist Group, 2001) and others in the genre of Latina *testimonio*—is the contention that the generation and sharing of knowledges and suppressed stories are acts of political urgency and political action.

With several texts exploring the linkages between storytelling and social change, we searched for texts that examined the methodological and pedagogical complexities of story production. The Oral History Association has developed significant resources for educators in oral history, with regard to methodologies and pedagogies particularly helpful for practitioners interested in learning how to use oral history with their students or in communities. They are solid resources appropriate for learning the nuts and bolts of how to conduct oral history projects. Similarly, *Digital Storytelling in the Classroom* (Ohler, 2008) provided foundational knowledge for teachers to support students' creation of digital stories, and the possibilities for using this tool for teaching and learning. Lanman and Wendling's (2006) *Preparing the Next Generation of Oral Historians* is also a resource for educators seeking to enliven history for students at all levels. The anthology opens with chapters on the fundamentals of oral history and its place in the classroom, but its heart lies in nearly two dozen essays by educators who have successfully incorporated oral history into their teaching. The chapters include step-by-step descriptions of the projects, and practical suggestions on creating curricula, engaging students, gathering community support, and meeting educational standards. However, this volume does not reach beyond oral history as a storytelling methodology, nor does it emphasize critical history as a critical social justice approach.

Despite the existing body of scholarship, the curious absence of interdisciplinary texts from a social justice perspective that acknowledge the intersections across pedagogies and methodologies of knowing and representation motivated us to draw together scholars and educators in the fields of Communications, Education, Sociology, History, and Ethnic Studies. *Crafting Critical Stories* explores the challenges and possibilities for critical (hi)storytelling as a form of culturally relevant, critical pedagogy. As a body of work, the scholarship in the following pages addresses the intersections and distinctions across disciplines, and between the work of educators utilizing different forms of critical storytelling methods and teaching practices. It engages in the discussion of the connections of critical storytelling pedagogy to culturally relevant teaching and social justice education. By bringing together critical pedagogues in conversation around issues of representation, methodology, meaning, and impact, *Crafting Critical Stories* invites educators to see how power dynamics across multiple people and/or borders can be mediated in the classroom and in the community. The volume highlights various critical storytelling approaches (critical family, digital, *testimonio*, and oral history) across disciplines, and brings them into conversation with one another.

More Possibilities of Inclusion

This book aims to highlight different ways in which oral history, digital storytelling, *testimonio*, and critical family history have been used in the classroom; and have been used in, used with, or written by marginalized communities. As pedagogues who practice these "signature pedagogies" (Benmayor, 2012) we include chapters that speak to each of the genres, so as to explore the overlapping and/or intersecting tenets across them. Rather than being a "how to" or methodology book, *Crafting Critical Stories* examines the tensions related to the production and representation of critical stories, and capitalizes on their specific use in K–higher education classrooms and in communities. The contributors to this volume answer some of the following questions: How are teachers drawing from cultural and familial sources of knowledge? What are the struggles of integrating children's community and/or family histories into schools? Does the integration of pedagogies of the home and family histories necessarily disrupt educators' pedagogical practices? What does the process of integrating one's silenced, ignored, and/or excluded history into school mean for underrepresented, marginalized, silenced students? How do we shift our disciplinary knowledges by seeking out silenced (hi)stories? Through self-reflexivity, the contributors explore how they were shaped by, and influenced, critical stories.

While this book explores the possibilities of critical (hi)story pedagogies and methodologies, the significance of new technologies and access to digital archives have been influential in their increased use. New media have created more opportunities for exploring, creating, and sharing our critical (hi)stories and experiences across various social and geographic borders. Hence, within this collection, there are examples of critical (hi)story pedagogies rooted in the use of digital media that cultivate bridges between home and school, between White students and students of color, between adults and children, and across language divides and community cultures.

The book is organized in three sections. The first section, "Striving for Critical Consciousness: Excavating (Hi)stories of Privilege and Oppression," explores questions, methodologies, and tensions experienced by educators who have complicated, or facilitated practices by which students examine and address their legacies of oppression and privilege through critical storytelling. In Chapter 1, Christine Sleeter illustrates how racist roots of contemporary unequal relations can be made visible through critical family history research. After describing her methodology, she excavates and explores the implications of the "footholds" and "cushions" that she, as a White person, inherited. In Chapter 2, Ellen Correa explores her performance or "positioning" (Davies & Harré, 1990) as a White Puerto Rican teacher in the classroom. She looks at how her affective performance of identity, particularly the oppressive influence of shame, impacts her teaching. She proposes that self-reflexivity and the examination of teacher performance of racial and/or ethnic identity can help improve teaching and learning in the classroom. In Chapter 3, Jane Van Galen analyzes the genre of digital storytelling as a tool for exploring and complicating education students' understanding of social class, social mobility, and education. Next, Barbara Kessel and Kim Hackford-Peer focus on the use of critical education history in the context of an Introduction to Gender Studies course. Through the use of what they call, "critical education history," they examine their experiences facilitating students' reflexivity about their education experiences, and the schooling conditions of women and LGBTQ students. In the last chapter of section one, Judith Flores Carmona and Aymee Malena Luciano share self-reflexivity as an essential practice in critical pedagogy, and particularly in a *testimonios* course. The authors propose *testimonio* pedagogy to move us toward an understanding of suffering, not as an individual experience, but as a communal process of teaching and learning, and as a way for people to read, connect and engage with, draw upon, and become inspired to share *testimonios* in education.

Part two of the book, "Bridging Diverse Community Knowledges Through Critical Storytelling" includes chapters that speak to the complexities of bridging community knowledge(s) through research, teaching, and community-engaged learning. In Chapter 6, Sherick Hughes and Kate Willink examine coreflexive critical dialogues as a significant, collaborative methodology for critical (hi)storytelling across gendered, raced, classed, and cultured lines. The coauthors explore two crucial moments in field research through critical dialogues, and speak to how this methodology enriched their lived experiences of culturally relevant, critical pedagogy and qualitative fieldwork. DeeDee Mower's chapter argues for the significance of integrating oral histories within Social Studies curricula. She illustrates how community members' stories help students grasp multiple and conflicting perspectives on historical events, and formulate critical questions about their representation. Mower's analysis of how ideologies of childhood serve to maintain silences and support dominant and narrow perspectives on historical events will be particularly relevant to those working with young people. In the final chapter of part two, Kristen Luschen writes about the Educational Histories/Education Hopes digital storytelling project designed within a course-based collaboration between middle school and undergraduate students. Luschen explores the complexities and possibilities of facilitating critical consciousness and transformative co-learning relationships across communities of difference through personal storytelling.

The third section of the book, "Knowledge(s) of Resistance," builds from understanding that the histories and lives of students of color, immigrant students, and marginalized communities have not been well represented in educational research and curriculum. This section explores the significance of these knowledge(s) of resistance, and emphasizes an assets-based, bottom-up approach to teaching, researching, and engaging with historically marginalized communities. In Chapter 9, Sundy Watanabe interrogates interactional tensions in rhetorics of presence and performance occurring between selected Native and non-Native persons within a large, research-intensive university context. Interactional tensions arise, she argues, because these participants hold discrepant beliefs concerning the role national, tribal, and rhetorical sovereignty should and/or does play in community and self-determination. She posits that if American Indians are to be more successful in completing higher education degrees, university personnel and programs must address these tensions and negotiate to more fully indigenize the academy. In Chapter 10, Hilton Kelly addresses the significance of oral history methodology for qualitative inquiry. Drawing upon his research with Black educators who taught in legally segregated schools in the South, the author illustrates how oral history in qualitative research can unearth subjugated knowledge as a critical intervention for progressive social change. Kelly's chapter offers readers a window into how he employed historical methodologies to revise a long-held, dominant story of the inferiority of Black schools in the South prior to school integration, making visible Black people's stories of struggle and perseverance. In Chapter 11, James H. Adams and Natalie G. Adams present oral histories as a way to illuminate how, long before Critical Race Theory (CRT) materialized in law schools as a critique of traditional civil rights discourse, Black teachers and principals developed their own collection of strategies and discourses to deal with the practical and everyday consequences of civil rights litigation. In the last chapter, J.Luis Loya Garcia argues that cultural linguistics is a potent tool for empowering Latina/o students in Spanish classes designed for Heritage Speakers. He uses "pedagogies of the home," oral histories, cultural linguistics, and the archeology of words, to illustrate the linguistic dislocation, in English and Spanish, that Latina/o students suffer due to their direct or indirect ties with indigenous, non-Western views of the world.

Among social justice educators, the call to narrate, craft, share, and explore critical stories—*testimonios*, pedagogies of the home (Delgado Bernal, 2001), oral history, and critical family history (Sleeter, 2008)—has gained urgency in recent years. As standardized curricula and assessments saturate the everyday lives of teachers and students, the spaces of learning with and from each other in culturally informed and critical ways are constrained or eliminated. There is urgent need to bridge the disconnection between schools and communities, between dominant epistemologies and those that have been ignored or suppressed. The genres of critical storytelling in this volume seek to illuminate counternarratives that disrupt claims of neutrality, objectivity, color blindness, and meritocracy in society and in classrooms. These genres also seek to preserve knowledge(s) that are not learned in schools, as a way of illuminating and preserving epistemic and pedagogical community tools and assets (Flores Carmona & Delgado Bernal, 2012).

Crafting Critical Stories: Toward Pedagogies and Methodologies of Collaboration, Inclusion, and Voice engages the meaning of innovative critical (hi)storytelling for critical pedagogy in the twenty-first century. Our hope is that pedagogues, educators, students' consciousness, and practice will be impacted at multiple sites and in meaningful, transformative ways.

Bibliography

Barone, T. (1992). Beyond theory and method: A case for critical storytelling. *Theory Into Practice, 31*(2), 142–146.

Bell, L. A. (2010). *Storytelling for social justice: Connecting narrative and the arts in antiracist teaching.* New York, NY: Routledge.

Benmayor, R. (2012). Digital testimonio as a signature pedagogy for Latin@ studies. *Equity and Excellence in Education, 45*(3), 507–524.

Davies, B., & Harré, R. (1990). Positioning: The discursive production of selves. *Journal for the Theory of Social Behaviour, 20*(1), 43–63.

Delgado Bernal, D. (2001). Learning and living pedagogies of the home: The mestiza consciousness of Chicana students. *International Journal of Qualitative Studies in Education, 14*(5), 623–639.

Dyson, A. H., & Genishi, C. (1994). *The need for story: Cultural diversity in classroom and community.* Urbana, IL: The National Council of Teachers of English.

Flores Carmona, J., & Delgado Bernal, D. (2012). Oral histories in the classroom: Home and community pedagogies. In C. E. Sleeter & E. Soriano (Eds.), *Creating solidarity across diverse communities: International perspectives in education* (pp. 114–130). New York, NY: Teachers College Press.

Jackson, M. (2002). *The politics of storytelling: Violence, transgression and intersubjectivity.* Copenhagen, Denmark: Museum Tusculanum Press.

Lanman, B. A., & Wendling, L. M. (2006). *Preparing the next generation of oral historians: An anthology of oral history education.* Lanham, MD: Rowman & Littlefield.

The Latina Feminist Group. (2001). *Telling to live: Latina feminist testimonios.* Durham, NC: Duke University Press.

Ohler, J. (2008). *Digital storytelling in the classroom: New media pathways to literacy, learning, and creativity.* Thousand Oaks, CA: Corwin Press.

Parkinson, R. (2009). *Transforming tales: How stories can change people.* Philadelphia, PA: Jessica Kingsley.

Razack, S. (1998). *Looking White people in the eye: Gender, race, and culture in courtrooms and classrooms.* Toronto, Canada: University of Toronto Press.

Sleeter, C. (2008). Critical family history, identity, and historical memory. *Educational Studies, 43*(2), 114–124.

Solinger, R., Fox, M., & Irani, K. (2008). *Telling stories to change the world: Global voices on the power of narrative to build community and make social justice claims.* New York, NY: Routledge.

PART I

Striving for Critical Consciousness: Excavating (Hi)stories of Privilege and Oppression

1

Inheriting Footholds and Cushions: Family Legacies and Institutional Racism

Christine Sleeter

"I didn't own slaves, why should I feel guilty?" This is a common response of White people to hearing about racism today (Trainor, 2005). Essentially, such a response objects that slavery, as well as theft of Indigenous peoples' land, happened so long ago that attending today to violent forms of racism in the distant past evokes only anger and guilt, rather than helping us to transcend racism.

In this chapter, using the methodology of critical family history (Sleeter, 2011), I show how racial privilege, rather than being a relic of the past, is a living inheritance. Those of us who are White, particularly if our ancestry in the US extends back at least three generations, have inherited material and psychological resources that I will describe as *footholds* and *cushions*. Footholds enable opportunity; cushions protect from misfortune. Both enable White people as a whole to retain continued disproportionate control over the nation's resources. While laws that had supported White supremacy have been overturned, inheritances built on the basis of those laws continue to be passed from one generation to the next.

Understanding Contemporary Racial Disparities

Surveys have found a gradual liberalization of White adults' attitudes about racial integration (such as where people can live), and a gradual decrease of genetic explanations for racial disparities (Hunt, 2007). While this shift represents progress in racial attitudes, the dominant White perspective today—that race does not matter (and should not be focused upon)—contrasts with perspectives among African Americans and Latinos, and enables Whites to stop meaningful efforts intended to close gaps across racial lines, while viewing themselves as nonracist (see Bonilla-Silva, 2010).

White adults are much more likely than African American and Latino adults to explain disproportionately high rates of poverty among people of color in terms of lack of individual motivation, and are less likely to do so in terms of systemic racial discrimination (Bonilla-Silva, 2010; Hunt, 1996, 2007; Kluegel & Smith, 1986; Schuman & Krysan, 1999). White adults are also much more likely to oppose government remedies for racial discrimination, such as affirmative action—particularly Whites who have a superficial understanding of racism and a strong concern about White deprivation (Shteynberg, Leslie, Knight, & Mayer, 2011). Bonilla-Silva (2010) argued that, while Whites tend to regard President Obama as symbolizing a transcendence of racism, African Americans regard him as symbolizing the possibility of doing so one day. The election of the first African American president seemed to validate Whites' belief that race no longer matters, ironically at a time when progress in closing economic and other gaps between Whites and people of color had stalled, and in some cases reversed.

The perceptions held by White adults in general are common among teachers. St. Denis and Schick (2003), for example, writing of their experiences as antiracist Canadian teacher educators, described three deeply embedded ideological assumptions among mainly White preservice teachers: while culture matters somewhat, race does not; everyone now has equal opportunity; and, what counts are individual actions coupled with good intentions.

Similar patterns emerge in studies of young people. For example, Epstein (2001, 2009) interviewed students in grades 5, 8, and 11 about U.S. history, finding growing disparities between White and Black children. Although White fifth graders, for instance, believed that the Bill of Rights gives rights to everyone, about half of the African American children pointed out that not everyone has rights. While White fifth graders described the US as being built on progress, democracy, and opportunity for all, African American fifth graders were beginning to articulate a sense of racial oppression. By the time they reached high school, the African American students, rather than viewing the US in terms of individual rights, as the White students did, spoke of systemic racism from which African Americans continue to struggle for emancipation.

While people of color see and experience racial discrimination today—as they saw and experienced it in the past—among Whites there is a strong belief that giving too much attention to race and racism prevents racism from fading away, and that there has already been sufficient governmental work (particularly legislation) to ensure that everyone has equal opportunity, regardless of race. The belief that the US is now *postracial* paves the way for enabling disregard for the negative impacts on people of color of policies and practices such as home foreclosures, and the support of racist policies such as voting restrictions and anti-immigration legislation.

Data on family wealth and the role of inheritance in maintaining racial disparities challenge White beliefs that race no longer matters. Wealth, according to Lui, Robles, Leondar-Wright, Brewer, and Adamson (2006), refers to "economic assets. A family's net worth is their assets minus their debts" (p. 5). While most people are at least vaguely aware of racial disparities in wealth, it is commonly assumed that disparity gaps are gradually closing. According to the U.S. Census Bureau (2012), in 2007 the median wealth of White, non-Hispanic families was $170,400, while that of non-White or Hispanic families was only $27,800—less than one-sixth the median wealth of White families. Data from the 2004 census (U.S. Census Bureau, 2011) further disaggregated by race. In 2004, the median net wealth of White, non-Hispanic families was $113,822; of Black families, just $8,650; of Hispanic families, $13,375; and of Asian families, $107,690 (data on Asian families lump together widely varying ethnic groups that include very wealthy immigrants). Note that the median White family's wealth was *13 times* that of the median Black family, and 8.5 times that of the median Hispanic family. While the wealth of African Americans tends to be concentrated in homes and cars, the wealth of Whites is much more diversified, and includes income-producing investments (Hodge, Dawkins, & Reeves, 2007).[1]

Wealth tends to be passed from generation to generation through both inheritance and "family financial aid" (Lui et al., 2006). As Shammas, Salmon, and Dahlin (1997) documented in *Inheritance in America*, "The bulk of household wealth in America, perhaps as much as 80 percent of it, is derived from inheritance, not labor force participation" (p. 3). Lui and colleagues (2006) concurred: "Most private wealth in the United States was inherited. And even for people who do not inherit money after their parents' deaths, their family's education and social contacts and financial help from living relatives makes a big difference" (p. 5). In addition to direct inheritance, Lui and colleagues (2006) pointed out that large disparities in family wealth produce disparities in "family financial aid" to offspring, such as contributions to a down payment on a house, or help with college tuition. Family financial aid serves as footholds and cushions extended to next generations, to the extent that families can afford to do so. About half of White families can afford this kind of aid, compared with only about one-fifth of Black families (Lui et al.,

2006). The case study I report in this chapter shows how this process of inheritance and family financial aid works.

Critical Race Theory (CRT) offers a theoretical perspective for connecting legalized racial disparities in the past and ongoing racial disparities of the present. A major tenet of CRT is that racism is endemic to the structure of U.S. society, and that rather than asking whether or not racism is at play, a more productive question to ask is *how* racism is at play. Of particular relevance to this chapter, CRT examines how, through the commodification of land and people for profit, Whites established the basis for Whiteness as property, which maintains White economic supremacy through inheritance. According to CRT legal scholar Cheryl Harris (1993), both slavery and seizure of Indian land "established and protected an interest in whiteness itself, which shares the critical characteristics of property" (p. 1724). Whiteness guaranteed legal entitlement to freedom, gradually taking the form of an object protecting one's personhood, giving Whites a vested interest in maintaining it. In the establishment of the colonies that became the United States, the conditions for amassing family wealth on the basis of race were established by law. Over time, these legalized conditions diminished as the slave trade was ended, slavery itself was ended, and gradually Jim Crow laws at the state and local levels were overturned. Yet, as Lui and colleagues (2006) showed in detail, the U.S. government continued to assist White people in ways that excluded people of color (such as farm aid, unemployment insurance that excludes domestic workers and farm workers, and Federal Housing Administration regulations that benefited White home buyers). Even when regulations imply racial fairness, deeply embedded, racially discriminatory practices often still occur, such as in the mortgage industry (Ross & Yinger, 2002).

What White people usually do not recognize is how the combination of laws historically benefiting White people, ongoing inheritance laws, and everyday taken-for-granted practices combine to create and maintain racial disparities in wealth. The remainder of this chapter illustrates how these processes work, based on an analysis of my own family.

Data on Family Wealth Historically

This study is part of a larger study of four-plus generations of my own family history. For both the larger study and the study in this chapter, two types of data were collected: family-related data, and historical contextual data. For this chapter's family data, I used U.S. Census statistics, supplemented by online family trees. I gathered data regarding land acquisition mainly from deeds in county courthouses (such as in Jonesboro and Madisonville, Tennessee), and other land records available on Ancestry.com. I gathered data on land values, where I could, from deeds records and, in the case of central Illinois, newspaper articles and a research study about Illinois land values over time (Dovring, 1977). I located original wills, wills on microfiche, and transcribed wills.

I used historical accounts to interpret family data in a wider context. I sought accounts that were written at the place and time when specific family members lived, if these were available. I also sought accounts written by contemporary historians and sociologists that shed light on the acquisition and transfer of financial assets.

Situating the Problem

I was born into a professional class family, as a daughter of a father who was a physician and a mother who stayed home to raise her four children. When I was six, my father died suddenly of a heart attack. My mother's parents came to our financial rescue: between them and my father's life insurance, we were able to keep our home, and my mother was able to continue to stay home to raise us. The cushion my grandparents could offer enabled us not only home security, but also continued access to public schools attended by other middle and professional class children.

Later my grandparents, whom I had never regarded as wealthy, constructed a series of footholds that benefited me (and my siblings). They helped put us through college. My mother's father's will divided his assets among his two daughters and four grandchildren; my share helped fund my graduate education. My mother's mother established a trust in her will that gave my mother and her only sibling (my aunt) financial security for the rest of their lives. When my mother died, I inherited a share of my grandmother's trust, which served as a down payment on my house. I inherited an additional portion of the trust when my aunt died, which helped me pay off the mortgage on my house.

Until I delved into the research reported in this chapter, I had not given much thought to the question of where the financial resources for these footholds and cushions came from. I knew that all my grandparents had worked hard, although the one who passed on the largest inheritance had not held a job that I am aware of. The research reported below highlights the significance of inheritance. While in some cases inheritances were squandered, the predominant story is one of White ancestors profiting from land taken from Indigenous peoples (in some cases profits augmented by slave labor) generations ago, then passing down footholds and cushions to next generations, in historical contexts that legally favored Whites.

Seizure and Sale of Indigenous Peoples' Land

Writing about the process of the seizure and sale of Indigenous peoples' land in Tennessee, Phelan (1888) summarized a pattern that was replicated repeatedly:

> The general groundwork was the same in all cases. Indian lands were taken possession of and then improved. The Indians entered into hostilities, and were eventually defeated and compelled to sue for peace. Treaties were made and increased territory given to the whites, and new boundary lines were established, which were again overstepped. Act after act was passed to legalize usurpations, and all the worst features of civilization were brought into play to win a field for the foundation of a government. (p. 51)

My ancestors were among the Europeans or Euro-Americans who were recruited to buy land that was seized from Indigenous peoples. In this section, I examine whose land my ancestors acquired; in the next section, I trace how my generation still benefits from those acquisitions.

Table 1.1 details the acreage that my European and Euro-American ancestors acquired as a direct result of policies to expel Indigenous peoples from their land, and to recruit prospective White landowners. The table specifies

1. The Indigenous tribe or nation that had lost the land;
2. The county or White settlement in which it is located;
3. When my ancestor(s) acquired the land;
4. How many acres they acquired;
5. From whom they purchased the land; and
6. How much they paid, in 2010 dollars.

Initials rather than names were used to protect family privacy. Empty cells indicate data that I do not have. Many of the families that appear on this table also acquired additional land, but I included only acreage bought directly from the state or federal government following expulsion of Indigenous peoples, or in a couple of cases, acquired directly from someone else within ten years of purchasing from the state or federal government.

In researching the history of how my ancestors took possession of land, I found the recurring pattern that Phelan (1888) had described to be striking. Initially, hunters and trappers entered land and began to trade with the Indigenous peoples who were there. For example, Hatley (1995) described a border area in the Carolinas between the Cherokee and White settlements that was a site of active trade. As the British, then the U.S. government

Table 1.1. My Family's Acquisition of Indigenous Peoples' Lands

Whose land?	Where?	When?	Acquired by whom?	Acres	Acquired from whom?	Price (in 2010 $)
Arrohattoc tribe of Algonquin	Henrico Co, VA	@1670	H.B.	200		
Arrohattoc tribe of Algonquin	Henrico Co, VA	1702–1730	H.B., II	700	State of Virginia (for bringing colonists)	
Cherokee, ceded in 1760	Long Cane Creek, SC	1764	H.B., III or IV	200+		
Cherokee	Knob Creek, TN[2]	1772–1775	D/M	704	State of N. Carolina	
Cherokee	Washington Co, TN	1798	B.H.	100		$7,518
Cherokee	Washington Co, TN[3]	1783–1788	D.McC./W.N.	760	State of N. Carolina	
Cherokee, ceded in 1805	Roane Co, TN	Before 1812	A.B./E/D.			
Cherokee	Monroe Co, TN	1827	G.C.H./S.McC.	160	State of Tennessee	$2,238
Cherokee	Monroe Co, TN	1828	W.McC.	67	Bought from trader who had bought from Cherokee	$4,897
Creek	Baldwin Co, AL	Before 1820	L.H./E.W.			
Caddo	Hempstead Co, AR	@1838	B.J.H.		From wife's first husband who bought from State of Arkansas	
Kickapoo, ceded in 1819	Macon Co, IL	1849–1853	W.H.S.	200	U.S. Government	
Kickapoo	Cass Co, IL	1830s	K.G. J.	480		
Kickapoo	Cass Co, IL	1854	H.J.	40	State of Illinois	Warrant
Ute	Routt Co, CO	1880s	O.McC./C.F.H.			

began to express interest in acquiring land for expansion, the government began to exert pressure (including military pressure) on tribes to cede their land. Treaties established boundaries between British or U.S. government land and tribal land. But White settlers, initially in small numbers, would trespass the boundaries, setting up permanent establishments on tribal land. For example, during the 1770s, streams of English and Scots-Irish people trespassed onto Cherokee land in the area of what later became Washington County, Tennessee. Similarly, in what is now Southeastern Iowa, in the late 1820s, White settlers began to build houses on land that still belonged to the Sauk.

As tribes tried to protect their land from White encroachment, the British or U.S. government sent in the military to protect White families, even when they had trespassed negotiated boundaries. The government also began largely unsuccessful attempts to convert tribes to individual farming. The Cherokee, more than any other nation, tried to anticipate White Americans' definitions of what it meant to be "civilized" as a way to protect themselves from conquest. During the 1820s, the Cherokee codified their language into an alphabet that the entire population quickly learned to read with the help of a Cherokee-run printing press. The Cherokee also established numerous businesses, such as 62 blacksmith shops, eight cotton machines, 18 schools, and several public roads and ferries (Yates, 1995).

Indigenous peoples' attempts to protect their lands from growing incursions by Whites were always met with conflict, ramped up U.S. military pressure, and rewritten treaties in which the tribes were forced to cede more land to the U.S. government. Usually a "last straw" incident, such as a massacre or discovery of gold on tribal land, precipitated the U.S. military expelling the remaining tribal members. While this was happening, in an effort to build up a White population, states worked with land and transportation companies to actively recruit prospective White farmers or plantation owners. As soon as the U.S. government gained control over land, surveyors divided it into plots, usually of 40 acres, to sell. The Homestead Act of 1862 escalated this process, allowing a settler to exchange five years of living on public land for 160 patented acres, paying only the cost of the patent and surveying. Although, theoretically, any citizen could purchase land, little of it was actually sold to African Americans; the vast bulk was sold to Whites (Williams, 2000).

How did my ancestors interpret the expulsion of Indigenous peoples from land they bought? Possibly, some were only dimly aware of what had happened. For example, W.H.S. purchased land in Illinois in 1849 and 1853, more than 20 years after the Kickapoo had been expelled. Others actively participated in the process of expulsion. For example, as part of his military service in the War of 1812, G.C.H. was a sergeant in the company that was part of the brigade that attacked the Creek Indians in what later became central Tennessee (Kanon, 2007). When the U.S military expelled the Cherokee from Southeastern Tennessee in the infamous "Trail of Tears" in 1838, some of my ancestors had already bought land ceded by the Cherokee, and many Cherokee families still lived in the area. It is probably fair to say that while some ancestors may not have had a clear idea who was being dispossessed, how, and why, most probably did, and condoned the project of creating a White nation, as well as the rules that enabled them to build family wealth.

Transmitting Wealth

I was able to locate enough data to draw some linkages between cushions and footholds I inherited, and profits derived from land transfers generations ago, along with (in some cases) slave labor. Below, I describe some linkages from my father's side of the family, then from my mother's side. In both sets of descriptions, I call attention to the roles of inheritance and family financial aid in making footholds and cushions available. Individuals needed to decide what to do with resources made available to them, and some ancestors made very bad decisions. But the system of inheritance and family financial aid offered cushions to those affected by individual mismanagement of wealth, as well as by the early death of a spouse.

Germans in the Midwest

My father descended from German immigrants to the Midwest, mainly Illinois and Iowa. As noted in Table 1.1, great-great grandfather W.H.S. was granted 40 acres in Macon County, Illinois from the U.S. government in 1849, then another 160 acres in 1853, from which the Kickapoo had been expelled in 1819. According to U.S. Land Office records, both transactions were "cash-sale" entries; both documents also state that the land was "given and granted" to him. I do not know how much he actually paid for the land (or whether he paid for it all). To estimate the land value, I used Dovring's (1977) estimate of farmland value in Illinois in 1850, which was $8.00 per acre, calculating the 200 acres to be valued at $1,600 ($41,409 in 2010 dollars).[4]

One generation previously, another German ancestor, K.G.J., had purchased 480 acres in Illinois; I lack detailed information about that land. One of his sons, great-great grandfather H.J. (who likely inherited some of his father's land), bought 40 acres in Cass County from the State of Illinois in 1854, using a land warrant (granted to military veterans for their service; see Hageman, 2006–2008; Illinois State Archives, n.d.). He and his family later sold that land and bought acreage in Macon County, Illinois.

One of the sons of W.H.S., W.P.S. (who married a daughter of H.J.), in 1894 acquired 160 acres that had been his father's, then sold those same acres in 1896 for $372,297 (2010 dollars), or slightly more than 11 times their 1850 value ("All Going to Iowa," 1896, p. 8). The family farms had been prosperous, according to various local newspaper articles; W.P.S. had also gained enough social status to have become a county supervisor.

W.P.S. used proceeds from the sale of those 160 acres to purchase 360 acres in Iowa for $465,371 (2010 dollars). That purchase turned out to be unfortunate, however—the Iowa land was swampy, and he died two years later, leaving his wife and four children, one of whom was my grandfather. However, his family was cushioned from the loss his death created. His widow, in addition to inheriting what was left of his estate (I have no data on that), also inherited the 2010 dollar equivalent of about $75,000 from her father, H.J., when he died a few days later ("Will Probated," 1898, p. 6). For her and the four children, the inheritances from both father and husband served as important cushions. The family stayed in Iowa until all four children had completed school, then she and the two youngest moved back to Illinois, where she bought a house.

My grandfather stayed in Iowa, attending Iowa State University where he earned a Bachelor of Science degree, then an MD degree. He practiced medicine until his death at the age of 55; his wife, my grandmother, stayed home raising their two sons, both of whom also became physicians. Both generations of physicians had been afforded footholds through their families that enabled them to complete MD degrees. Thus, I was born into a professional class family.

Southeastern Tennessee

My mother's mother descended from the Appalachian Mountains; growing up, I had assumed them to be relatively poor. A perusal of Table 1.1, however, suggests a different story, since most people on that table were ancestors of my mother's mother. Here, I will trace the legacy of wealth inherited from the G.C.H./S.McC. family, and the W.McC. family.

G.C.H. can be described as a land speculator; the 160 acres he bought from the state of Tennessee in 1827 was only part of his portfolio. Deeds records in Monroe County, Tennessee show a pattern of him buying and selling land continuously. One should note that buying and selling land in Tennessee (and the rest of the South) during that time period was mainly restricted to White people. By 1860, the family wealth (real estate + other property) was listed in the census at $30,000 ($719,152 in 2010 dollars). Between the 1830s and the Emancipation Proclamation, he also owned between three and six slaves (in the 1850 census, the configuration looks like a family).

G.C.H. and his first wife, S.McC., had about 14 children. One of their eldest, B.J.H., from whom I descend, went to Arkansas where he obtained land for a small plantation worked by six or seven slaves. (I cannot tell whether he bought the land, or took possession of it on the death of its owner, since he was administrator of the estate; he also married the widow of the land's former owner). When B.J.H. and his wife's three children were still small, he died from injuries sustained in a duel ("Arkansas Ties," 1846). As it turns out, the only thing he left behind were debts, since apparently he had managed the assets he had very badly (Reed and wife et al., 1861).

The three children (one of whom, D.E.H., is my ancestor) were sent to Tennessee to live with their grandfather, G.C.H. and his second wife, which served as a very important cushion for them. The will of G.C.H. divided his estate equally among his children and the offspring of children who had died. On the basis of having been raised by a wealthy grandparent, then inheriting a portion of his estate, D.E.H. was able to complete his education, buy a small farm, and later become County Clerk. One of his daughters was my great-grandmother, who married a descendant of W.McC.

W.McC. was a neighbor of G.C.H. In 1828, he purchased 67 acres from a trader who had earlier purchased the land apparently from the Cherokee Nation. Like G.C.H., W.McC. also expanded his holdings, although not as aggressively, and without purchasing slaves. By 1860, the W.McC. family wealth (real estate + other property) was listed in the census at $9,000 ($215,746 in 2010 dollars). The will of W.McC. directed that his wife and children each be given $700 ($16,766 in 2010 dollars) plus an equal share of his estate after other bequests had been made.

One of the sons of W.McC. was my great-great grandfather, J.H.McC. In 1860, W.McC. deeded 132 acres to his son, J.H.McC., for the equivalent of about $40,000 (2010 dollars). At some point, J.H.McC. had a two-story brick house built on the farm (which is still standing). One of his sons, my great-grandfather, O.McC., married D.E.H.'s daughter, C.F.H.

Great-grandparents O.McC. and C.F.H. left Tennessee right after they were married, stopping for a few years in Routt County, Colorado (from which the Ute had just been expelled) before going on to the San Francisco area. Despite footholds his family would have been able to offer, O.McC. drifted from job to job (such as ranch hand, clerk, and carpenter), eventually abandoning the family and later ending up in prison. Great-grandmother C.F.H., however, who was renting a house in San Francisco after her husband left, managed to accumulate money. Her parents had died shortly after O.McC. had abandoned the family. Neither parent left a will that I have been able to locate. I suspect that they transferred financial assets to their daughter while they were still alive when it became apparent that her husband was an unreliable source of family support.

The eldest daughter of O.McC. and C.F.H. was my mother's mother. Both she and my grandfather built wealth by investing in property (as well as the stock market) in the San Francisco Bay area; these were the grandparents that helped my family when my father died, put me through college, and established trusts that supported my mother and later helped me. Since my mother's mother did not hold a job outside the home, I can only surmise that the money she had available to invest came from her mother.

My grandparents' investment activity needs to be understood in the context of the rampant racial discrimination in the buying and selling of property. Discriminatory practices have included restrictive covenants to prevent people of color from buying into White neighborhoods, real estate practices that steer buyers of color away from White neighborhoods, redlining of neighborhoods where banks refuse loans and where people of color are concentrated, and mortgage discrimination by banks. Although passage of the Fair Housing Act in 1968 purported to make such discriminatory activity illegal, it persists and is well-ingrained (see Ross & Yinger, 2002), partially because it had been sanctioned by the federal government earlier. The Federal Housing Administration (FHA), created by the federal government in 1934 to help lift families out of the Depression by offering loans, was specifically constructed to keep people of color from buying in White neighborhoods. Following World War II, a good 98% of FHA and Veterans Affairs home loans went to Whites (see Hodge et al., 2007; Loewen, 2005). So, when my grandparents were building wealth by buying property, they were making use of regulations and processes that explicitly benefited White home buyers.

Discussion and Conclusion

This investigation explores links between the relative material advantages that White people have today, ongoing inheritance practices, and institutionalized racism in the past, specifically seizure and sale of Indigenous lands to White people, slavery, and racial discrimination in property buying and selling. I used a methodology that I have termed "critical family history" (Sleeter, 2011) that situates one's individual family history within a broader historical, cultural, and sociocultural context. In the case of this study, by tracing my ancestry and focusing on ancestors' property acquisitions, I was able to document a considerable transfer of Indigenous lands to them from the late 1600s to the mid-1800s, in a context in which most buying and selling of property had been restricted to White people. Through deeds records, old newspaper articles, and records of wills, I was able to trace the flow of wealth built on the land, in some cases augmented by slave labor, over generations through both inheritance and family financial aid. While the history of my family cannot be generalized to all White families, the research process I followed can be replicated by other people to explore the roots of their own legacies.

The concept of footholds and cushions was particularly useful for this analysis because, rather than overlooking the role of hard work, on the one hand, or indolence and poor judgment on the other, footholds direct our attention to opportunities resources make available, and to cushions, or ways in which families shield themselves from the impact of crises. For example, my grandfather who became a physician in Iowa worked hard for his education, and worked throughout his adulthood until his untimely death at the age of 55. At the same time, he was able to attend school as an adolescent and young adult, rather than having to go to work to help support his mother and younger siblings, because of cushions his mother inherited when W.P.S. died suddenly. Inherited footholds and cushions, while they might replace work in some instances, usually interact with work, policies, and laws, enabling successes that otherwise might not have been possible. But, race structures access to inherited footholds and cushions.

I am aware of having transgressed a taboo on speaking publicly about family finances. In my experience, White people rarely discuss inheritance publicly, in much detail. But I suggest that maintaining silence about family financial wealth, including small nest eggs that are commonly passed from one generation to the next, supports historical amnesia about where inherited wealth came from in the first place, and the role of institutional racism in generating a significant portion of White family wealth. I encourage others, particularly White people, to examine how their own family wealth (or lack thereof) was shaped historically. White people whose ancestry goes back several generations may very well be benefiting, without realizing it, from the seizure of Indigenous people's land in much the same way that I have described here. Those whose ancestors immigrated more recently may still be benefiting from policies that favored White home buyers, as well as other policies such as U.S. farm aid or union exclusion of non-Whites. As Ross and Yinger (2002) illustrated in their analysis of ongoing mortgage discrimination, even legislation directed at eliminating racial discrimination may be ineffective when it lacks clear standards or enforcement.

What about the guilt that White people commonly express on learning about White privilege? The person who asserts that he or she did not own slaves is not only attempting to distance him or herself from a mentality that condones slavery, but also from the implied expectation that he or she has some responsibility for racial inequality now. For me, at least two implications flow from awareness of inherited cushions and footholds. First is the need to discard the assumption that my advantages rest solely on hard work. While people in my family tree have worked, many very assiduously, through processes of inheritance and family financial aid, they had resources to work with. Even when disasters struck, family members cushioned each other financially to minimize the disaster's impact.

Second is the need to seek actions that help to close the racial family wealth gap. Since this study examined the continuing White benefit of theft of Indigenous lands, I will suggest actions that can help to address today's legacy of that theft. The land base of most tribes today is inadequate; work is being done to address that problem. Within the boundaries of many reservations, the U.S. government sold or transferred control of plots of land to non-Indians, resulting in a checkerboard pattern of land under tribal control, a situation that creates economic difficulties for tribes as well as difficulty in building tribal sovereignty. Other tribes lost their land entirely during the Termination period of the 1950s, and are trying to reclaim that land. To these ends, there are several Indian-controlled organizations seeking financial donations, including:

- o The Indian Land Tenure Foundation (http://www.iltf.org/get-involved/community-funds/land-recovery-funds). This foundation works with various organizations to address loss of land in Indian Country. One such Indian-controlled organization is the Indian Land Capital Company that helps tribes consolidate and expand land holdings. Another is the Klamath Fund that works to reclaim 692,000 acres the Klamath lost during the Termination period. A third organization is the HONOR Fund (which stands for Honor Our Neighbors' Origins and Rights) that was begun by non-Natives during the 1980s to help tribes purchase land within their tribal boundaries that they do not own, and has been folded into the Indian Land Tenure Foundation.
- o White Earth Land Recovery Project (http://welrp.wordpress.com) works to help recover the original land base of the White Earth Indian Reservation in Minnesota.

o The Lakota Lands Recovery Project (http://villageearth.org/global-affiliates/pine-ridge-reservation); this grassroots organization works to consolidate tribal control over the land and resources of the Pine Ridge Reservation.

There are other small but significant actions that one can take, such as offering scholarship aid to students from non-White communties, rather than keeping financial aid within the family, or working to increase inheritance taxes to help fund public institutions such as schools and health care. The point is seeking out meaningful ways of reversing the racial family wealth gap, particularly access to footholds and cushions. Footholds and cushions are not themselves biased resources. The bias arises when White people have overwhelming access to them because of their historical construction and because of our present-day amnesia about that history.

Notes

1. Finding comparable data about American Indian family wealth proved elusive.
2. To calculate 2010 dollar equivalencies, I used the Inflation Calculator, retrieved from http://www.westegg.com/inflation/
3. Knob Creek, Washington County is presently in the state of Tennessee. Prior to Tennessee's admission to the Union in 1796, however, Washington County was part of North Carolina.
4. Same as above.

Bibliography

All going to Iowa. (1896, February 25). *Decatur Daily Republican*, p. 8.

Arkansas Ties. (1846, March 30). B. J. Harris. *Arkansas Gazette News* (No. 1–Whole No. 1369). Retrieved from www.ArkansasTies.com

Bonilla-Silva, E. (2010). *Racism without racists: Color-blind racism and the persistence of racial inequality in the United States* (3rd ed.). Lanham, MD: Rowman & Littlefield.

Dovring, F. (1977). The farmland boom in Illinois. *Illinois Agricultural Economics*, *17*(2), 34–38.

Epstein, T. (2001). Racial identity and young people's perspectives on social education. *Theory Into Practice*, *40*(1), 42–47.

——— (2009). *Interpreting national history: Race, identity, and pedagogy in classrooms and communities*. New York, NY: Routledge.

Hageman, P. (Transcriber). (2006–2008). Cass County, Illinois public domain land tract sales. Retrieved from http://www.genealogytrails.com/ill/cass/land-j.htm

Harris, C. I. (1993). Whiteness as property. *Harvard Law Review*, *106*(8), 1707–1791.

Hatley, M. T. (1995). *The dividing paths: Cherokees and South Carolinians through the era of revolution*. New York, NY: Oxford University Press.

Hodge, M. E., Dawkins, M. C., & Reeves, J. H. (2007). A case study of mortgage refinancing discrimination: African American intergenerational wealth. *Sociological Inquiry, 77*(1), 23–43.

Hunt, M. O. (1996). The individual, society, or both? A comparison of Black, Latino, and White beliefs about the causes of poverty. *Social Forces, 75*(1), 293–322.

———. (2007). African American, Hispanic and White beliefs about Black/White inequality, 1977–2004. *American Sociological Review, 72*(3), 390–415.

Illinois State Archives. (n.d.). Illinois public domain land tract sales. Retrieved from http://www.cyberdriveillinois.com/departments/archives/databases/data_lan.html

Kanon, T. (2007). *Regimental histories of Tennessee units during the War of 1812.* Retrieved from http://www.tennessee.gov/tsla/history/military/1812reg.htm

Kluegel, J. R., & Smith, E. R. (1986). *Beliefs about inequality: Americans' views of what is and what ought to be.* New York, NY: Aldine de Gruyter.

Loewen, J. W. (2005). *Sundown towns: A hidden dimension of American racism.* New York, NY: New Press.

Lui, M., Robles, B., Leondar-Wright, B., Brewer, R., & Adamson, R. (2006). *The color of wealth: The story behind the U.S. racial wealth divide.* New York, NY: New Press.

Phelan, J. (1888). *History of Tennessee: The making of a state.* Boston, MA: Houghton Mifflin.

Reed and wife et al. vs. Ryburn et al. (1861). *Arkansas Supreme Court,* Vol. 023, p. 48–49. Retrieved from http://opinions.aoc.arkansas.gov/WebLink8/DocView.aspx?id=247710&page=2&dbid=0

Ross, S. L., & Yinger, J. (2002). *The color of credit: Mortgage discrimination, research methodology, and fair-lending enforcement.* Cambridge, MA: MIT Press.

Schuman, H., & Krysan, M. (1999). A historical note on Whites' beliefs about racial inequality. *American Sociological Review, 64*(6), 847–855.

Shammas, C., Salmon, M., & Dahlin, M. (1997). *Inheritance in America: From colonial times to the present.* Galveston, TX: Frontier Press.

Shteynberg, G., Leslie, L. M., Knight, A. P., & Mayer, D. M. (2011). But affirmative action hurts us! Race-related beliefs shape perceptions of White disadvantage and policy unfairness. *Organizational Behavior and Human Decision Processes, 115*(1), 1–12.

Sleeter, C. E. (2011). Becoming White: Reinterpreting a family story by putting race back into the picture. *Race, Ethnicity and Education, 14*(3), 421–433.

St. Denis, V., & Schick, C. (2003). What makes anti-racist pedagogy in teacher education so difficult? Three popular ideological assumptions. *The Alberta Journal of Educational Research, 49*(1), 55–69.

Trainor, J. S. (2005). 'My ancestors didn't own slaves': Understanding White talk about race. *Research in the Teaching of English, 40*(2), 140–167.

U.S. Census Bureau. (2011). *Median value of assets for households, by type of asset owned and selected characteristics: 2004.* Retrieved from http://www.census.gov/hhes/www/wealth/2004/wlth04-1.html

——— (2012). *Family net worth—Mean and median net worth in constant (2007) dollars by selected family characteristics: 1998–2007.* Retrieved from http://www.census.gov/compendia/statab/2012/tables/12s0721.pdf

Will probated. (1898, July 27). *The Herald-Dispatch,* p. 6.

Williams, T. (2000). *The Homestead Act: A major asset-building policy in American history.* St. Louis, MO: Center for Social Development, Washington University.

Yates, D. N. (1995). *The bear went over the mountain.* Princeton, NJ: Cherokee Press.

2

"I Knew When You Said Your Name in Spanish!":
On Being a White Puerto Rican in the Classroom

Ellen Correa

> **Teacher:** "Have you ever thought a person was one race and then they told you they were a different race?"
> **Student 1:** "Yes, you!"
> **Teacher:** "You didn't know I was Puerto Rican when I came in?"
> **Student 1:** "Not until you told us."
> **Student 2:** "I knew right away!"
> **Student 3:** "I knew when you said your name in Spanish!"

This was an interaction I had with sixth graders during the first in a series of media literacy workshops where we were discussing the meaning of race. One of my goals for this introductory workshop was to complicate the definition, to suggest that race is not a biological category—and therefore not easily identifiable by skin color—but rather a social construction. This was not the first time in my life that someone had questioned my racial or ethnic identity, yet I was caught off guard when a student immediately used me as an example of the difficulty of identifying a person's race simply by looking at them. Her immediate response, and the enthusiasm with which several other students joined in the discussion of my enigmatic racial and ethnic identity, told me that it was a subject that had been on their minds since I had introduced myself to them at the beginning of the workshop.

The purpose of this chapter is to explore my performance, or as Davies and Harré (1990) have termed it, "positioning," as a White Puerto Rican teacher in the classroom. I am a light-skinned woman of Puerto Rican descent who was raised in a predominantly White, U.S. mainland community. In the tradition of other antiracist scholars (Alexander, 1999; Chacon, 2006; Cooks,

2003; Jay, 1997; Johnson, 1999; Johnson & Bhatt, 2003; Mitchell & Rosiek, 2006; Morgan, 2004), I examine the pedagogical implications of the ways I was positioned racially and/or ethnically, in relationship with my Puerto Rican students. In this chapter I examine how my performance of ethnic identity may have influenced teaching and learning in a series of workshops in which the sixth-grade participants were predominantly Latin@. Werry and O'Gorman (2007) suggested that engaging *affect* might "work against the more intractable theoretical impasses that beset both performance and pedagogy scholarship and practice" (p. 215). With this in mind I begin to look at how my affective performance of identity in a particular classroom may have influenced teaching and learning. I take up this discussion through the use of autoethnography, as modeled in Werry and O'Gorman's (2007) "Shamefaced: Performing Pedagogy, Outing Affect," and draw from Davies and Harré's (1990) theory of positioning, and theories of identity and pedagogy.

I begin this chapter by briefly describing the pedagogical setting, and then portray several classroom interactions in which my performance of a White Puerto Rican identity may have had particular salience for teaching and learning. Throughout, I intersperse vignettes related to my own ethnic and cultural identity development. Davies and Harré (1990) took what they called an "immanentist view" when they asserted that

> Similarities between various conversations are to be explained by reference only to whatever concretely has happened before, and to human memories of it, which form both the personal and cultural resources for speakers to draw upon in constructing the present moment. (p. 1)

The personal stories point to past experiences which have contributed to forming and understanding the "personal and cultural resources" from which I draw my performance of a White Puerto Rican teacher. I conclude the chapter by suggesting how this kind of self-reflexive examination of teacher performance of racial and/or ethnic identity may help me to improve teaching and learning in the classroom, and perhaps encourage other educators of color to continually reflect on their own positionality and pedagogy.

The Media Watchdog Project

The setting was a series of media literacy workshops provided to sixth graders at a state classified "underperforming" middle school in a predominantly low-income Latin@ New England community. The workshops were designed and facilitated by me (a graduate student) and two undergraduate students as a service-learning project offered by our university, and titled "The Media Watchdog Project." My coteachers were two White undergraduate women in their early twenties, and I am a middle-aged Latina of Puerto Rican descent. Our task was to provide a series of four one-hour workshops in which we encouraged students to use critical thinking to identify and critique racial and ethnic stereotypes prevalent in popular media. Although I had taught lower-division Communication undergraduate courses for several years, this was my first experience teaching middle-school students, and I was concerned with presenting the material in a way that was both understandable and relevant to their experience. The dialogue that introduces this chapter ensued early in the first session, after the university guest teachers and middle-school students introduced themselves (name, hometown, race and/or ethnicity, and favorite TV show), and the students brainstormed definitions for the word, *race*. The class consisted of 12 students about equally divided between boys and girls. The students were between the ages of 11 and 13; one student was White, one was African American, and the rest were Latin@s, mostly Puerto Ricans.

"I Speak Some Spanish."

> My mother tells a story about me when I was a toddler. My grandmother, her mother, is in the kitchen cooking at the stove and I'm tugging at her skirt insisting, "arroz, arroz, arroz." Or, in my baby language it comes out more like "aho, aho, aho." Abuelita is delighted with her precocious grandchild asking for her favorite dish of white rice. What strikes me now as I'm studying about what whiteness means in this country and what it has meant in my life, is that this word, certainly one of the first words I ever uttered, was in Spanish. I'm surprised by this story, because I did not grow up speaking Spanish. When my grandmother died a few months later, my parents moved to an all-White rural neighborhood. My friends were White. My teachers were White. My parents spoke to me only in English. I grew up mainstream.[1]

I told the sixth graders that I am Puerto Rican. *I am like them*. This explicit claim of an ethnic identity was the first step in positioning myself as Puerto Rican. In many contexts I cannot rely on being recognized as Puerto Rican. I must position myself by explicitly asserting my ethnic identity in relationship with the students. Davies and Harré (1990) explained that

> An individual emerges through the processes of social interaction, not as a relatively fixed end product but as one who is constituted and reconstituted through the various discursive practices in which they participate. Accordingly, who one is is always an open question with a shifting answer depending upon the positions made available

within one's own and others' discursive practices and within those practices, the stories through which we make sense of our own and others' lives. (p. 2)

This is particularly true of my ethnic identity. I must choose to position myself (or not) as a Puerto Rican through my discursive practices. In many settings my relatively light skin and native English accent position me as socially privileged. In some situations I can "pass" as a White person, but for many years I have chosen not to exercise this "option." In my everyday life I choose discursive practices that mark me as a person of color—as a Latina. But something was different in this sixth-grade class. From the first moment, I sensed not just surprise but pleasure from the students. They were delighted to find that I am Puerto Rican; that I am like them. And I found myself choosing to mark my Puerto Rican identity in more frequent and varied ways. I searched (although, as will be seen, I was not always successful) for ways to be the "Puerto Rican teacher," to connect with them, and to help them connect to each workshop topic in ways that were, in this context, uniquely available to me. I was aware of my own pleasure in the situation. I had never felt so Puerto Rican in my life, and it felt good.

> I'd admitted that my Spanish was limited, but then a boy in the back of the room kept raising his hand, eager to participate in our discussion of negative stereotypes of Latin@s in the media. Luis's[2] English was slow and labored, and he frequently paused and peered into my eyes asking me to supply the English word he vainly sought. "D'ilo' en Español," [sic] (say it in Spanish) I said. It was a risk. What if I couldn't understand him? What if his rapid version of Puerto Rican Spanish failed me after living for years with the slower pace of Mexican Spanish in California? But I had at least some resources at my disposal that could encourage this child eager to learn and teach, and I wanted to try to use them in his interest. Luis immediately switched to eloquent and impassioned Spanish. And although I didn't catch every word, I was relieved that I understood the gist of it: his sophisticated sense of the ways Latin@s are portrayed on TV, as gangsters, prostitutes, or at best, poor but honest people. He was outraged at not just the negative stereotypes, but the lack of knowledge about the richness of his culture exhibited in English-language TV programs. I summarized his comments in English for the few in the room who did not understand Spanish, and we continued the discussion at an elevated level thanks to Luis's contribution.

According to Davies and Harré (1990),

> A particular strength of the poststructuralist research paradigm...is that it recognizes both the constitutive force of discourse, and in particular of discursive practices and

at the same time recognizes that people are capable of exercising choice in relation to those practices. (p. 2)

Although I always identify myself as Puerto Rican, or usually as a Latina of Puerto Rican descent, I do not usually choose to speak and encourage others to speak Spanish, an important marker of that identity. Rather, my limited Spanish-speaking skills mark me as a *pocha*, a wannabe White girl. So speaking Spanish among other Latin@s is a risky choice for me. But in this interaction the choice seemed clear. Perhaps it was Luis's courage that inspired me. He had something to say, and shame or false pride was not going to keep him from expressing his ideas regarding Latin@ stereotypes on TV. How many times had his English been criticized by teachers and derided by other students? I was not conscious of all this in the seconds it took me to encourage the student to "dílo en español"; it is only now that I consider that Luis's willingness to try to express himself in a foreign language gave me the courage to converse with him in Spanish for those few minutes.[3]

Davies & Harré (1990) theorized the way I have come to understand my interaction with Luis.

> If we are to come close to understanding how it is that people actually interact in everyday life we need the metaphor of an unfolding narrative, in which we are constituted in one position or another within the course of one story, or even come to stand in multiple or contradictory positions, or to negotiate a new position by 'refusing' the position that the opening rounds of a conversation have made available to us. With such a metaphor we can begin to explain what it means to 'refuse' to accept the nature of the discourse through which a particular conversation takes place. (p. 4)

Davies and Harré (1990) also discussed Erving Goffman's concept of "footing" as a means to discuss how our positions change in the midst of conversations. "A change of footing implies a change in the alignment we take up to ourselves and to the others present as expressed in the way we manage the production and reception of an utterance" (Goffman, 1981, p. 128, as cited in Davies and Harré, 1990, p. 4). In that discursive moment, Luis's labored English utterances influenced me to change the language in which we were conversing, and that change in footing may be perceived as a means to engage a liberatory, or at least less oppressive, pedagogical approach in an interaction with a student for whom the Spanish language was dominant. In that moment, at least, I was able to risk being positioned as a *pocha* and encourage Luis to express himself in his native language.[4]

"Are We Good Students?"

> I think I'm in the fifth grade. It's elementary school anyway. I'm talking to a White boy, although I don't think of him in those terms. We haven't just met; we've known each other for a while; probably ride the bus to school together every day. I don't know why the topic comes up, but I'm not surprised when he asks me,
>
> "What are you?"
>
> "Puerto Rican," I say, and watch with a familiar sense of satisfaction as the look of disbelief comes over his face.
>
> "But you're not a real Puerto Rican. I think of you just like a White person."
>
> "Thanks," I say quickly.
>
> Years later, in high school, I was on the "college prep" track. Not in the popular crowd, but accepted as one of the "smart" students. There were Puerto Ricans in my high school but they weren't my friends. None of them were in college prep. I don't know what possessed me during our field day senior year to go up to a group of Puerto Rican girls and start talking to them. They asked me my name and
>
> "What are you?"
>
> "Yo soy Puertorriqueno [sic]," I told them. Except I didn't pronounce the ñ and I used the masculine form.
>
> "Yeah right, you're 'Puertorriqueno'" they shot back.
>
> Their laughter stung. This was my punishment for 17 years of thinking of myself as a White girl.

Throughout my childhood important others have positioned me as "just like a White person," and my hurried "thanks" in that early encounter indicates that as a child I was aware that Whiteness was considered a good thing; superior to being Puerto Rican. And later, in high school, the sarcastic, "Yeah right, you're '*Puertorriqueno*' [sic]" positioned me as "too White." What have I learned from being continually positioned as "White enough" by White people and "too White" by family members and other Puerto Ricans? When I am no longer the student but the teacher, how do these pervasive messages influence teaching and learning with a group of Puerto Rican middle-school students? Could the way I make sense of these experiences help me to empower my students to resist internalizing negative views of their racial and ethnic identity? According to Davies and Harré (1990), "Among the products of discursive practices are the very persons who engage in them" (p. 2). What kind of Puerto Rican teacher have these experiences helped to constitute?

> While I was working one-on-one with a student, she volunteered that she hated school.
>
> "Why do you hate school?" I asked.
>
> "All my friends hate school," she replied. "It's boring and the teachers are mean to us. Besides, I'm just not a good student."
>
> I asked, "Lettie, what makes you think you're not a good student? You're doing good work on this project."
>
> Lettie turned to her classroom teacher who was working at the computer a few feet away.
>
> "Mister, are we good students?"
>
> He didn't seem surprised by the question.
>
> "You all have potential if you'd just apply yourselves," he answered. "Your problem is that you don't apply yourselves."

Lettie's use of the pronoun "we" was telling. When I asked her why she hated school she answered: "All my friends hate school." It was not just Lettie who hated school, but rather all the Puerto Rican students she knew. When I asked why she thought she was not a good student she did not ask her teacher if *she* was a good student, but rather, "are *we* good students?" Lettie was teaching me a lesson. If she and her friends were not good students it was because their teachers believed—and communicated—this positionality. She showed me that she and her classmates were positioned as students who "don't apply yourselves," a code understood as meaning they were not good students. Lettie's interaction with her teacher demonstrated Davies and Harré's (1990) contention that discourses influence who we become. At least some of the discursive practices of the middle-school teachers, and subsequently the students themselves, constituted the Puerto Rican children as poor students. Perhaps this was not this teacher's intent. However, he undoubtedly believed that the students arrived at the school "unmotivated," and that teacher-student interactions had nothing to do with constructing this positionality. Education scholar Herbert Kohl (1994) explained,

> If you look at a child through the filter of her or his environment or economic status, and make judgments through the filters of your own cultural, gender, and racial biases, you'll find the characteristics you expect. You'll also find yourself well placed to reproduce failure and to develop resistance in some children, a false sense of superiority in others. (p. 44)

And similarly, Morgan (2004) asserted that,

> There are no neutral spaces in schooling, no ways to insulate oneself from the social consequences of one's activities. Standardised tests, psychometric models, reading methodologies, constructs of language proficiency, 'scientific' research on

> bilingualism—all are interconnected, in some key way, with power relations. To apply these technologies or instruments uncritically or without regard to the prior learning experiences of a particular group of students is to hasten the likelihood of academic underachievement and social marginalization for minority students. (p. 176)

Lettie gave me a knowing look after her teacher's comment, and we went on with the activity of identifying negative stereotypes of people of color in the media. But how could this activity have any positive effect on her self-esteem in the face of the real-life negative stereotype to which she had just been subjected? And why did I not draw on my experiences of being racially positioned by others to help Lettie resist the messages of inferiority communicated by her teacher? In discussing the education of children of Mexican origin in a school in Texas, Kohl (1994) asserted that "equity would mean their children would be honored for the people they were and welcomed to participate in a complex democracy that had high regard for them" (p. 94). As a teacher committed to evincing a high regard for my students, how can I use my own experiences of being positioned as inferior, or as superior to the extent I could perform Whiteness, to develop the means to help them resist their positioning as bad students? Again, according to Kohl, the outcome of such positioning seems startlingly close to the ways Lettie and her friends perform "unmotivated students" for their teachers. "I have encountered willed not-learning throughout my thirty years of teaching and believe that such not-learning is often and disastrously mistaken for failure to learn or the inability to learn" (Kohl, 1994, p. 2). At the very least, my silence in the face of the teacher's negative comment failed to interrupt the student's positioning as "not motivated." How did my own experiences of shame, as well as a false sense of superiority, influence my failure to help Lettie resist becoming, to use Davies and Harré's term, a "product" of her teacher's negative discursive practices? Did my silence position me as an ally to those who view ethnic Puerto Ricans as "unmotivated"? Certainly, it did not benefit the student. Rather, my silence benefitted the teacher, in that I did not challenge his negative portrayal of the Puerto Rican students.

"I Feel Bad When I See That on TV."

> It was one of those moments of raw, painful honesty that catches you unawares while you're doing something mundane, like cooking dinner with your mother. We'd never talked much about why she and my father had decided to move to a White community when my brother and I were babies, about why they decided to teach us only English, about why we'd grown up "White." Or that's not exactly right. What we never talked about is the effect these decisions had on my brothers and me. About how those decisions

influenced the people we became. I've turned my life upside down to devote myself to exploring these issues on a daily basis as a student and a teacher, yet we don't talk about it. But one day I did bring it up.

"What was it like for you growing up in New York City?" I asked her.

"When I was younger we lived in a Jewish neighborhood and I went to school with mostly White kids. I had friends and did well in school. But then we moved to a Puerto Rican neighborhood and it was terrible. Kids didn't care about school. There were drugs and violence everywhere," she said.

"Is that why you wanted to move to the country when you got married?"

She knew where I was going with this. It was the proverbial elephant on the table.

"Listen, I used to come home from school and have to step over the drunks and drug addicts passed out in the apartment building hallway. Why wouldn't I want to leave? Why wouldn't I want to be different? Why wouldn't I run away from 'my people' as fast as I could?"

Maybe it had to do with the ordinary chores we were engaged in: she was washing vegetables at the sink; I was setting the table in the pretty kitchen in my middle-class home. Maybe it was the exact words she used that day, or the fact that I was somehow, finally, open and ready to deal with what I had long suspected. Whatever the reason, those few sentences hit me hard. I couldn't respond to her rhetorical questions. I could barely choke back the tears. I realized that though she'd never been so explicit before, her view of Puerto Ricans was mine, too. They were poor, uneducated, drug addicts. They. We. It was a visceral feeling. It was a sense of shame; deep, enduring shame, and it is in me.

How do I perform the shame that is related to my ambiguous ethnic identity and the reasons for that ambivalence? How do I perform shame in the classroom? For me, the shame comes from being "liberated" (to some degree) from my ethnic and class background. My family's hope of liberation from socioeconomic oppression has resulted in (among other things) a deep and abiding shame in my loss of connection with my racial and ethnic heritage. And I know, too, that another kind of shame comes from ubiquitous messages of the inferiority of Puerto Ricans that I internalized as a child and continue to experience as an adult. Yet, I continue to find myself in situations where that shame will manifest. In a sense, I seek out such experiences. Not the experience of shame that often catches me by surprise, but relational experiences with "my people." I seek ways of relating to those who have not been "liberated" of their culture and heritage, and who suffer unjustly as a result. How can I connect with other Latin@s in an honest way, where I can both account for the borrowed White privilege I experience, and perform a sense of respect and dignity for the person I am today? How might I perform a White Puerto Rican identity that benefits and empowers my Puerto Rican students?

> It was the last day of the workshop series and I was working with a small group of students on writing and filming a public-service announcement critiquing media stereotypes. The class was humming with the excitement of the students in the other groups, but my group was quiet.
> "But what do we write?" one student asked. "We don't know what to write."
> Reluctant to drive the process, I finally suggested that each student talk about how they felt when they viewed negative stereotypes of Latin@s and other people of color on TV. The students lined up uncomfortably against the wall and each one, eyes cast to the floor, mumbled their piece.
> "I feel bad when I see only White people with long blonde hair living in rich houses," one little girl whispered.
> I tried in vain to animate them, to encourage them to speak louder so they could be heard on the film. But, it was just too much—and after a few tries we gave up.

This experience provoked my thinking about performing shame in the classroom. My students could not wait until the ordeal (of performing their shame?[5]) was over, and neither could I. I did not want to project my ambivalent racial position on the students in that workshop. Yet, I wonder to what extent their Puerto Rican teacher's relationship to shame may have influenced the way they positioned themselves during that exercise? They were to identify the ways people of color are stereotyped—negatively positioned—in the media. The objective was to provide the means and context for students to identify and *resist* such positioning, but is it not possible that their response might, rather, have been shame? My goal was to empower the students. But to the extent that they and their teacher have internalized these messages, is it not possible that the exercise might have had the opposite, unintended consequence? My heart sank when I viewed that video. At best, it seems their teacher did little to help her students to articulate the injustice of the ways they and theirs are negatively positioned in media depictions. Werry and O'Gorman (2007) mused that "it is perhaps no surprise how frequently shame coagulates around race in the classroom" (p. 223), and they proposed that these experiences can be used to invoke important, teachable moments. They went on to say that, to recuperate shame, likewise, is not to celebrate it, but rather to recognize its fundamental role in the unmaking and making of our socialized selves and the connectivities, histories, and relations of force that constitute them. It is, ideally, to turn that role to progressive ends. (Werry & O'Gorman, 2007, p. 228)

For Werry and O'Gorman, "the goal, then, is not to make shame *better*, but to look shame in the eye—to say, there you are, *what are you doing here?*" (p. 218).

Conclusion

Communication scholars Thomas Nakayama and Judith Martin (2007) urged that White intercultural communication teachers and researchers evince a "postcolonial reflexivity...[and] engage in self-reflexive inquiry into the ways that their Whiteness has influenced and guided their research and teaching" (p. 125). Christine Sleeter (2008), too, "recommends that preservice teachers examine their own backgrounds and experiences to identify assumptions, beliefs, and values, as well as cultural contexts in which they grew up, which impact on how they understand schooling and students" (p. 114). Carmen Montecinos (1995) brought teachers of color into the conversation when she said, "[We] cannot assume that teachers who are members of a minority group can translate their cultural knowledge into culturally relevant pedagogy and content" (p. 110). And Brian Morgan (2004) advised that, "if we are to make teachers aware of identity as having pedagogical implications, then we should attempt to convey that information in ways closely related to teachers' own pedagogical experiences and ways of knowing" (p. 177).

In this chapter I engage in self-reflexive inquiry into some of the ways Whiteness influences and guides my performance of a Puerto Rican identity and hence my teaching in a predominantly Puerto Rican classroom. I use autoethnography to help uncover the ways my pedagogical experiences are linked to my ways of knowing; to reflect on the ways I may have explicitly and inexplicitly positioned myself as a White Puerto Rican in three classroom experiences, which served variously—in my view—to help and hinder the achievement of my pedagogical goals. Morgan (2004) suggested that, "identity negotiation, against this backdrop, is not easily isolated or measured. To date, there are no 'identity benchmarks' or task descriptors...that adequately capture its holistic features" (p. 176). Hence this chapter is not, cannot be, a scientific analysis of the influence of my performance of ethnic identity on classroom teaching and learning. Rather, it is the use of what might be called critical (auto)ethnography to, as Diversi and Moreira (2009) said, "produce knowledge that is inevitably open-ended, about possibilities of being for more people" (p. 185).

I want to emphasize that I do not mean to suggest that I possess either an essentialized Puerto Rican or White identity. On the contrary, I mean to demonstrate that teacher identity in the classroom is a complex performance influenced by the teacher's discursive history, as well as the ways she or he is perceived by the students. For example, the powerful sense of Puerto Ricanness I experienced in that sixth-grade classroom is not usually manifest in the college-level courses that I teach. I perform Puerto Ricanness and Whiteness differently in a classroom of predominantly White young adults than I do in a classroom of middle-school Puerto Rican students. In other words, the differences in the ways I perform a Puerto Rican identity both construct and are partly a consequence of how particular students and groups of students perceive me.

I view the process of writing this chapter as a step toward improving teaching and learning in my classroom. The self-reflexive inquiry of teachers of color as well as White teachers should not stop at the inquiry stage, but rather, should be positively engaged in the classroom. I want to take the lessons learned through self-reflexive examination of these experiences to move toward performances of identity that will help me achieve liberatory pedagogical goals, on behalf of and with my students. If my encouragement to "dílo en español" resulted in a liberatory moment in the classroom, I hope to replicate that behavior in appropriate contexts. And I hope that understanding the meaning and effects of my silence when a teacher ascribed a negative stereotype to a student of color will encourage me to identify effective strategies to join with students in interrupting and challenging negative discursive constructions in the performative moment. According to Cooks (2003), "As participants in one another's storylines, individuals, through discourse, either explicitly or implicitly make subject positions available that may (or may not) be taken up by another." As Cooks saw it, I must "look at position[6] and the possibilities for movement and agency" (2003, p. 249) in the classroom as I discursively take up certain storylines and reject others.

The third classroom vignette presents a more complex challenge for me, as I do not know exactly whether or how my performance of a White Puerto Rican identity may have created or exacerbated the students' sense of shame regarding the stereotyping of people of color in the media. Again, my goal here is not to provide evidence that the students that day were indeed acknowledging their shame, as opposed to being disengaged from the activity for any number of unrelated reasons. Since I offer this vignette (and indeed the chapter as a whole) as a personal reflection and not an empirical study, I ask readers to accept my experience of shame in that classroom, as well as my fervent sense that I must reflect on and engage the emotions—including shame—that arise for me as a White Puerto Rican teacher, and consequently influence teaching and learning. Here I might heed Werry and O'Gorman (2007) when they urged, "To talk about shame is not to ratify or (re)produce it, but to intervene into the mechanisms by which it is circulated, intensified, and privatized, precisely through its unspeakability" (p. 228). Perhaps the act of breaking my shamed and shameful silence, and encouraging the students to do the same will help in "resisting the defensive or ameliorative maneuvers, those that transmute shame into blame, pain into anger or self-loathing" (Werry & O'Gorman, 2007, p. 228).

Although I do not yet know how to do this—what this will look like in a particular context—I view this reflection as a step towards breaking my shamed and shameful silence in the classroom. And I conclude that recovering a different understanding of the role shame plays in my performance of identity in the classroom, and, consequently, inviting shame into classroom discussion, will assist my students in better understanding and resisting the imposition of negative positionalities, and in constituting their identities as excellent students in discourse with their White Puerto Rican teacher.

Notes

1. A version of this vignette was first published as part of a coauthored article: Correa and Lovegrove (2012).
2. Student names have been changed.
3. I was aware that if there was no formal school policy, speaking Spanish during classroom instruction was considered inappropriate.
4. I realize that the risk was not so great with a group of 12-year-olds as it would have been with a group of adults. My decision to switch to Spanish was undoubtedly influenced by this.
5. For a compelling discussion of Latin@ identity and negative affect see Cristina Beltrán (2012).
6. Cooks (2003) used the term, *position*, "as a metaphor for discussing the ways individuals are constituted and reconstituted through social interactions and discursive practices" (p. 249).

References

Alexander, B. K. (1999). Performing culture in the classroom: An instructional (auto)ethnography. *Text and Performance Quarterly, 19*(4), 307–331.

Beltrán, C. (2012). Racial shame and the pleasure of transformation: Richard Rodriguez's queer aesthetics of assimilation. *Aztlan: A Journal of Chicano Studies, 37*(1), 37–64.

Chacon, R. M. (2006). Making space for those unruly women of color. *Review of Education, Pedagogy, and Cultural Studies, 28*(3–4), 381–393.

Cooks, L. (2003). Pedagogy, performance, and positionality: Teaching about Whiteness in interracial communication. *Communication Education, 52*(3–4), 245–257.

Correa, E., & Lovegrove, D. (2012). Making the rice: Latina performance *testimonios* of hybridity, assimilation, and resistance. *Equity and Excellence in Education, 45*(2), 349–361.

Davies, B., & Harré, R. (1990). Positioning: The discursive production of selves. *Journal for the Theory of Social Behaviour, 20*(1). Retrieved from http://www.massey.ac.nz/~alock/position/position.htm

Diversi, M., & Moreira, C. (2009). *Betweener talk: Decolonizing knowledge production, pedagogy, and praxis*. Walnut Creek, CA: Left Coast Press.

Jay, G. S. (1997). Taking multiculturalism personally. In G. S. Jay, *American literature and the culture wars* (pp. 103–135). Ithaca, NY: Cornell University Press.

Johnson, J. R., & Bhatt, J. A. (2003). Gendered and racialized identities and alliances in the classroom: Formations in/of resistive space. *Communication Education, 52*(3–4), 230–244.

Johnson, K. (1999). *How did you get to be Mexican?: A White/Brown man's search for identity*. Philadelphia, PA: Temple University Press.

Kohl, H. (1994). *'I won't learn from you' and other thoughts of creative maladjustment*. New York, NY: New Press.

Mitchell, R., & Rosiek, J. (2006). Professor as embodied racial signifier: A case study of the significance of race in a university classroom. *Review of Education, Pedagogy, and Cultural Studies, 28*(3–4), 395–409. Retrieved from http://dx.doi.org/10.1080/10714410600873274

Montecinos, C. (1995). Multicultural teacher education for a culturally diverse teaching force. In R. J. Martin (Ed.), *Practicing what we teach: Confronting diversity in teacher education* (pp. 97–116). Albany, NY: State University of New York Press.

Morgan, B. (2004). Teacher identity as pedagogy: Towards a field-internal conceptualization in bilingual and second language education. *Bilingual Education and Bilingualism, 7*(2–3), 172–188.

Nakayama, T., & Martin, J. (2007). The 'White problem' in intercultural communication research and pedagogy. In L. M. Cooks & J. S. Simpson (Eds.), *Whiteness, pedagogy, performance: Dis/placing race* (pp. 111–137). Lanham, MD: Lexington Books.

Sleeter, C. (2008). Critical family history, identity, and historical memory. *Educational Studies, 43*(2), 114–124.

Werry, M., & O'Gorman, R. (2007). Shamefaced: Performing pedagogy, outing affect. *Text and Performance Quarterly, 27*(3), 213–230.

3

Mediated Stories of Educational Mobility: Digital Stories in Teacher Education

Jane Van Galen

It is the first night of class, and I am talking about the culminating assignment on the syllabus. I see arms begin to fold, and a sure and quiet wariness settles over the room. The course, *Education and the American Dream*, examines the distinctively American myth of unlimited opportunity through schooling, even as social class continues to shape life chances. I have just explained that they will each create and share a digital story about a moment in their own schooling in which social class shaped their dreams, their access to learning, and their sense of where they fit in the world.

It has taken some time to understand what I was seeing in such moments of critical teaching. For years, I had joined colleagues in lamenting teacher education students' resistance to talking about privilege, inequality, and justice. But over the years, I began to hear in our shared laments how often we would casually invoke the shorthand of "White-middle-class" to describe our teacher education students, and how often we had speculated that they were resisting from positions of uncomplicated privilege. Yet, I could not help but notice that little actual evidence of class backgrounds (theirs, or ours) was ever apparent. But then, as I began teaching more about how social class shapes access to education, I began to notice that in many of my classes, the resistant, folded arms belonged to bodies that are the first in their families to go to college.

Knowing this, however, made it no easier to talk about their backgrounds as poor and working-class students. Many of these students assume, as do most U.S. Americans, that they are simply "middle-class," regardless of the economic and social status of their families (Bettie, 2003; Furman, Kelly, & Nelson, 2005; Jones, 2007; Kelly, 2007; Sacks, 2007). In popular and political discourse, even in the classrooms of critical educators, class is often invisible, even when it may be strongly in play (Lindquist, 2004, p. 190). My goal for this course was and is to make class visible.

The students in this elective course are seniors or graduate students. Most are early-career teachers or aspire to become teachers. Approximately 75% of the students who take the course are the first in their families to attend college. Most of the students are White; the small numbers of students of color are typically second-generation Asian or Latina/o immigrants. Typically, 75% of the class are women, and many are "nontraditional" aged students.

While some middle-class students do take this course, my interest in this chapter is in the students who are navigating college on their own, unable to draw on family for financial support. As Sleeter (Chapter 1, this volume) has noted, 50% of White students and a much higher proportion of students of color receive *no* "footholds and cushions" from families. From economically vulnerable poor and working-class families, these students are investing in education as their hope for economic opportunity. As seniors and graduate students, they are positioned at the very point of transition between the *promises* of success through school and as-yet-unrealized rewards.

Reading and talking weekly about social class, the course requires these very students to confront the reality that the odds are still stacked against them, regardless of how hard they have worked. Getting past their initial resistance would mean that students would have to acknowledge what school had taught them not to be. Most would have learned long ago to silence the linguistics styles, tacit class identification, or social capital that they have learned have no place within the middle-class norms of the academy (Linkon, 1999, p. 8; Mack, 2006, p. 58; Payne-Bourcy & Chandler-Olcott 2003, p. 18). And now, in this assignment, I was asking them to speak publicly of these very things as a condition of success in my class.

I came too slowly to understand the pain that would come as I tapped into these silences, trained as I am to intellectualize social experiences. I should have known better: I am a first-generation college student myself, and my work on these projects was based in theoretical positions that define class as not just about income or occupational status, but as embodied in the slights and conceits of everyday social interactions in a stratified society (Bourdieu, 1984). Sayer (2005) elaborated:

> Class matters to us not only because of differences in material wealth and economic security, but also because it affects our access to things, relationships, experiences and practices which we have reason to value, and hence our chances of living a fulfilling life… Condescension, deference, shame, guilt, envy, resentment, arrogance,

contempt, fear and mistrust, or simply mutual incomprehension and avoidance typify relations between people of different classes. (p. 1)

As poor and working-class children, the complexities of their lives were likely invisible to middle-class teachers and peers. They learned that approval was bestowed upon those most like their teachers, and that winning their teachers' approval would be their one best shot at earning the basic control over their lives that had eluded nearly everyone that they knew (Lucey, Melody, & Walkerdine, 2003; Robillard, 2003; Walkerdine, 2003). They bought into the dream, and made it through college against considerable odds,[1] when family and friends did not.

And likely, by the time that they have reached my class, they have come to sense that "opportunities for mobility are rarely clean" (Fine & Burns, 2003). Equally likely, little in their schooling prepared them for the class borders that stood between them and their ambitions (Dews & Law, 1995; Muzatti & Samarco, 2006; Welsch, 2005). Critical scholars, their attention focused on the deep, structural obstacles to economic and educational opportunity, have yet to theorize about the psychosocial processes of becoming one of the few who "got away" (Fine & Burns, 2003; Reay, 1997a). Invisible as poor and working-class children in the formal curriculum of their public schooling, their social experiences of upward class mobility through success in school are now largely invisible in teacher education.

My students had every reason to resist telling their stories, had they even begun to untangle them. Yet, I believed that their stories would be richly telling. To have made it this far, these first-generation students had to have been deeply *changed* by school, change that may have come at considerable human cost (hooks, 2000). Lucey et al. (2003) explained:

What is so clearly at stake [in pursuing educational mobility] is the loss of identity, control, status (within the family perhaps), the community, belonging, safety: all major ego losses, any one of which can unconsciously constitute a threat to our very survival. (p. 286)

Yet few have had the educative space to pause mid-course in the "complex social trajectory" (Reay, 1997a, p. 25) of upward mobility to tally what they have gained *and* lost. And so, with Valerie Walkerdine (2003, p. 243), I have come to realize that upward mobility has a "deeply defensive aspect." I have come to understand the tightly folded arms at talk of class stratification as one sign of how much may be at stake for these students, and as *only* the first step toward eventually knowing—and telling—their own stories.

The Course

The first-generation students who enroll in *Education and the American Dream* are uniquely entangled within the myth of mobility through schooling, simultaneously banking on it being true, yet far from certain of the promised economic and social rewards. It is understandable that these students, many of whom are precariously balancing jobs, school, and family, would fold their arms in resistance at the very idea that social class still will matter in the end.

Julie Lindquist (2004) has argued that middle-class educators may easily misread students' reactions to critical pedagogies:

> pedagogies informed by critical and cultural theory have treated class less as a complex affective experience than as a set of social issues to be addressed through systematic analysis... We understand class as a problem of distribution of resources, but we experience it affectively, as an emotional process. (pp. 190, 192)

Many adherents of critical pedagogies, she explained, fail to understand what is at stake for first-generation students "accepting new ways of interpreting their lives" (Lindquist, 2004, p. 191). Thus, my goals for the class are twofold. First, I want students to develop a broad intellectual understanding of how social class shapes access to education and opportunity at the intersections of gender, ethnicity, immigration, and sexuality. Second (and most importantly, for this chapter), I wanted the first-generation students to come to a more complicated understanding of their own positions as those who had succeeded in school against the odds. Expecting that they come to class driven by hope in hard work and its just rewards, I wanted them to also question why the odds had been so stacked against them to begin with. In opening these conversations about social class and constrained opportunities, I knew that analytical academic writing would never be enough.

Multimedia and Identity Construction

Digital Storytelling is positioned squarely at the intersections of intellect and affect, of which Lindquist and Walkerdine wrote. Bass and Eynon (2009) elaborated:

> new media technologies promoted the expansion of what we have come to call *embodied pedagogies*, inducing learning that engages affective as well as cognitive dimensions, not merely through the role of emotion, but through creativity and intuition, through expressions of self-identity and subjectivity as the foundation of intellectual engagement. (para. 1)

As Hull and Nelson (2005, p. 225) explained, creative multimodal projects "can afford not just a new way to make meaning, but a different kind of meaning," what Benmayor (2009) described as "a different, more visible, and perhaps more polysemic space" for embodied theorizing (para. 1).

Digital story production supports the difficult work of examining and reexamining one's own interpretation of life experiences, and then telling that story publicly (Carpentier, 2009; Lambert, 2006; Lundby, 2008; The Visible Knowledge Project, 2002). In creating their digital stories, students write first-person narratives of transformational moments in their schooling, record their narratives, and then use video-editing software to incorporate images, artwork, video clips, animation, transitions, pans and zooms, sound, and silence into a multimedia story of schooling as a classed being. As they write and revise, choose images and music, and make the multiple technical and aesthetic decisions of production, they visit and revisit the story that they will tell. Produced over several weeks near the end of the course, the stories are revised multiple times as they frame their experiences within new contexts of class readings and discussions. They work within creative constraint: they can write no more than 500 words, and use no more than a dozen images.

Students also write final, reflective essays on their production processes, in which they tie their production decisions to what they learned from course readings and conversations *and* their learning in the reflective spaces of story creation. The core challenge for me as their teacher is to support their creation of stories that move beyond "what happened" to the more vital question of "what happens next" (Robillard, 2003, p. 84). Coming to know one's own story is one element of this process; forming "new political relationships" with one's experiences through collective telling of stories is the deeper goal (Lindquist, 2004, p. 191).

My decisions to employ Digital Storytelling then, were grounded in two goals: (a) to provide new tools by which these class "border-crossers" could distinctively represent their "complex social positioning as a complicated amalgam of current privilege interlaced with historic disadvantage" (Reay, 1997b, p. 225); and (b) to support the deeply reflective process of creating personal narratives, in order to complicate what Adair and Dahlberg (2001, p. 174) have termed a cultural "impulse to frame class mobility as a narrative of moral progress."

Contextualizing Stories About Class and Schooling

The creation of stories is supported by work throughout the course that challenges the core belief of policy and practice in the United States, that success in school will be rewarded. We discuss Bourdieu, analyze data on labor markets and college attainment, and deconstruct education policy documents. To decenter the analytical, middle-class voice of much academic writing, we open each week with the voices of those from the poor and working class: we read the poetry of Ana Castillo, Phillip Levine, and Patricia Dobler. We listen to Bruce Springsteen and Drive-By Truckers. Students analyze popular films such as *Good Will Hunting*, *Real Women Have Curves*, and *Rushmore* through the lenses of the course reading and discussions.

We listen deeply for the metaphors within this work that describe childhood experiences characterized by early restlessness for a new kind of life. We hear of being singled out by teachers as "better" than siblings and classmates, and consequently, being distanced from them. We hear of being invisible. Sometimes, we hear of schooling as salvation. Lindquist (2004, p. 189) wrote of the "paradoxes of nostalgia and ambition" in working-class lives, and we work to honor each while working against sentimentalizing both home life and academic success. And then, we craft our stories.

Digital Stories of Mobility

As I write of what I have learned from five years of student stories,[2] I will foreground the work of three students: Alicia, Lisa, and Jessica. From their stories, I will draw connections to the themes that I see woven through many of the stories of the poor and working-class students. I will first introduce the students, briefly describe their stories, and then discuss their own perspectives on what they learned from these multimedia representations.

Alicia. When she took the class, Alicia, a Latina, had just started teacher education after five years of working in another profession. As I introduced the project to class on the first day, Alicia grew visibly annoyed, and insisted that she did not want to tell her story. She asked me to publicly confirm that she would not be required to tell it as a condition of passing the course. I explained that she could not possibly tell her whole story in this short project, and that she was free to tell any parts that she chose.

Yet, within weeks, she began making powerful connections between course readings and her childhood. Her questions often moved class discussions to important, deeper places, and students frequently sought her out during class breaks to share their own stories with her.

Her digital story, "From the Beginning," opens with a black screen, over wistful, solo piano chords. The screen then fades up to an image of her as a smiling, small child that fades to a large road sign, marking the border between Texas and all that lies beyond. In a wistful voice, she tells in both English and Spanish of driving for days with her mother and siblings to join her military father in a distant state. They arrived in the middle of the night, and got up the next morning to go to their new school. In the first few minutes of her story, she tells of seeing White children in her class for the first time. Misunderstanding something she heard from her grandmother, she assumes that White children are called "Bobs." When she joyfully points out all the Bobs at an open house a few weeks later, her mother is deeply embarrassed. The story then turns to her telling of her mother's efforts to make Alicia more middle-class and American.

Lisa. Lisa, a young, White, early-career teacher working in an upper-middle-class school, was adamant that she did not have a story to tell. Eventually, though, she told her story, "Change," of a terrifying night when she was in middle school when a strange woman came screaming to their front door trying to escape from an attacker. Her father let the woman into the house, and the whole family lost a night of sleep as the attacker (the woman's pimp) screamed obscenities outside. The police came, and the injured woman was taken away.

The next day, her exhausted father was seriously injured in a construction accident. He was then on disability pay for five years, "and we lost everything." Lisa had hated the woman for ruining her family. Her story traces her family's economic decline and her loss of the markers of status that had sustained her friendships.

Jessica. Jessica, a young, White, preservice elementary teacher, was also adamant in the first weeks of the class that there were stories that she would not tell. She had told the class that her father had recently been diagnosed with an aggressive, terminal cancer, and she eventually crafted a constrained story of his unwavering support of her success in school. The story opens with a brief image of a child's alphabet magnet board as she talks of her father's bragging to his working-class friends of her intellectual prowess from the time she started school. Next, we see what will be a recurring shot: a black and white photo of her as perhaps a 6-year-old, sitting on her father's lap near the beach, father and daughter alone in a chilly, misty landscape. She recounts times when she wanted to give up on education, and he encouraged her to believe that "she was the one who could make it."

The Stories of Upward Mobility

The stories that these students choose to tell are each highly personal, yet several common themes weave through them and those of their classmates.

Shame. A deeply internalized sense of shame permeates these stories of poor and working-class childhoods. The shame is evident in the many images of hand-me-down clothes or cheap food taken to school for lunch, and, more subtly, in stories of being "different" from the earliest years of school. Shame followed them to college; most explained that they had never spoken of their social-class backgrounds in any other course, in spite of their program's emphasis on honoring diversity.

Alicia was deeply aware that she had shamed her mother in misnaming the White children in the class, shame so deep that her relationship with her mother shifted to one of strategic correction. Alicia accepted her mother's efforts to navigate her through the middle-class norms of White schools, even while her mother herself was unsure of the rules of the game. Alicia was aware throughout her schooling that she could easily and innocently shame her family again.

After telling of her fear on the night that the screaming woman came into their home, Lisa's story moves slowly through images of a grove of trees transitioning through the seasons. She slowly narrates all of the things she lost in the months following her father's injury: swimming lessons, overnight field trips, clothes, parties, and eventually, friends who still had all of these things. She had just moved to "the good school," confident that this was where she belonged, but then found herself rejected by the very friends she had aspired to be like. Academic achievement had given her access to higher-status peers, but when she could no longer afford to keep up with them, she also rejected the academic. In the next segment of her story, we see tightly framed, black-and-white, close-up images of an angry young woman—pierced, screaming, punked-out—the identity that Lisa chose when the academic and social identity she had long sought had imploded.

In passing, Jessica mentioned in her story that her mother had left after her family had moved to a new neighborhood; privately, she explained more in her final essay. Her father had moved the family to a neighborhood that they could barely afford, to strategically move Jessica to better schools. Shortly after, her mother's addiction deepened, and Jessica was profoundly conscious of the burden of protecting this secret in her new school if she were to prove that she deserved the hard-won, new academic opportunities.

Shame is also woven in the telling of many of the stories that other students have told. In the rural Midwest, for example, Nora learned "proper grammar" from her first-grade teacher, and then took it upon herself to correct the language of her farmer father at the dinner table, at church, and in extended family gatherings. Her opening images are of an exuberant young child among endless open fields, and a weathered father in the dimming light of dusk.

Rhonda created a story of a road trip to deliver her daughter to college. This trip took them south on the interstate highway that Rhonda's father had helped build, moving his family north segment by segment from one temporary home to another. Rhonda shows a black-and-white photo of her childhood bike parked in front of her family's trailer in a mobile home park. She then washes the image with cartoonish color, as she tells of her embarrassment that her father so often tried to convince others that they were better off than they were.

Elizabeth's story was also set in a school open house. She described parents who were not self-aware enough to notice how they were embarrassing her, an excellent student in the class. In trying to fit in, her parents had feigned arrogance. "We were trying to live in a world that we were not born into," Elizabeth narrates. "We did not have the natural-born awareness of it to navigate it," although she, as a fourth grader, sensed how misguided her parents' efforts were.

The pervasive shame was a reminder to students that their identities as successful students were never secure. Robillard (2003), writing of first-generation college students, observed:

> The social structure of the working class is such that there is no sense of stability. There is general, vague feeling of having no control, of uncertainty. One's life need not actually be out of control; the threat only needs to loom large. (p. 85)

Doing well in school was often the only thing that these children could control in their lives, and being a good student was often part of their deliberate but precarious identity construction as someone who would become someone better. All the while, many of their parents, who may have applauded their children's ambition, watched as they slowly lost control of their own children, who internalized middle-class judgments of people like them (Walkerdine, 2003).

Isolation. The complex amalgam of shame and emerging academic success often left these children straddling two worlds, a second common theme running through the stories. Lucey et al. (2003) noted that navigating social mobility "involves the construction and the constant policing of internal and external 'boundaries', where competing and conflictual people, behavior, identifications and ideas must be kept apart" (p. 293). These are complicated gymnastics for young children, who are simultaneously learning that they and their families are "the Other," but that only *they* have earned the right to aspire to "move up."

After the story of the open house, Alicia's story moves through a series of images of her and her brothers grinning broadly as they carve Halloween pumpkins and visit a White Santa. She narrates that Spanish was no longer spoken in her home after that day. The final, lingering image in Alicia's story is of her in her high school graduation regalia, smiling and laughing. She says: "It worked. It worked better than my parents had hoped. I became a stranger in their homes. A stranger in my own family." Alicia then pulls back on her image until we see that she is standing with two blonde, White girlfriends also in graduation robes, laughing in the bright sunshine, as the plaintive solo piano continues to play. There is no family in the picture at this turning point in her life, as she stands intimately close to her friends, mimicking their poses.

Earlier, as we were work-shopping scripts, Alicia had told the class that she had never told her parents that she was applying for college. She explained that she simply came down with her suitcase one morning to announce that she was leaving. She had had only strained contact with her mother since.

Conversely, Lisa constructed a school identity after her father's accident that consciously rejected her parents' aspirations for her. As her images shift from the vulnerable, small girl to the screaming, pierced adolescent, she narrates: "My grandmother died of lung cancer, so I began to smoke," and of her satisfaction with being welcomed by the "bad kids."

Jessica's story, crafted at the very time that her father was dying, reflected the urgency she felt to simultaneously separate from and also pay tribute to her father's role in her becoming educated. Privately, she had told me that she was considering leaving school to care for him as he died, since there was no money to hire help for him. Publicly, she told in her story about how doing well in school was part of his lifelong dream of her being "the one" in his family who could "make it."

In her voice-over, she says: "Maybe he saw parts of himself in me, more so than in my siblings." She ends her story with images of the two of them having beers in a bar, the most public photo of them together that we have seen. She tells of being embarrassed as he introduced her to his friends as a college graduate. In the process of creating her story, she made the decision to stay in school to honor his urgent dream of being the father of an educated daughter, rather than leave school to play the more private role of daughter to a critically ill father.

Many of the other stories tell of isolation within families as the students became more immersed in the life of school. Anna, an early-career, White teacher pregnant with her first child, created a story in which she is touching her father in every single image—from being propped high on his shoulders as a toddler, to dancing with him at her wedding. In shot after shot (she went well beyond the expectation of only a dozen images), he is sheltering and protecting her, smiling proudly at her. Her narration, meanwhile, tells of vicious, ongoing fights over her decision to attend college to become a teacher, and turn away from the family's tradition of manual labor.

Adam, a young, White man new to teaching, told of his fear, home alone waiting for his single mother to pick him up, that she was late because her aged car had died. They were due at a school conference where his placement in the college track would be affirmed, and his seventh-grade self understood how deeply important this meeting would be for his mother's sense of herself as a successful parent.

The struggles to navigate academic identities and family relationships resonate through many of the stories. Many students in my class had been tracked, physically separated from friends and siblings who were left behind in other classrooms. By high school, many also began working long hours to pay for college, leaving them further isolated from family and friends. In college, they could not afford the social activities taken for granted by those being supported by their families.

Many felt the weight of being the public face of their family's dignity, even as few of their parents were positioned to support their academic success. These things were never discussed in school. Their teachers saw only their nascent academic success.

Seeing class. Finally, through many revisions of their stories, many students publicly owned their identities as classed individuals, and finally acknowledged classism. While it would be important to remember that these are not comprehensive autobiographical essays, but short emblematic *stories*, this moment of coming to more fully understand their social class backgrounds typically was, as Lindquist (2004) cautioned, a deeply emotional experience.

Alicia explained in her reflective essay that she was at last reclaiming her own version of the story from the mythical version created by her family:

> I found that [in first drafts] what I was writing were the words I had heard over and over again told by my family. Their story is that I gladly accepted the challenge of learning English. In my family's version, of the story, I learned English with

lightening speed, I loved to walk to school every day for the free breakfasts, and made so many friends that the fact that I did not become prom queen puzzled them.

In my own memories, I hated learning English, dilly dallied my way to horrific free breakfasts, hid behind books in hopes of never becoming prom queen.

Alicia then wrote:

> I realized what a force my mother has been in my life. She was the one who woke us for school, made our meals, fought for us to be in class, for us to have a future…we all made decisions that were not what they expected of us, and I realized this quarter how painful that must have been for her.

She had barely spoken to her mother in years. To even get copies of her childhood photos for the project, she negotiated a meeting in a public space through a sibling. But there was, at last, a meeting between her and the mother who had invested so much in what she understood to be necessary for her daughter's success.

Lisa wrote of now realizing that there were rifts with her family that still needed to be healed. "I had never looked at this situation from his point of view until we started interpreting the poems, songs, and essays in class," she wrote. "This has made me look at my family history from a different angle. I had never thought of my father as working class, but he had no power over his status." Her digital story ends with the words, "Thank you to my dad," slowly coming into focus.

The ending was more complicated for Jessica. Her father's impending death left her with few opportunities to reconcile the many roles she had played in his life. Instead, she wrote of staying in school, not only for him, but also with the hope that she and her fiancé, who worked in a dangerous trade, might have the economic security that her father had never had.

Nora, who had diligently corrected her father's grammar, explained that she realized only later that he must have understood the personal cost of educating his daughter to become someone who would look down on him. At the end of her story, she used the word *ain't* ironically and repeatedly, as she narrated her commitment to instilling pride in family within her own students.

Rhonda wrote that she cried repeatedly while writing her story. "I have worked so hard to give my daughter a life better than the one I had," she wrote. Yet, just before her own college graduation, she realized also that she was still far from the life that she has aspired to, the life that she had mistakenly thought had been available to her parents, had they only made other life choices.

Adam wrote that he cried when reading his story to his wife. Elizabeth wrote that she had to rerecord her voice-over repeatedly, as she cried as she told her childhood story and realized that she was not yet in a position to provide a better life for her own son.

Each had come to understand how social class had shaped their families' lives, and continued to shape their own. They more fully understood the constraints that had shaped their parents' choices, and the many ways in which their schooling had worked against their eventual success. Especially as they viewed everyone's stories on the last night of class, they saw that what they had long understood as their own and their parents' individual choices were instead artifacts of deep social stratification in the US. For many, this enabled them to forgive and to heal.

Stories as Critical Pedagogy

Critical pedagogies that work to instill in teachers an understanding of structural inequalities would seem to ask very different things of middle-class students and those from poor and working-class backgrounds. For middle-class students, becoming critical may be primarily an intellectual and moral endeavor. For poor and working-class students, much more is at stake, as we ask them to rethink their trajectories to college (Lindquist, 2004, p. 191). Accepting critical perspectives on their lives requires them to acknowledge the precariousness of much in which they have placed their hope: the promise of reward for lifelong sacrifice, of vindication of their families through their success, the ease of just being able to make the rent without drama.

As they have spent hours sorting through childhood photos, reliving painful memories, and reframing much of what they have understood of their own trajectories through the lenses of class, these students have opened the conversation about the multiple obstacles to upward mobility. As they have publicly told their stories, often for the first time, they have also come to see themselves and their families apart from the judgmental middle-class gaze. They have seen, often for the first time, the strength, resilience, and complicated love of their childhoods. Telling their stories has enabled them to explain their distinctive identities first to themselves and then to others (Lambert, 2006).

In their multimodal metaphors of desolate road signs, tension-filled solo piano music, and images of smiling children not yet feeling the pain narrated by their adult selves, these students have created stories of schooling as classed beings. The lives of students on the margins have become visible, finally projected on the screen of a classroom and amplified through the speakers, as we cry and laugh together on the last night of class.

They have begun a process of complex bridging of multiple, conflicting identities (Mack, 2006) that they have long kept apart. They are more clearly connected to their own stories, they have unfolded their arms, and they have been heard, often for the first time in the symbolic setting of school. My hope is that they are also now positioned to better hear the stories of their own students.

Notes

1. Rates of college enrollment and retention are significantly lower for the children of parents who did not attend college than for the children of parents with college degrees, even among high achievers (Choy, 2002; Karen, 2002; NCES, 2005a; Sacks, 2007). The highest-achieving, low-income eighth graders are only as likely to complete college as the lowest-achieving students from high-income families (NCES, 2005b, p. 50).
2. Writing about these stories is challenging. Had this been a conventional written assignment, I could analyze student meaning here with only verbal quotes. But I cannot quote the juxtaposition of images, the pacing of their voice-overs, their uses of silence and music that together convey the students' meaning. I instead do my best to describe the multimedia productions without privileging only the written parts of their stories.

References

Adair, V., & Dahlberg, S. (2001). Cutting class in the multicultural literature classroom. *Pedagogy*, *1*(1), 173–175.

Bass, R., & Eynon, B. (2009, January 7). Capturing the visible evidence of invisible learning (Part III). Academic Commons. Retrieved from http://academiccommons.org/commons/essay/capturing-visible-evidence-invisible-learning-3

Benmayor, R. (2009, January 7). Theorizing through digital stories: The art of 'writing back' and 'writing for.' Academic Commons. Retrieved from http://academiccommons.org/commons/essay/theorizing-through-digital-stories

Bettie, J. (2003). *Women without class: Girls, race and identity*. Berkeley, CA: University of California Press.

Bourdieu, P. (1984). *Distinction: A social critique of the judgement of taste* (R. Nice, Trans.). Cambridge, MA: Harvard University Press.

Carpentier, N. (2009). Digital storytelling in Belgium: Power and participation. In J. Hartley & K. McWilliam (Eds.), *Story circle: Digital storytelling around the world* (pp. 188–204). West Sussex: Wiley-Blackwell.

Choy, S. (2002). Access and persistence: Findings from 10 years of longitudinal research on students. Washington, DC: American Council on Education. Retrieved from http://www.acenet.edu/bookstore/pdf/2002_access&persistence.pdf

Dews, C. L. B., & Law, D. L. (Eds.). (1995). *This fine place so far from home: Voices of academics from the working class*. Philadelphia, PA: Temple University Press.

Fine, M., & Burns, A. (2003). Class notes: Toward a critical psychology of class and schooling. *Journal of Social Issues, 59*(4), 841–860.

Furman, F. K., Kelly, E. A., & Nelson, L. W. (2005). *Telling our lives: Conversations on solidarity and difference*. Lanham, MD: Rowman & Littlefield.

hooks, b. (2000). *Where we stand: Class matters*. New York, NY: Routledge.

Hull, G. A., & Nelson, M. E. (2005). Locating the semiotic power of multimodality. *Written Communication, 22*(2), 224–261.

Jones, S. (2007). Working-poor mothers and middle-class others: Psychosocial considerations in home-school relations and research. *Anthropology and Education Quarterly, 38*(2), 159–177.

Karen, D. (2002). Changes in access to higher education in the United States: 1980–1992. *Sociology of Education, 75*(3), 191–210.

Kelly, E. A. (2007). A house made of words: Class, education, and dissidence in three lives. In A. Scott & D. J. Freeman-Moir (Eds.), *The lost dream of equality: Critical essays on education and social class* (pp. 205–232). Rotterdam, The Netherlands: Sense.

Lambert, J. (2006). *Digital storytelling: Capturing lives, creating community*. Berkeley, CA: Digital Diner Press.

Lindquist, J. (2004). Class affects, classroom affectations: Working through the paradoxes of strategic empathy. *College English, 67*(2), 187–209.

Linkon, S. L. (1999). Introduction: Teaching working class. In S. L. Linkon (Ed.), *Teaching working class* (pp. 1–11). Amherst, MA: University of Massachusetts Press.

Lucey, H., Melody, J., & Walkerdine, V. (2003). Uneasy hybrids: Psychosocial aspects of becoming educationally successful for working-class young women. *Gender and Education, 15*(3), 285–299.

Lundby, K. (2008). Introduction. In K. Lundby (Ed.), *Digital storytelling, mediatized stories: Self-representations in new media* (pp. 1–17). New York, NY: Peter Lang.

Mack, N. (2006). Ethical representations of working-class lives: Multiple genres, voices, and identities. *Pedagogy, 6*(1), 53–78.

Muzatti, S. L., & Samarco, V. (Eds.). (2006). *Reflections from the wrong side of the tracks: Class, identity, and the working class experience in Academe*. Lanham, MD: Rowman & Littlefield.

National Center for Education Statistics (NCES). (2005a). First-generation students in postsecondary education: A look at their college transcripts (NCES Report 2005–171). Washington, DC: Author. Retrieved from http://nces.ed.gov/pubs2005/2005171.pdf

———. (2005b). Youth indicators, 2005: Trends in the well-being of American youth (NCES Report 2005–050). Washington, DC: Author. Retrieved from http://nces.ed.gov/programs/youthindicators/

Payne-Bourcy, L., & Chandler-Olcott, K. (2003). Spotlighting social class: An exploration of one adolescent's language and literacy practices. *Journal of Literacy Research, 35*(1), 551–590.

Reay, D. (1997a). The double-bind of the 'working class' feminist academic: The success of failure or the failure of success. In P. Mahony & C. Zmroczek (Eds.), *Class matters: 'Working class' women's perspectives on social class* (pp. 18–29). Bristol, PA: Taylor & Francis.

———. (1997b). Feminist theory, habitus, and social class: Disrupting notions of classlessness. *Women's Studies International Forum, 20*(2), 225–233.

Robillard, A. (2003). It's time for class: Toward a more complex pedagogy of narrative. *College English, 66*(1), 74–92.

Sacks, P. (2007). *Tearing down the gates: Confronting the class divide in American education.* Berkeley, CA: University of California Press.
Sayer, A. (2005). *The moral significance of class.* Cambridge, UK: Cambridge University Press.
The Visible Knowledge Project. (2002, September). Digital storytelling: Some selected on-line resources (VKP Newsletter, Georgetown University). Retrieved from http://crossroads.georgetown.edu/vkp/newsletter/0902/resources.htm (no longer accessible).
Walkerdine, V. (2003). Reclassifying upward mobility: Femininity and the neo-liberal subject. *Gender and Education, 15*(3), 237–248.
Welsch, K. A. (Ed.). (2005). *Those winter Sundays: Female academics and their working class parents.* New York, NY: University Press of America.

4

Here I Stand: College Students' Critical Education Narratives

Barbara Kessel and Kim Hackford-Peer

This chapter focuses on the use of critical education narrative and the centering of personal experience in the context of an Introduction to Gender Studies course. The course was aimed at challenging students to be more reflective about their education experiences and the schooling conditions of women and LGBTQ students. Sleeter's conceptualization of Critical Family History "applies insights from various critical theoretical traditions to an analysis of how one's family has been constructed historically within and through relations of power" (Sleeter, n.d., para 10). Informed by Sleeter, and drawing upon poststructural feminist and queer theories, we use what we call *critical education narrative* to explore students' histories and experiences with/in relations of power in institutions of education.

We see as our contribution to this volume the queering of the use of narrative by resisting the "drive to sum up one's self, one's learning, and the other as directly, developmentally, and inclusively knowable and identifiable" (Miller, 1998, p. 371). We describe how we queered the production of narratives utilizing a layered approach that allowed for multiple and contradictory tellings. These layers included an initial self-portrait, an educational autobiography, journals, interviewing one another, and an end of semester self-analysis of students' educational autobiography. Additionally, we discuss how we see the use of such narratives as having the potential to queer education more broadly. This involves moving beyond developing critical consciousness and questioning relations of power. Specifically, we suggest that critical education narratives can work to queer education, calling into question normalcy by embracing and capitalizing upon the possibilities to reimagine and rework pedagogy, course content, and often-taken-for-granted power relations.

In the spirit of the class and our pedagogical commitments, we offer our version of a narrative telling of what unfolded in the class. Throughout the chapter we engage in narrative writing and critical self-reflection, highlighting incoherencies that emerged. We interweave details about our pedagogical goals, what engaging in this kind of teaching means to us, insights from students' critical educational narratives, and reflections on our experiences as facilitators.

Week 1: What a Queer Class!

> Most students have been educated in contexts that do not address how social difference is fashioned by relations of power and how relations of power govern the self. Most have not had sanctioned opportunities to discuss subjects like feminism, gay and lesbian rights, anti-racist conduct, or what it means to construct one's own racial, gendered, and sexual identity. (Britzman as cited in McKoy, 2000, pp. 252)

Our students were like most on the first day of our Intro to Gender Studies class. The ten of them shuffled in, found seats, and waited for some sort of official beginning. We started the semester in a somewhat conventional way, with attendance and handing out the syllabus, but in many respects, even those acts were not carried out as they are in most classrooms. Instead of going down a list and calling out names, students introduced themselves. Most shared their name, year, major, where they grew up, and what kind of schools they had attended.

When we handed out the syllabus we instructed them to take it home, read it, and come back with questions, comments, or suggestions for changes. We announced that we would discuss it in earnest the next day. They flipped through the pages anyway, perhaps taking note of the amount of work involved in the class. Then a student raised her hand while saying, "I have a question." She continued, "You have the word, queer, all over in the syllabus. Can you say something about that? What does it mean?" Kim responded by asking the class what they thought the word *could* mean and what kinds of responses it was triggering.

Some students were initially uncomfortable with the word *queer*, familiar only with its pejorative usage. One part of the conversation, then, was discussing how the word has been reclaimed to critique the idea that there is a "normal" against which different, weird, or queer can be clearly defined and made to be "less than." Over the next 40 minutes we collected an array of ways to think about the word *queer* while also talking about words—their power, inadequacy, and how their meanings are fluid and change over time and across contexts. We eventually settled on not settling on a singular, all-encompassing definition for *queer*, queering the notion that words have clear and absolute meanings, while at the same time claiming a commitment to the notion that *queer* is about questioning, resisting, and rethinking norms.

These students were particularly good at recognizing and naming normative ideas and practices. Perhaps because many of them had spent their lives living on the margins: the students claimed a variety of racial and ethnic identities;[1] few currently engaged in practicing the dominant LDS (Latter-Day Saints or Mormon) religion, and several had left the LDS Church; half were older, "nontraditional" students; most were first-generation college students; about a third identified as gay or bisexual; a third had children; and most knew (and shared) their families' stories of coming to Utah as immigrants (some documented, some not), refugees, or Mormon pioneers. They had already spent a lifetime bumping up against norms, and most were well versed in negotiating the norms that tried to structure their lives. They had also learned, to varying extents, how to resist them, but most, as Britzman (1993) suggested, had never before been asked to interrogate, challenge, and resist norms in an educational space. Yet, here we were, in this increasingly queer classroom, two White instructors with our own histories of bumping up against institutional barriers, asking them to challenge and interrogate the norms of institutions of education from within the very walls of the institution.

On that first day we started engaging in this project of recognizing, naming, interrogating, grappling with, and resisting norms. In addition to the critical practices of questioning power, we also began queering the meanings of words and norms, and reimagining possibilities that might exist if we left meanings open or read them in multiple ways. There were also other ways that we got a little bit queer in our approach to the class. For example, the students pointed out that the space we met in was not a "normal" classroom. We met in the Gender Studies lounge, a room with two avocado green walls and two light lilac walls; a rickety table; overflowing bookshelves; a brown chalkboard; and a small, sleek, black coffee table around which we sat on an array of seats, including a mauve love seat, a grey couch supported by a brick where the frame was broken, chairs covered in turquoise vinyl, and plastic brown and green chairs. There was a gender-neutral bathroom across the hall, and a small kitchen two doors down where we stored snacks for class. The students honed their critical skills when they expressed with certainty that they liked the classroom space, and wondered why a building that houses the Gender Studies Program is known as "Building #44." They wavered between finding the unnamed nature of the building a troubling message about the university's lacking commitment to Gender Studies, and finding it exciting because "Building #44" could mean anything. They identified possibility and queerness wrapped up in almost everything about the physical space of our classroom. In other words, their critical skills allowed them to question, and their ability to take a queer approach to the space allowed them to see its "difference" from their other classroom settings and imagine how this might open up possibilities for a different kind of class. Indeed, one of the students explicitly commented in an assignment that since this was not a "normal" class/room, she found a sense of freedom in thinking about what she could possibly expect from her education.

Of course, some norms were easier to get queer with—those we already questioned or that did not work for us were obvious targets. Others were normal to us in ways that felt comfortable, safe, and natural, and were less likely candidates for queering. The content of the class itself was something that the students identified as closer to queer than other classes they had experienced, because it overtly included taboo topics such as desire, sexuality, and race, and therefore resisted the normative expectation that these are not topics to be discussed in school. In fact, it went one step farther, by asking students to consider, from their own experiences, how such topics had an impact on their education. The curriculum asserted that these are indeed topics to be discussed in school, because they play a significant role in the lives of students.

At the same time, students were less comfortable with making suggestions about amending the course content; when we asked for feedback about the syllabus or suggestions for changes, we got none. Here, students maintained normative ideas about the distinction and power imbalances between professors and students. However, students did begin to post videos and articles for their classmates to view or read on our online forum. They were not asked to do so, nor were they required to engage with one another's posts, but they did. So they found ways to add to the content, and move the class in ways they wanted it to go. They often began talking about these videos and articles before class began, and these discussions spilled over into and mixed in with the day's discussion. Perhaps these insertions were more comfortable ways for them to queer the content, since they fell outside of the formal syllabus.

With our malleable definition of the word *queer* as "the ability to rework and reimagine norms and stereotypes," we engaged with another main component of the class. The class was designed to bring into conversation gender studies (with a strong focus on intersectional aspects of identity) and education (as a process, an institution, an ideal, and a personal experience). The class worked through two approaches as we engaged with the topics; we created and grappled with our own critical education narratives, and we began to learn about discourse. We looked for the ways that various discourses were wielded in the texts we worked with, our own conversations, and our writing, emphasizing how these discourses limited the ways that we thought and talked about ourselves and education. Deborah Britzman (1995) argued that discourses work through cultural logic to contain ideas and make them comprehensible in particular ways. She saw the imperative of education to move beyond these limits: "It is precisely this centripetal force, a cultural insistence to put back into place boundaries at all costs, that education is obligated to exceed" (pp. 151–152). In identifying the discourses each of us used in our narratives, we also pointed to the power they have to structure our stories, and worked at reimagining how we might queer our narratives by exceeding their discursive boundaries.

It is important to note, then, that our (students' and instructors') oral and written stories were always positioned as primary texts in the course. This, too, was an opportunity for us to get queer with the class. As Miller (1998) suggested, autobiography as a curricular practice can be a queer intervention when incorporated in ways that invite incoherence, fracturedness, unknowingness, and fluidity. She cautioned that much of the time autobiography

> reinforce[s] classroom representations of a knowable, always accessible conscious self who progresses, with the help of autobiographical inquiry, from ignorance to knowledge of self, [and] other.... Such normalized versions of autobiography serve to limit and to close down rather than to create possibilities for constructing permanently open and resignifiable selves. (p. 367)

Our goal was to work against these familiar and tempting ways to tell our education narratives. This is how most of us learned to tell stories—stories about ourselves and others, and stories based in experience or woven out of our imaginings. But the linearity and certainty of the approach did not allow us room to move, question, be critical, or get queer.

We structured the course so that we could play with different approaches to, or layers of, our critical education narratives. As a class, we read the layers (created in various formats) up next to, against, over, and through each other. The name of the class, "Here I Stand: An Introduction to Gender Studies," was one layer. At first glance it seems to reference a forward-moving journey toward a singular time and place, and a final complete and coherent self (Here I Stand) and field of study (Gender Studies). However, there are other, more queer, ways to read the title as well, and continually (re)reading the course, the texts, and our own narratives was our project throughout the semester. For example, "Here I Stand" came to mean something much more fleeting and less certain, which centered narrative as a critical queer pedagogy. Additionally, our engagement with Gender Studies included intersectional aspects of our identities, and applied to our exploration of our educational experiences.

In working against traditional notions of narrative, we built into the class multiple ways for students to tell their stories. We began setting the pedagogical stage for layered tellings in the first week of the class. First, we asked the students to create portraits that reflected themselves as students. We gave these directions along with blank paper and a selection of writing and drawing utensils:

The rules are simple—find a way to represent yourself as a student. This can be how you see yourself, how others see you, how you want to be seen... You can draw an actual portrait of yourself, you can create a word cloud, you can draw a timeline, you can make a map, you can draw a cartoon, you can... (You get the idea—do it however it makes sense for you!). Once you're done take a few minutes to journal about what you did and why. We'll use these drawings to begin to introduce ourselves to one another—so be prepared to share at least some of what you draw with your classmates.

Their creations were varied, and as we took time to share them, it became apparent that they were but momentary glimpses. Students referenced them as "what I made that moment," implying that they might create something different in a different moment. They used other phrases like, "So, that's what is on the paper," or, "Anyway, that's a little bit about me," which indicated that there was much left unsaid, unrevealed on the paper. It also suggested that students were performing but a piece, a particular fragment of themselves in that moment. We used this to talk about the project of creating our own critical education narratives throughout the semester, and we explained that these portraits were one of the many layers of our narratives.

The second thing we did to set the pedagogical stage was to begin to introduce the students to outside texts that could be read as critical education narratives. One of the first readings the students engaged with was Lee's (2001) essay, "Beyond Bean Counting." In the essay, Lee discussed her own personal (including political and academic) experiences with feminism, which she described as "an uneasy balancing act between the imperatives of outreach and inclusion on one hand, and the risk of tokenism and further marginalization on the other" (p. 67). The essay took up the ways that students, particularly in classes that purport to be at least a little bit about them, look for themselves in the curriculum, their classmates, and the professors, and is critical of the continual absence of what so many students are looking for. Lee wrote of her Feminist Studies 101 class, "A class about women, I thought, was a class about me, so I looked for myself everywhere, and I found nothing" (p. 68).

Lee's narrative immediately resonated with the students, and it became one that we revisited as a class many times throughout the semester. It was an example of a critical education narrative that was also queer, as it was teeming with questions, critiques turned to uncertain grapplings, and personal experiences portrayed through multiple readings and new imaginings. Additionally, this piece was important because it signaled another way that we could get critical and queer in the class; it sent the message that even the discipline of Gender Studies was up for interrogation, reimagining, and reworking. In our case, the fact that the first piece we read complicated the very subject matter around which the class is built opened up the possibility for students to pose and take up questions about power relations within the class, the university, their previous schools, their families, their churches, and other entities within the community. This in turn allowed possibilities for writing what might have been unwritable in other spaces, for considering what might have otherwise been unconsiderable, and for saying what they knew was unsayable in other classes.

These queer reconsiderations enhanced our processes of engaging with our critical education narratives. As instructors, we drew heavily from Britzman's (2012) questions and assertions:

> What makes normalcy so thinkable in education? How might pedagogy think the unthought of normalcy?... Queer theory transgresses the stability of the representational; pedagogy situates the problem of normalcy in classroom sites and worries about the social production of the learning self. (p. 293)

Our intention was to put the layers together, pull them apart, and rework them to see what we as a class could learn about ourselves and our ideas regarding, and experiences with, schooling and education.

As this introduction to the class suggests, from the beginning, the classroom was a space in which meaning was struggled over and co-constructed. While this was always our intention, students' questioning of the word *queer* and the dialogue that ensued set the stage, early in the semester, for a high level of critical engagement and reconsideration of the norms we take for granted. Students talked about their families, communities, schools, teachers, friends, the media, and popular culture, and their stories became texts that we critically analyzed and grappled with in the class in order to discuss power relations in society broadly.

Assignment 1: Critical Educational Narratives—
Our Stories as Texts

> In critical approaches to self-examination, personal and family experience is the beginning of a research process rather than the culmination. (Sleeter, n.d., p. 115).

In the first graded assignment for the course, due the third week of class, students were asked to write an educational autobiography. Specifically, they were asked to:

> *Consider, for example, how your sense(s) of self (or your identities) were influenced by your experiences in school and how your identity influenced how you viewed (and currently view) education and schooling. Include how you developed your sense of yourself in relation to school. What messages did you get about the role of school in your life and from whom or where did these messages come? Were these messages ever in conflict with one another and, if so, how? If you received similar or compatible messages, discuss that. Discuss how your experiences with education have shaped your identity in terms of how you see yourself as a student and in the ways education is a part of your life and future.*

Beginning the class with students writing their critical education narratives was purposeful. Highlighting students' narratives was part of the pedagogical staging discussed earlier. Their written education histories were an important layer of students' narratives. These written accounts allowed students to expand upon the moment-in-time self portraits that they had done the first day of class, and pushed them to begin thinking about their education histories more broadly and critically.

The use of educational narratives as the first assignment had three main purposes:

1. Provoke students to reflect upon their educational experiences;
2. Formally center and integrate students' experiences into the curriculum as "academically legitimate" grounds from which to begin our exploration of power relations in education and society; and
3. Instruct students in how to write personal narratives as a form of scholarly writing.

Scheduling this as the first assignment signaled to students their significance to the class, and indicated that the class would not be about abstract discussions of education. As the directions suggest, students were asked to reflect upon their personal experiences with/in education, in terms of messages they received about who they were and could be as students. This required them to draw upon the multiple identifications they took up, as well as those others mapped onto them, and consider if and how these were part of their experiences. Students' educational narratives were a starting point from which we delved into a critical analysis of schools as institutions.

We (Kim and Barb) also wrote educational autobiographies, and while the students did not formally share their pieces with one another, we shared ours with everyone in the class. We wanted to make it clear to students that this kind of writing is meaningful, and that we would not ask them to take risks with their writing that we were not willing to take. We shared our narratives with the students before theirs were due as a way to prime them to bring their whole—spiritual, intellectual, cultural, racial, ethnic, sexual—selves into their writing and into the classroom. We also hoped to illustrate how to integrate analysis and personal experience through narrative. We did worry that our narratives could be read as examples of "how to do the assignment," and therefore limit the students' approaches to their own narratives. However, our narratives were stylistically different, and we used this to emphasize that there is no "one way" to write this kind of paper.

Students were asked to view education through their own experiences as part of this written assignment, while also integrating concepts and theories from class readings. In this way, students critically engaged in analyses of schools and educational institutions, as well as other spaces where "education took place"—like homes, churches, and other community spaces—from their own experiences, (re)considering both the importance of local and/or personal context and broader implications. For example, recalling their own experiences, students disrupted romantic notions of schools as equal playing fields, and as neutral and objective places. These memories were sometimes painful, yet they became powerful ways for students to make connections between their lives and the critical texts we read for class. By drawing upon their experiences in relation to the texts, we hoped to illustrate how personal experience can be a way to understand and explore power relations, as well as how theories that critique and analyze power relations can be used to think about their life experiences.

In their writing, we pushed students to draw upon the texts used in class to consider their own experiences and the experiences of others, and to support their ideas by integrating concepts they had learned. This was not a simple or easy process for any of us. Laurel Richardson (1997) wrote of

> work[ing] in a highly complex period: on the one hand, poststructuralism calls us to greater play, reflexivity, and ethical responsibility about our writing. On the other hand, institutions that hire us may adhere to older canons of writing practice. How, then, do we write ourselves into the texts with intellectual and spiritual integrity? (p. 2)

Richardson's question is important for our students and for us. As instructors, we know that our desire to bring personal experience and history into the classroom is contradictory to common classroom practice in higher education generally and within our institution. Our queering of classroom pedagogy and reimagining critical educational narratives as playful, creative, fluid, *and* scholarly had to benefit, and not come at the expense of, students. We take our role in facilitating students' success at the university seriously, and knew that in asking them to write personal narratives as a form of scholarly writing, we would also have to instruct them in how to do so in a way that would build writing skills that would be recognized in more traditional classrooms. The tension in this contradiction was increasingly apparent, as we struggled to provide feedback that both affirmed and privileged their stories and challenged them to integrate more of the outside readings.

Later, we asked students to revisit their narratives and identify discourses about education that circulate in their lives, and to identify the sources of these discourses. Students were asked to explore their relationships to education based on a multitude of factors. Similar to Sleeter's work on Critical Family History, this assignment asked students to consider how power works to constitute limitations and possibilities in their lives. While Sleeter's focus is to explore family history to illustrate how power relations work to construct disparities of wealth and privilege, we asked students to consider relations of power through educational experiences. Specifically, our use of critical education history is a tool to help students grasp, in a personal way, how wealth, privilege, and marginalization shape and are shaped by institutions of education. This intersects with Sleeter's work in researching personal family history, as students also consider their families' experiences with, expectations from, and access to education across generations. Indeed, in the narratives students produced, family was central, but was one of many components of their educational histories that students explored. Their narrative tellings highlighted the complexity of their educational experiences, and the convoluted power relations that impact them. Their raced, classed, and gendered experiences became central to their critical assessments of power relations within and beyond institutions of education.

Writing their experiences also gave students a way to begin to bring their own critiques of power relations into dialogue with one another. We agree with Nash's (2007) assertion that:

> Certainly, our students want competence, fairness, compassion, intellectual stimulation, and enthusiasm from us as educators. In my own opinion, though, they want something else equally as important. They want to be understood, and to be heard, from the nucleus of the stories they are living. They want to make a claim for some unchartered time to engage in honest, heartfelt narrative dialogue with us and with one another. Writing personal narratives in a scholarly setting is one way to achieve this desire. (p. 3)

The dialogues in which students (and we as instructors) engaged queered education by allowing for a rethinking and reimagining of what educational equity might mean. By week three, when students were writing their critical education narratives to turn in, they had begun to form relationships with us and with one another, but in their written narratives, they shared memories and experiences that they had not shared in class.

This highlights the importance of students having a place to share parts of their stories in a less public way (i.e., with us as instructors, but not with the whole class). Writing allowed a place for more private reflections. Writing their narratives as part of a structured assignment also bridged the divide that discounts personal experience as not "scholarly" or "academic." By structuring assignments around students' storying of themselves, they earned "credit" for their narrations, and their stories became a pedagogical tool for teaching scholarly narrative writing. As the semester proceeded, many of the students shared more vulnerable parts of their written stories in class dialogues. They commented on feeling like others in the classroom understood them. Several said that they learned much from their peers in class and from hearing about experiences that were different than their own, or about experiences that were similar in some ways, but different in others. We suggest that the actual writing of their experiences with/in education was an important layer of their stories, because it provided a space in which they could perform their narratives differently for a different, more private, audience. It gave them more time to reflect and, through the assignment instructions, guided them in particular directions. Finally, it provided an inscribed layer to return to as their narratives shifted over the semester.

Tensions in Production—Shifting Narratives

> [There are] clashing investments in how stories are told and of the impossibility of telling everything. There is that excess, that difference within the story, informing how the story is told, the imperatives produced within its tellings, and the subject positions made possible and impossible there. (Britzman, 2000, pp. 37–38)

We found, as students produced narratives about their educational experiences, that several tensions emerged. We briefly discuss three of these tensions:

1. The tensions that students identified as they wrote and talked about navigating institutions of education;
2. The tensions and contradictions between the layers of their stories; and
3. The tensions that developed between teacher and student expectations.

As the semester progressed, students drew upon memories of and examples from their own experiences. They identified tensions that existed between school as an ideal and what they and/or their parents expect from school and their experiences in school. As mentioned earlier, romantic notions of school as an equal playing field fell away as students wrote about being bullied by teachers, afraid to ask for help, and tracked into remedial-level classes, or not given information about how to pursue higher education. These memories were often in contradiction to students' views about what education should provide. At the same time, they talked about schools as places where they had friends and select teachers who recognized their talents and abilities. They grappled with knowing that they were capable, yet understanding that schools were not always places where their capabilities would be identified and/or valued. These tensions were also highlighted as students wrote about what they hoped getting a college education might mean to their future possibilities. Education was discussed as having the potential to help them fulfill goals and dreams, but school was a place where they had also experienced marginalization.

The second tension unfolded as students narrated their experiences differently, and sometimes contradictorily, in their various assignments. Their different iterations revealed their struggles with what they came to term as "boxes" that they were put in and, at times, put themselves in. Several times in class and in their writings, students discussed the limitations of identity categories that failed to signify how they see themselves in the world. They were frustrated by categories of race, sexuality, religion, and gender that they were expected to check on university and scholarship applications, for example, and/or categories that the university placed them into in order to account for them. These categories inadequately expressed their multiple and shifting identities. They were eager to queer widely accepted identity categories, yet could not escape them. However, students also expressed very clearly their desire to claim identity categories for themselves. There were tensions between wanting to claim, know, and understand themselves and maintain connections to families[2] and communities that identified in particular ways, and feeling boxed in by the ways in which these identifications essentialized them.

They expressed these tensions in varying ways in different layers of their narratives. For example, many shared stories of being racially and/or ethnically misrecognized. As they shared these experiences in class and in their writings, the students worked to employ both their critical and their queer lenses. They questioned the necessity of simplistic, essentializing identity markers, and highlighted the ways in which they did not work for them, either because they are mixed-race, or because people commonly assume their identity to be something other than what it is. They complicated the normative drive to claim a coherent identity by sharing a wide range of feelings about being misrecognized. One biracial student talked of her ability to pass in many different racial and/or ethnic circles due to what she termed her "racially ambiguous appearance." She claimed that this helped her gain access to and find acceptance in multiple communities. At the same time, though, she expressed pain in being unidentifiable as belonging in the very community that made up "half" of her identity, and she wavered between staunchly claiming this piece of her identity and embracing her "ambiguity."

Identity categories and the way students took them up also came into tension in class discussions. In one discussion, spanning multiple sessions, students talked about understanding the need for outreach services for marginalized groups on campus, but expressed limitations associated with the assumptions that were made about them, their needs, and who could best provide services to them as students. They worried about the tokenism that Lee (2001) discussed, but also understood that within systems of education, where they are still on the margins, outreach services provide essential resources. The metaphor of the box, which they used over and over throughout the class, reflected both the boxes that they were supposed to check to indicate "who they are" for the university, and also the sense of being put in a box that they could not get out of. This became particularly salient as they critiqued the essentialism inherent in identity categories, and the suggestion that these categories allow us to really know anything about someone. What became clear was that although identity categories are insufficient to describe their multiple and shifting selves, students both employed and contested them in the layers of their narratives. That is, while students often rejected identity categories in class dialogues, they utilized them, mostly unproblematically, in their critical education narratives, and usually reworked or complicated them in their drawings, self-portraits, and class presentations.

Finally, the third tension was students' resistance to traditional aspects of assignment structures and deadlines. While we were already flexible with deadlines and expectations, students pushed back, and reworked assignments for their own purposes. As noted earlier, students often brought in popular culture and current events as a way to talk about their lives and issues that were important to them. Oftentimes, this diverted class discussions from outside texts that they were assigned to read for class, and/or shifted the discussions we had planned. As instructors, we tried to refocus the discussions, and at other times, went in the directions students had taken the dialogue, and tried to work in the materials or particular concepts we planned to discuss. This was exciting and frustrating. Just as we pushed students outside of their comfort zones, they did the same with us. This meant that sometimes tensions developed, particularly when we employed our power as instructors to redirect the conversation, or to insist that they complete overdue assignments. In our concluding section, we offer reflections about what we learned from the class—lessons we take into our future endeavors as teachers, and that we believe provide insight for other educators looking to use critical histories and narratives in classrooms.

Dialoguing Final Thoughts

Writing hurts. (Behar, 1995, pp. 23)

The final assignment for the class was for students to revisit their written critical education narratives to examine the discourses that they employed in telling their own stories. We asked them to analyze their narratives, considering the concepts and theories we had talked about over the semester, as well as dialogues from class. In some ways, students were deeply engaged in and savvy about critiquing power relations and discourses, but we had to challenge them in (re)reading and reworking their own narratives. As part of this process, students were required to meet with one of us so that we could discuss the themes in their stories and provide individual mentoring on specific aspects of their writing.

Still, it was difficult for them to identify the hegemonic discourses they relied upon in telling their own stories. As instructors, we struggled through these tensions, debriefing with each other after each class, discussing assignments, and continually strategizing about how to meet the needs of students while also working to accomplish goals we had set for the class. The following reflection occurred via e-mail as we thought about our experiences:

Kim: So I think that to some extent our desire as instructors was to get them to a place where they were at least for moments reading their own narratives queerly (see Britzman, 1995 pp. 164–5), but I don't know that any of the students got there... I think that there were brief moments of slippage where they went there in their speaking, but not in their writing. What does this say about critical education histories as written artifacts that might reify rather than queer and what does this mean for us as educators?

Barbara: And also, I think, what does it say about writing as scary? Dangerous? In that once something is inscribed (and handed in) it becomes cemented, unchangeable—a commitment that perhaps students weren't willing to make in defining themselves because it then becomes another box. Words in conversation can be more fluid and moving. Does/can 'writing oneself into existence' defy queerness and fluidity, limiting the existences that are then possible?

When we met later and discussed this in more detail, we concluded that as instructors committed to bringing our own and students' personal experiences, histories, and narrative writing into our classrooms it is essential to find balance between structure and flexibility. In attempting to queer classrooms, we must always be ready to not be ready for the ways that students will both resist and work to queer classrooms. Particularly in trying to break down traditional teacher-student power relations, we realized that students' visions of what this looks like were sometimes different from our own as instructors. We are left with the necessity of balancing our students' needs and desires, our responsibilities to provide tools to help them to succeed in higher education, and our own desires to reimagine, rework, and queer education.

The tensions between breaking apart and rethinking education while at the same time preparing students to succeed within the walls of a traditional institution are problematics that we cannot get around or understate. It is the central tension of living in a world where the queer and poststructural feminist theories we employ and espouse offer us possibilities of a different kind of education that is more respectful and inclusive of our students' knowledges, while at the same time existing in a world, nation, and campus where hegemonic rules remain firmly in place. We strive to prepare our students to face the realities of higher education, while also offering the vision that there can be different ways of teaching and learning.

We are left convinced of the importance of queering narratives and the usefulness of such narratives for the broader purpose of queering education. Specifically, we found that a multilayered approach in which students developed multiple tellings of their stories provided rich and critical narratives. These narratives were not linear or seamless, and they did not suggest a coherent storyline. However, we believe that they provided room for students to express the complexity of their lives, experiences, and identities.

The queering of educational narratives also facilitated and was facilitated by the queering of education more broadly. For example, conducting the class in a different space, and positioning ourselves as colearners in the class, made it possible for students to rethink the way they learn and the ways they are taught in school. Positioning students as central to the course of study and asking them to engage in the construction of course materials (i.e., their narratives as texts), and to take a more active role in determining how the class would proceed, was a way of queering education.

Finally, we recognize that each classroom will be different. Each instructor has different pedagogical styles and varied goals, in terms of content and objectives. This chapter is not meant to be prescriptive, but, rather, to suggest how critical education histories and narratives can allow for movement and flexibility in meeting the needs of educators and their students.

Notes

1. Students at times embraced and at other times critiqued racial categories as ways to identify themselves. Several described themselves as having complex, hybrid identities. This will be taken up later in the chapter. However, specific identifications will not be detailed, in order to protect the confidentiality of the students in the class.
2. We note here that students in the class talked about family in varying ways. At times, family was talked about as biological families (though not necessarily in traditional Western terms of nuclear biological families). There were also times when students talked about families more fluidly to include chosen families.

References

Behar, R. (1995). Introduction: Out of exile. In R. Behar & D. Gordon (Eds.), *Women writing culture* (pp. 1–29). Berkeley, CA: University of California Press.

Britzman, D. (1993). Beyond rolling models: Gender and multicultural education. In S. K. Biklen and D. Pollard (Eds.), *Gender and education: Ninety-second yearbook of the*

National Society for the Study of Education (pp. 25–42). Chicago, IL: University of Chicago Press.

———. (1995). Is there a queer pedagogy? Or, stop reading straight. *Educational Theory*, *45*(2), 151–166.

———. (2000). The question of belief. In E. St. Pierre & W. Pillow (Eds.), *Working the ruins: Feminist poststructural theory and methods in education* (pp. 27–40). New York, NY: Routledge.

———. (2012). Queer pedagogy and its strange techniques. In E. R. Meiners & T. Quinn (Eds.), *Sexualities in education: A reader* (pp. 292–308). New York, NY: Peter Lang.

Lee, J-Y. (2001). Beyond bean counting. In B. Findlen (Ed.), *Listen up: Voices from the next feminist generation* (pp. 67–73). Seattle, WA: Seal Press.

McKoy, K. (2000). White noise—The sound of epidemic: Reading/writing a climate of intelligibility around the "crisis" of difference. In E. St. Pierre & W. Pillow (Eds.), *Working the ruins: Feminist poststructural theory and methods in education* (pp. 237–257). New York, NY: Routledge.

Miller, J. L. (1998). Autobiography as a queer curriculum practice. In W. F. Pinar (Ed.), *Queer theory in education* (pp. 365–373). Mahwah, NJ: Lawrence Erlbaum.

Nash, R. (2007). *Liberating scholarly writing: The power of personal narrative*. New York, NY: Teachers College Press.

Richardson, L. (1997). *Fields of play: Constructing an academic life*. New Brunswick, NJ: Rutgers University Press.

Sleeter, C. (n.d.). *Critical family history theory*. Critical Family History. Retrieved from https: //sites.google.com/a/christinesleeter.org/critical-family-history/Home/critical-family-history-theory

5

A Student-Teacher Testimonio: Reflexivity, Empathy, and Pedagogy

Judith Flores Carmona and Aymee Malena Luciano

In this chapter, we employ self-reflexivity as a crucial element to our pedagogical practices in a *testimonios* course taught at a predominantly White campus. We look back at our participation in the course, *Testimonio*: Chicana and Latina Epistemology and Pedagogy, across two semesters, Fall 2010 and Fall 2011. During the first offering, we were involved as student (Aymee) and teacher (Judith), but shifted to coteachers in the subsequent semester. This course was taught at a small, private, liberal arts college in New England. In the course, we asked students to become critically conscious, to achieve conscientization, or what pedagogue Freire referred to as *conscientização*. This concept, developed by Brazilian pedagogue and educational theorist, Paulo Freire, and grounded in Marxist critical theory, focuses on achieving an in-depth understanding of the world. Grounded in the philosophy that individuals have "the right to *say his or her own word, to name the world*" (Freire, 1995, p. 15), as educators our purpose is to make it "possible for people to enter the historical process as responsible Subjects" in order to achieve *conscientização* (Freire, 1995, p. 18). Rarely, however, do we as educators move toward this conscientization and "new awareness," not only of our pedagogical practices, but also an awareness of "self." Critical consciousness also includes taking action against the oppressive elements in one's life that are illuminated by that understanding. In our course, the reading and writing, telling and sharing of *testimonios* challenged the facilitators to reflect on the potential for our pedagogical practices and the use of *testimonio* in academia to contest power relations in the classroom.

In this chapter we ask, through teaching a *testimonios* course, how did we become transformed? How did we move together toward critical consciousness and toward *conscientização*? We will elaborate on the two semesters Judith taught the *testimonios* course. In Fall 2010, Aymee took the course as a student, and in Fall 2011, Aymee was the teaching assistant for the course. We share self-reflexive pieces combined with a reflection of our teacher-student pedagogical practices. Was *testimonio* epistemology and pedagogy a successful pedagogical practice in achieving conscientization? Through the production of digital *testimonios*, informed by Chicana/Latina feminist theorists, how did the students "theorize" their lived experience, their "theory in the flesh" (Moraga, 2002, p. 21)?

Our pedagogical insights as student and teacher will be presented in this chapter by first sharing how we both arrived at the small liberal arts college, and how we personally draw from pedagogies of the home in educational settings (Delgado Bernal, 2001). We first situate our positionality in the course and at the institution where the course was taught. We then share our reflections about the course during Fall 2010 and in Fall 2011 and discuss how we employed *testimonio* pedagogy in the classroom. We conclude by sharing our thoughts about the pedagogical possibilities that the genre of Latina *testimonio* affords us in the classroom, and we attempt to answer the questions we pose above.

The Campus

Hampshire College, located in Amherst, Massachusetts, is an independent, innovative, liberal arts institution and member of the Five College consortium. The sister campuses include Amherst College, Mount Holyoke College, Smith College, and the University of Massachusetts, Amherst. This small, private, liberal arts college is recognized for its progressive, student-centered educational approach. There are no traditional majors, and students embark on self-created and self-designed educational pathways or programs of study (Wenk & Luschen, in press). For example, students can merge Latina/o Studies and Feminist Studies or Queer Studies and educational issues to create a concentration—an interdisciplinary focus of study may resemble a traditional major, though it is not field specific.

According to the Hampshire College website, in the 2011 academic year there were 1,500 students enrolled, and the student-faculty ratio was twelve to one. The average size of class is 18, and the population of students of color is listed as 18 percent. Six percent are designated as international students.[1] In Spring 2012, the faculty demographics for Hampshire College were described as follows:

Faculty with a work visa would be counted as international. Faculty with dual citizenship, resident aliens, or naturalized citizens are all counted as domestic faculty. Among all full-time faculty, 21.51% are faculty of color. Including non-full-time faculty, 21.21% are faculty of color. The numbers are very different if we disaggregate based on rank. 34.38% of assistant professors are people of color, and 28% of associate professors are people of color. Only 3.23% of our full professors are people of color. In terms of sex, 51.14% of our faculty are female. The proportion is also higher at the level of assistant professors, where 56.24% of our faculty is female.[2]

The college has been making efforts to recruit and retain faculty of color, but it continues to be a predominately White institution with a predominately White faculty. The introduction of Chicana/Latina feminist thought through our course offered a new, and in some cases, challenging lens by which White students could read their experiences. For students of color, given their position in a predominantly White institution (PWI), this was a space of validation, a sense of home and belonging.

The Class and the Students

The *testimonios*[3] course was about the *testimonios* and autobiographical writings of and by Latinas in the United States and transnationally. Chicanas and Latinas have inscribed their lived experiences in academia as holders and creators of knowledge to counter the double jeopardy of racism and sexism (Delgado Bernal, 2002). Life stories are told through many forms: *testimonios*, memoirs, *autohistorias*, autobiographies and autobiographical fiction, oral histories and short stories, poetry and poetic prose pieces, essays, and audio stories. Drawing from these sources of knowledge, in this course we explored feminist epistemologies and their relation to pedagogy, and problematized traditional knowledge claims and objectivity. The course focused on Chicana/Latina feminist theories, the empirical educational research that draws upon these theories, and *testimonios* as method, epistemology, and pedagogy. Delgado Bernal, Burciaga, and Flores Carmona (2012) wrote the following on the genre of Latina *testimonio*:

> *Testimonio* is and continues to be an approach that incorporates political, social, historical, and cultural histories that accompany one's life experiences as a means to bring about change through consciousness-raising. In bridging individuals with collective histories of oppression, a story of marginalization is re-centered to elicit social change. *Testimonio* differs from oral history or autobiography in that it involves the participant in a critical reflection of their personal experience within particular sociopolitical realities. (p. 364)

Among the questions that we examined in the course are those concerning knowledge production, sexual politics, connections between mind-body-spirit, voice, and (re)presentation and truth. Using *testimonio* as a teaching tool, we explored the diversity and commonality of Chicana and Latina experiences. *Testimonio* pedagogy not only names the experiences of being Latinas in a nationalist, racist, ageist, classist, and sexist society, in which Latinas/os are generally seen as outsiders—"others"—but it centers the knowledge and our pedagogies of the home (Delgado Bernal, 2001). Pedagogies of the home, such as the wisdom passed on through oral history practices, extends critical pedagogies by placing "cultural knowledge and language at the forefront to better understand lessons learned from the home space and local communities" (Delgado Bernal, 2001, p. 624).

Testimonios allowed us to teach and learn from the stories that speak about colonization and migration, about being racialized, sexualized, and homogenized. *Testimonios* explain what it is like to inhabit more than one culture and language at the same time, to be a transnational, to negotiate responsibility, to name desire, and live one's sexuality. *Testimonios* allow us to speak about being daughters, mothers, romantic partners, providers, workers, social activists, thinkers, educators, leaders, role models, and creative artists. They celebrate and affirm commitments to family, community, and future generations. At the same time, they break with oppressive traditions and build new political, theoretical, artistic, and spiritual pathways toward wholeness, toward mind-body-spirit cohesion. *Testimonios* highlight how theorizing from one's own experience and writing one's own story have produced new knowledge(s), recognition, and forms of empowerment. As *testimonialistas*[4] we experience how memory, speaking, and writing are linked to identity transformations, empowerment, and social change. By teaching, sharing, and writing *testimonios*, as critical pedagogues, we draw out deeper meanings and theorizing from personal experience and insight.

The life stories or the autohistorias we read name the experiences of being and living in a nationalist, racist, and sexist society, in which we are generally seen as outsiders. Some of the texts we read include: *Borderlands/ La Frontera: The New Mestiza* (Anzaldúa, 1987/1999); *Telling to Live: Latina Feminist Testimonios* (Latina Feminist Group, 2001); *Speaking From the Body: Latinas on Health and Culture* (Chabram-Dernersesian & de la Torre, 2008); *Las Hijas de Juan: Daughters Betrayed* (Mendez-Negrete, 2006); *Latina: Women's Voices from the Borderlands* (Castillo-Speed, 1995); and *This Bridge Called My Back: Writings by Radical Women of Color* (Moraga & Anzaldúa, 2002). Part of every class dialogue was devoted to sharing our own life experiences with each other, writing about them, drawing out deeper meanings, and always connecting lived experience to the theoretical tools offered by the scholars.

One of the goals of *testimonio* pedagogy is that the individual *testimonio* becomes part of denouncing a collective, oppressive condition. As the facilitators of the course, we had to be willing to share our lived experiences with the class. To share our own *testimonios* is a pedagogical practice that allows for a feeling of solidarity to develop in the class community. The process of teaching this course necessitates our constant reflexivity, a deep reading of the assigned texts, a close and empathetic reading of the *testimonios* the students write as they are moved or inspired by the class readings, and a constant reframing of the pedagogical practices we employ as facilitators. In thinking and reflecting back on both courses taught, we, and specifically Judith, became acutely aware of how, as pedagogues, we must push ourselves toward *conscientização*.

Judith

I came to the genre of Latina *testimonio* in a course I took as an undergraduate with Dr. Rina Benmayor, in 1999. As a sophomore, still doubting that my knowledge was valid in higher education, the course opened my eyes and mind to recognize myself as a holder and producer of knowledge (Delgado Bernal, 2002). Since that first course, throughout my educational career, *testimonio* methodology and pedagogy have been instrumental in my development as a critical pedagogue. I employed *testimonio* methodology in my doctoral dissertation, and when I accepted the postdoctoral position at Hampshire College and had to design my courses, I knew I would teach a *testimonio* course.[5]

In Fall 2010, ten students participated in the *testimonio* course. This included one Dominican woman, one Puerto Rican woman, one mixed-race Latina (Cuban and Polish), a woman from Venezuela, one Salvadorian man, a second-generation Mexican American man, two Portuguese women, one Mexican Nicaraguan woman, and a Jewish woman who had worked for many years with and in Latina/o communities in the United States and abroad. One student came from Texas; all the others were from New England. The small, seminar-style class allowed for the students to almost immediately develop a sense of community, relationships of solidarity and familiarity with each other—they began to develop *confianza* (trust) as they intimately shared about their lives and co-facilitated class sessions. As a practice, in the middle of the semester, I meet one-on-one with each student to get to know them individually, and to find out how the class is going for them. In these sessions the students shared about their lives, about their overall academic progress, and about how it was the first time in their educational careers that they had ever taken a course that centered their epistemologies, and that drew from their pedagogies of the home. The course was allowing them to learn about and invoke "theory in the flesh" (Moraga, 2002, p. 21)—they were the primary source of knowledge, and they felt more than capable of successfully completing the course.

In the Fall 2011 semester, I had a different experience teaching the course. This time, I had a teaching assistant, Aymee, who had taken the course the previous year. When I walked into the classroom the first day of class, I must confess that I was struck by the number of students[6] and by the racial demographics of the class. This time, the class reflected the larger campus demographics—predominantly White and mostly women. Aymee and I realized that we had to rethink the syllabus and assignments, both because of the size of the class and the demographics of the students; we also had to think about how to employ *testimonio* pedagogy with a class of predominantly White students. We read more books and did more journaling rather than in-class sharing, and the students turned in more writing assignments. Focusing and drawing from the books was necessary because of the size of the class, and also to help the White students understand Chicana and Latina pedagogies of the home. The White students usually shared their thoughts and experiences in class discussion, while students of color shared among themselves or in meetings with me or with Aymee. The fact that students were not getting to know each other through the sharing of their *testimonios* in class did not allow them to create a sense of community until the end of the semester.

It was poignant to see the shift occur in the classroom and in the students. We had just finished reading *Speaking From the Body: Latinas on Health and Culture* (Chabram-Dernersesian & de la Torre, 2008) and the students, Aymee, and I were all able to relate to many themes in the book. Issues of chronic illness, body image, stress, pain, struggle, survival, familial expectations, among others, began to surface as topics of conversation. An overwhelming sharing of *testimonios* began to take place, emotions surfaced for the first time, and students who had not yet connected across their differences found that they had more in common than they thought. The students who had been afraid to share their personal stories suddenly opened up, and the relationships among the students developed into relationships of solidarity and shared struggle. At the end of the Fall 2011 semester, a White student shared the following in the course evaluation:[7]

As a student who had previously studied anthropology, this class opened my eyes to how much current ways of thinking and knowing are informed by colonialism. I appreciated the way in which we did not just conceptualize different ways of learning, but enacted them in student led presentations and self-written testimonios. However, I also found this class to be extraordinarily difficult emotionally because the readings and the stories were too painful. As somebody who is coming to terms with a highly traumatic personal history, I did not want to open myself up to being vulnerable. At first I didn't feel that the space was intimate or safe, and it was strange to bring my wounded parts into an academic setting, especially in such a large class. This class pushed me into an in between space, where I carried the rest of myself with me and I shared openly. I found the final paper especially helpful in organizing my ideas about testimonios and positionality. I am grateful to have had a chance to be in the course, and I am proud of my growth, academically and as a person. (Student, Fall 2011)

The fact that many of the White students shared from a source of pain and struggle showed the students of color that they had more in common than they believed throughout the semester.

In Fall 2011, the students had the option of producing a digital *testimonio* or a written piece, an illustration, poetry, or prose to be included in an anthology that would be printed and given to all the students. The pieces that would be included for the anthology could be submitted as "*anonima*/anonymous." After having read eight *testimonios* per student and helping many of them decide which piece to produce and/or publish I was emotionally exhausted from the painful stories, but also transformed by them. Most importantly, I changed my perspective about the "privilege" I had assumed was centered in the classroom. Based on salient identities, as teachers, we sometimes forget that students bring their "whole" selves into our classrooms, with many stories imprinted on their bodies. We must acknowledge their holistic lives, and not make assumptions about the privilege or oppression the students have experienced. I was moved to be self-reflexive, each week, each time I read their *testimonios*. I was not ready to read what the students had to share, and I was pushed to continually rethink my pedagogical practices in order to get to know the students and to be a better teacher. I wrote a piece for the anthology we produced in class. I wrote it right after I had read the last *testimonios*, and in this piece I admit to not being ready to read such painful trauma. This piece pushes me to continue being self-reflexive as an integral part of my pedagogy.

I Wasn't Ready for Your Truths. Professor Debra Busman wrote an essay titled, "You gotta be ready for some serious truth to be spoken" (2002):

I have to admit to her I wasn't ready!
I was not ready. *No estaba lista*
No estaba preparada para leer ni escuchar tu verdad, sus verdades[8]
I was not ready to read about pain so deep so tangible
When I experienced in my body, *el dolor*,[9] as I read your *testimonio*, I cried out loud and then I couldn't sleep
I was not ready to read that the White woman I thought of as privileged has endured *dolor y trauma tan profundo o peor que el mio*[10]
NO estaba lista para saber de la violación, de tus heridas, de tus sueños y pesadillas[11]
I was not ready to read
"I fell in love with my oppressor"
"I cannot sleep"
"I hate my body"
"I am confused"
"I am afraid"
"I was raped"
"I could be one of *Las Hijas de Juan*"
"My mother looked the other way"
"I detached myself from the pain, *anestesiado casi toda mi vida*"[12]
"ONLY YOU can read this Judith"
One day I had to be vulnerable like you and share my fears

I thank you for telling
If telling is healing, I hope we have all begun to *sanar nuestras almas y espíritus*[13]
Papelitos guardados ahora en mi corazón y en mi alma[14]
Gracias

Aymee

Going into this class in Fall 2010 I did not know what to expect. I did not know what epistemology or pedagogy meant, but I had read the description of the course, and I became very interested in drawing from the experience of oppressed groups to learn in the classroom, especially as an Afro-Latina from the Dominican Republic. This type of class is not one that I had experienced before, and I appreciated it very much. It allowed me to see how my experience and my life are validated as sources of knowledge and knowledge production.

Our class was very small. We were about ten students and most of us identified as students of color, Latina/os. We were eight women and two men. While some of us knew each other from outside of the class, some of us had never talked to each other. In order to share our stories we had to create a safe space. At first it seemed difficult to create a space where we could speak freely about our experiences and trust each other. I think that because it was such a small group it became easier for us to begin to share and open up in class. Also, for me it became easier to share because I was surrounded by other students of color who could easily relate to my experiences, and I could relate to theirs. Again, because the class was so small, it gave us all the opportunity to speak in class and share what was on our minds—how we were doing, what we thought about the texts, how we related to the text—and to talk openly and freely about different topics related to the readings and our experiences. We started each class by listening to each other's "how are you?" answers—Judith made sure to ask us each class session about our overall well-being and state of mind. This also gave us the opportunity to build community in the classroom, even the teacher.

The writing of our *testimonios* was a longer process in the Fall 2010 course than in the course in which I was the teaching assistant. We read fewer books and wrote less in Fall 2010. We concentrated mostly on in-class discussions during the semester, and ended up writing our *testimonio* during the end part of the semester. We all got the opportunity to facilitate class discussion one day of the semester. I felt that just through discussions, we learned so much from and about each other, and we all brought different topics to the table, from education, to immigration, sexual education, and other issues. It was interesting to see how most of our experiences of being Latina/os connected; we understood each other. In Fall 2010 I participated as a student, and I noticed that I had a space where I felt comfortable enough to speak up, and that what I had to say was valid. This was rarely true in previous courses, and even in other courses I was taking at the time. I was able to connect my own experience to everything we were reading and discussing, and it was a very empowering moment. As a student in the course, not only was I learning, but I was also teaching by sharing my thoughts and experiences. We all learned from each other.

Reflexivity on Being a Student in the Classroom

Hampshire College is very open to students taking whatever course they want to take. As a third-year student who just got back from studying abroad in Cuba, I had no idea which course I was going to choose to complete my list of courses for Fall semester 2010. I have always been interested in courses that examine the experiences of Latina/os in the United States, thus, the first week of classes my advisor recommended a course that had just been put on the list for Hampshire courses: *Testimonio*: Chicana and Latina Epistemology and Pedagogy. It had an interesting title, and it had to do with Latinas, why not? I signed up for the course without really reading the course description. All I knew was that we were going to be talking about the experiences and everyday life of Latinas, my type of course. In my opinion and experience, there are not enough Latina/o Studies courses at Hampshire

College, especially in this field of study and taught by Latina/o faculty. I was extremely excited about this one, even though I did not know the professor, since she was new to Hampshire.

The first day in that classroom, with about ten students, was completely different from any other courses I had taken at Hampshire, or the Five Colleges, or even in Cuba. For once, I was not the only student of color, and a few of my close friends were in the classroom. I felt safe. This was the first course where I was not quiet all the time, where I was open to sharing my stories and participating. This was the first time where I felt like the protagonist of the themes we were covering. I was able to relate to almost every reading and every discussion. I felt as though the course was created for ME, and for people like me. The readings and authors we covered empowered me, they helped me recognize the knowledge that exists in our Latina/o communities. Everything we did, read, wrote, and discussed got through to me and made me realize my position as an educated, immigrant Latina. I realized I had power, and it was in my voice. The course pushed me to talk about issues I had left in the dark because I preferred to cover up the oppressions (external and internal) rather than to bring them out. This had been the only class during my college experience where I felt comfortable enough to participate. I had stories to share, knowledge to impart, and knowledge to take in like a sponge.

Have you ever been in a classroom where you are not the minority? Where your stories are being shared and where you are the holder and creator of knowledge rather than the subject being studied? I was surrounded by students who looked like me, and I wanted to share and hear their stories. I did not fear being judged or someone taking pity on me. This was the perfect classroom. Small size in students, a professor who saw us as contributors to the classroom and did not see us as or make us feel inferior. She was also a professor who was willing to learn with us and from us. It was, and has been, the best experience I have ever had in a classroom in higher education. I always wished for more classes like these, but they are limited in a predominantly White institution.

Experience as a Teacher's Assistant in Fall 2011

My experience as a teacher's assistant was different from my experience as a student in the *testimonios* course. The number of students enrolled doubled, and I believe that the large number of students affected the way the students interacted with each other and with the texts and articles. As much as Judith and I wanted to create a safe space to share our stories and listen to each other closely, I think that the size of the class did not allow for us to completely do so.

The students in this course read and wrote more than I did when I took the course. The reading materials helped them to think about different experiences they might have had. Then they would write a one-to-two-page *testimonio* for every reading, which allowed them to have different *testimonios* to choose from for their final work. Unlike students in the first course, they were thinking and writing *testimonios* from early in the semester, which I believe made it a little easier for them to write their *testimonios* and theorize them.

The number of students of color in the course this time around was significantly smaller than the number of students of color when I took it. Maybe a quarter of the class was students of color. Remembering my extraordinary experience as a student in the previous course, I did not feel as comfortable as I did before. I think that if we would have created a space for all of us to talk more, maybe my level of comfort would have increased, but the class size did not allow for this communication. Alas, as a TA, I did not participate as much as I did as a student. However, students did approach me outside of class to discuss the midterm or the final.

On many occasions I wanted to let the students take the stage, rather than imposing my ideas, thoughts, and experience. Also, since the students facilitated in each class, the professor did not have as much participation as she had before. During the time I took the course she was able to speak more. Judith would provide us with the theoretical background, and the students would facilitate the readings more closely. The fact that we did not get to openly share our experiences meant that the professor alone read all the *testimonios*. I imagine how much knowledge of the students' experiences she gained, but then again, how stressful this could have been for her. I tried reading some of the *testimonios* myself, and I could not read them all. They were too powerful, too intense, and the stories some of the students were sharing were too strong for me to even read. The books we read in Fall 2011 included and addressed issues such as domestic violence, incest, trauma, body image and health, rape, and exclusion, to name a few. You can imagine, then, the testimonios that emerged from these readings exploring trauma.

If we had been able to share the *testimonios* openly in class, in a close, confidential, safe space, I think it would not have been so hard on the professor, and we would have been able to build community and work in solidarity. But then again, the topics were very heavy and strong. Having so many White students made me wonder if their experiences were considered *testimonios*, because I considered us, the students of color, the subaltern. I also realized how uncomfortable the students of color were with having so many White students in the class. I was uncomfortable myself, but I think this is where we can begin to build communities and solidarity. I realized that even though their skin gives them privilege, they still have marginalized identities. It was amazing to realize how we all were able to relate to one another through different experiences, even though we came from completely different backgrounds.

On Becoming a Teacher's Assistant. As a Division III student[15] at Hampshire College, I was required to TA a course. I had never felt prepared enough to TA any course at Hampshire College, no matter how well I had done in the course. When I realized that Professor Judith Flores Carmona was teaching the *testimonios* course again, I immediately messaged her about being her teacher's assistant. This was the only class in my Hampshire career that I felt completely prepared and comfortable enough to assist. Perhaps it was because of my comfort and confidence as a student in the classroom, or because I knew I could work very well with Professor Flores Carmona. Everything I learned when I took the course was still fresh in my head, plus I was creating a thesis using *testimonios*; therefore I found it helpful to talk to the students about the genre and re-listen to everything I was taught.

Testimonio as Sentipensante Pedagogy: Possibility to Connect Across and Beyond Differences

> Sentipensante pedagogy is integrative in the sense that it focuses on wholeness and non-duality. A key ontological principle of Sentipensante pedagogy is that it asks instructors to work with individuals as whole human beings—intellectual, social, emotional, and spiritual. (Rendón, 2009, pp. 134–135)

Testimonio as an example of *sentipensante* (sensing/thinking) pedagogy is about being able to grapple with and handle our secrets, our broken silences, and our truths. *Sentipensante* pedagogy, according to Laura I. Rendón (2009), "represents a teaching and learning approach based on wholeness, harmony, social justice, and liberation" (p. 132). In the course, students were asked to write themselves, to write about their experiences, to delve into the texts beyond the intellectual, and to make an emotional and spiritual connection to the *testimonios* they read. This connection allowed them to move beyond empathy, and to be able to write down their own *papelitos guardados*. The *testimonios* that were shared are stories about our bodies, about sexual violence, gender abuse, medicalization, body image, shame, illness, death, violence, *familia*, self-harm, trauma—all interwoven with hope, desire, imagination, re-claiming, resistance, self-love, growth, reflexivity, voice, and healing. Vizenor, in an interview with Coltelli (1990), said, "You can't understand the world without telling a story. There isn't any center to the world but a story" (p. 156). *Testimonio* guided us to hear an organic intellectual's knowledge that has not been privileged historically, or has been lost because of language barriers. These life histories, once narrated, help in the process of healing as the stories are uncovered to denounce inequitable treatment and allow us to connect across differences (Booker, 2002).

Teaching this course illuminates the difficulty and complexity of centering Latina epistemologies and pedagogy at a predominantly White campus, while also offering suggestions for how to build solidarity among students. As teachers, we foreground our approach to understanding feminist pedagogies and epistemologies in relation to education broadly defined, *educación*, and to our own subjectivities, lived experiences, circulating discourses, and pedagogical practices. We began the course by tracing the genealogy of *testimonio* and the characteristics of the genre of Latina *testimonio*, specifically. We read books that are about *testimonio* and that tell *testimonios*. Throughout the course we emphasized the *Latinidades*, the diversity in Latina/o communities, and we discussed our diverse epistemologies and pedagogical approaches.

The course was grounded in Chicana and Latina feminisms. Latina and Chicana writings have revolutionized and transformed feminist theory, and the genre of Latina *testimonio* has shifted our understanding of *Latinidades*. The concepts of the "borderlands," of simultaneous oppressions, of "new *mestiza*" and "*nepantla*" (Anzaldúa, 1999) identities and Latina feminisms grew out of Chicana and Latina writers reflecting on their experiences as women of color in the US. In the *testimonio* course, we explored the diversity and commonality of Chicana and Latina experiences, and we forged the possibility of engaging diverse students through *testimonio* sharing.

Testimonio pedagogy permits the teacher and the students to talk and move toward an understanding of our identities, our fragmented lives, and the ways that we constantly negotiate this bodily fragmentation. Students listen, connect, engage, and support one another by sharing their *testimonios* of pain, struggle, survival, trauma, and resistance. As noted in another student evaluation, *testimonios* center the voices of all who have been ostracized, or marginalized, and foreground lived experience in academia.

> It is the only course I have taken that has been effective in truly teaching that the personal is political and that the political is personal. I learned specifically and

rigorously about Latina identities and epistemologies, engaging in a wide variety of material by Latina feminists, and by women and queer feminists of color. I feel that I learned on an academic level about many issues including the genre of testimonio, the discourse around testimonio, its contested nature, historical origins, as well as about identity in terms of race, class, gender, sexuality, ability, and religion, as well as other themes such as marginalization, speaking from the subaltern, institutional oppression, internalized oppression, and reflexivity. I also learned on a deeply personal level, through undertaking personal storytelling projects that were transformative in my own life. (Student, Fall 2011)

Testimonio pedagogy allows people to connect across social positions, across differences, across language. *Testimonio* pedagogy facilitates opportunities to learn and perform aspects of *testimonio*, including issues surrounding reflexivity, collectivity, social awareness, and issues of power imbalance, to name a few. *Testimonio* can be viewed as a "pedagogy of possibility" (Aveling, 2001, p. 46, as cited in Sleeter, 2008, p. 116). It is interdisciplinary in nature; *autohistorias* become contextualized, lived experiences (body/mind and theory of the flesh), and learning takes place in a holistic way. This pedagogy of possibility lends itself to the development of critical consciousness, where the *testimonialistas* are able to bear witness to their realities using multiple mediums of expression. In doing so, their stories "tell how our bodies are maps of oppression, of institutional violence and stress, of exclusion, objectification, and abuse" (Latina Feminist Group, 2001, p. 12). When *testimonios* are heard and shared, the lived realities do not succumb to the "alchemy of erasure" (Latina Feminist Group, 2001).

Testimonio pedagogy lends itself to incorporating students' epistemologies, to creating spaces of solidarity, and to connecting across our differences. Through reading the work of Chicana and Latina scholars, all students are able to engage and search for their own *papelitos guardados*. This theory in the flesh, drawing from memory, allows all, students and the teacher, to connect empathically—the pain shared in *testimonios* helps us to listen to each other in different ways. The Mayan Tojolabales shared wise words about listening deeply: "*En lugar de decir yo te dije, dicen, yo dije, tu escuchaste*" (Lenkersdorf, 2008, p. 13)[16]—listening involves not being moved to speak but rather to listen intently for the lessons to be learned. "*El escuchar, pues, nos abre las puertas para entrar en otra cultura. Al hablar con la gente, nos pueden abrir su corazón, explicar sus problemas y alegrías y hacernos participar en el mundo que viven*"[17] (Lenkersdorf, 2008, p. 25). *Al escucharnos mutuamente, emprendimos un dialogo, nos emparejamos*[18]— when we listen to each other, we engage in dialogue and we become aligned—we listen to one another on equal ground. Indeed, to read and listen deeply we must "systematically [attend] to the many voices embedded in a person's expressed experience" (Gilligan, Spencer, Weinberg, & Bertsch, 2003, p. 157). According to Gilligan et al. (2003), we must engage in re-listening in order to get at the "collectivity of different voices that compose the voice of any given person" and the "myriad ways in which human society and history shape the voice and thus leave their imprints on the human soul" (p. 157).

While the students and the teacher may come from different social locations, when *testimonio* pedagogy is employed the sharing is conducive to building relationships not imagined in other spaces.

> I think I have grown a lot over the time of this course. The theories that we read about relating specifically to Latinas affected me on a personal level because I could connect to the readings. I gained confidence in speaking in class because my comments were always well-received and appreciated. The *testimonio* genre was something new at the beginning of the semester but it is now a form of art that I am very interested in especially as a tool for social change and storytelling. Some of the terms/concepts and theories that I am taking away from the course are nepantla, organic intellectual, pedagogies of the home, ethnography, and autobioethnography. (Student, Fall 2010)

Testimonio pedagogy moves us toward an understanding of suffering, not as an individual experience, but as a communal process of teaching and learning. This type of pedagogy allows a naming of ourselves, naming of our pain, naming of feelings and biases. The way that people read, connect, engage, draw, and get inspired to share their own *papelitos guardados* legitimizes the theory of *testimonio*—legitimizes organic knowledge(s) and an organic method of merging theory and practice into praxis. The *feminista* praxis of listening to stories of struggle, survival, resistance, and oppression forces the student and teacher to come inside the classroom as "whole"—we do not shed our identities at the door. *Testimonio* as *sentipensante* pedagogy (Rendón, 2009),

> [V]alues the individual's quest for knowledge yet also acknowledges the importance of dialogue and the shared construction of meaning. A sensing/thinking pedagogy also strives for balance and harmony; there is consonance between inner work, focusing on emotional and spiritual nurturance, and outer work, involving service and action in the world (p. 135).

This critical pedagogy comes out of the need to tell, and when connected to Chicana and Latina theoretical constructs, we are able to allow new theories of the flesh to spring from our bodies. *Testimonio* is often seen as a form of expression that comes out of intense repression or struggle. Through *testimonio* one can denounce the brutal abuses toward family and community. For example, *testimonio* challenges silence and reclaims space and discourses often silenced or marginalized by dominant discourses. *Testimonio* pedagogy emerges out of oppression to legitimize our realities and experiences, our ways of knowing and ways of telling, a way of telling to live (Latina Feminist Group, 2001).

Concluding Thoughts: Reflections on Pedagogy

Through *testimonio* we continue to become critically conscious teachers. To teach the genre of Latina *testimonio* means that we trace the history and legacy of *testimonio*, and that we embark on a *sentipensante* pedagogical approach that bridges the mind-body-spirit split in Western education. For students and for the "teacher," *testimonio* recognizes and asserts our epistemologies in academia. We are able to connect across shared *testimonios*. There is an intimacy in the pedagogy—or a connection between the private and public spheres. Together, teacher and students simultaneously and collectively create wider meanings through *testimonio*.

The *testimonios* course transformed our pedagogy, as we connected and empathized when we listened to each other's pain and theory in the flesh. Especially in Fall 2011, we moved together toward critical consciousness and toward *conscientização* when Aymee and Judith employed self-reflexivity each day and after the course was over. *Testimonio* epistemology and pedagogy can be a successful pedagogical practice in achieving conscientization, because students and teachers can "theorize" and draw from lived experience. We center our knowledge(s) at the core of the teaching and learning. This embodied learning grants us pedagogical possibilities with White students and communities of color alike.

Testimonio validates the lived experience and epistemologies of historically oppressed groups, and the *testimonio* itself moves into becoming a counterstory that disrupts master narratives that are often seeking a single, positivist "Truth" in educational spaces (Solórzano & Yosso, 2002). Further, "*testimonio* emphasizes the validity of experiential or lived knowledge" and produces knowledge, "not as empirical facts, but as a strategy of cultural resistance and survival," and offers a way for the subaltern to "talk back" to dominant intellectuals (Brabeck, 2003, p. 256; hooks, 1984; Solórzano & Yosso, 2002). We understand *testimonio* pedagogy as a culturally specific tool for teaching and learning—that serves as a bridge for students and teachers across differences and toward relationships of solidarity. *Testimonio* as a pedagogical tool lends itself to healing and reconnecting people who have been fractured because of unethical relationships of power, and forces a reinvention and a radical repositioning of learner and teacher.

Notes

1. http://www.hampshire.edu/admissions/12331.htm
2. This quotation is from a report examining campus demographics sent to faculty at Hampshire College on March 2, 2012 by Jaime Davila, Special Presidential Assistant for Diversity.
3. See Delgado Bernal, Burciaga, & Flores Carmona, 2012 for readings on *testimonio* methodology and pedagogy.
4. *Testimonialistas* tell, write, and share *testimonies*.
5. As a doctoral student, I took a *testimonios* course with Dr. Dolores Delgado Bernal, and cofounded a student organization at University of Utah, called Latinas Telling *Testimonios*.
6. The class had doubled in size in comparison with the Fall 2010 semester.
7. The student quotes in this chapter came from end of semester course evaluations.
8. I was not ready, I was not prepared to read or listen to your truth, your truths.
9. The pain.
10. Profound pain and trauma maybe worse than mine.
11. I was not ready to know about the rape, about your wounds, about your dreams and nightmares.
12. Sedated, anesthetized most of my life.
13. To heal our souls and spirits.
14. Tucked away papers, secrets now in my heart and soul. Thank you.
15. A student in their final undergraduate year.
16. Instead of saying I told you, they say, I told, you listened.
17. When we listen we open doors into other cultures. When we talk and listen to people we open their hearts, we are able to listen to their struggles and joys, we begin to engage in their world with them.
18. When we listen to each other we engage in dialogue, we become aligned with one another.

Bibliography

Anzaldúa, G. (1999). *Borderlands/la frontera: The new mestiza* (2nd ed.). San Francisco, CA: Aunt Lute Books.

Booker, M. (2002). Stories of violence: Use of testimony in a support group for Latin American battered women. In L. H. Collins, M. R. Dunlap, & J. C. Chrisler (Eds.), *Charting a new course for feminist psychology* (pp. 307–321). Westport, CT: Praeger.

Brabeck, K. (2003). *Testimonio:* A strategy for collective resistance, cultural survival and building solidarity. *Feminism & Psychology, 13*(2), 252–258.

Busman, D. (2002). You gotta be ready for some serious truth to be spoken. *Social Justice, 29*(4), 150–152.

Castillo-Speed, L. (Ed.). (1995). *Latina: Women's voices from the borderlands.* New York, NY: Touchstone.

Chabram-Dernersesian, A., & de la Torre, A. (2008). *Speaking from the body: Latinas on health and culture.* Tucson, AZ: University of Arizona Press.

Coltelli, L. (1990). *Winged words: American Indian writers speak.* Lincoln, NE: University of Nebraska Press.

Delgado Bernal, D. (2001). Learning and living pedagogies of the home: The *mestiza* consciousness of Chicana students. *Qualitative Studies in Education, 14*(5), 623–639.

———. (2002). Critical race theory, Latino critical theory, and critical raced gendered epistemologies: Recognizing students of color as holders and creators of knowledge. *Qualitative Inquiry, 8*(1), 105–124.

Delgado Bernal, D., Burciaga, R., & Flores Carmona, J. (Eds.). (2012). Chicana/Latina testimonios: Methodologies, pedagogies, and political urgency [Special issue]. *Equity and Excellence in Education, 45*(3), 363–372.

Flores Carmona, J. (2010). Transgenerational *educación*: Latina mothers' everyday pedagogies of cultural citizenship in Salt Lake City, Utah (Unpublished doctoral dissertation). University of Utah, Salt Lake City, UT.

Freire, P. (1995). *Pedagogy of the oppressed*. New York, NY: Seabury.

Gilligan, C., Spencer, R., Weinberg, M. K., & Bertsch, T. (2003). On the listening guide: A voice-centered relational method. In P. M. Camic, J. E. Rhodes, & L. Yardley (Eds.), *Qualitative research in psychology: Expanding perspectives in methodology and design* (pp. 157–172). Washington, DC: American Psychological Association Press.

hooks, b. (1984). *Feminist theory: From margin to center*. Boston, MA: South End Press.

The Latina Feminist Group. (2001). *Telling to live: Latina feminist testimonios*. Durham, NC: Duke University Press.

Lenkersdorf, C. (2008). *Aprender a escuchar: Enseñanzas maya-tojolabales*. México, D.F., Mexico: Plaza y Valdés.

Méndez-Negrete, J. (2006). *Las hijas de Juan: Daughters betrayed*. Durham, NC: Duke University Press.

Moraga, C. (2002). Entering the lives of others: Theory in the flesh. In C. Moraga & G. E. Anzaldúa (Eds.), *This bridge called my back: Writings by radical women of color* (Rev. 3rd ed., p. 21). San Francisco, CA: Third Woman Press.

———, & Anzaldúa, G. E. (Eds.). (2002). *This bridge called my back: Writings by radical women of color* (Rev. 3rd ed.). San Francisco, CA: Third Woman Press.

Rendón, L. I. (2009). *Sentipensante (sensing/thinking) pedagogy: Educating for wholeness, social justice and liberation*. Sterling, VA: Stylus.

Sleeter, C. (2008). Critical family history, identity, and historical memory. *Educational Studies, 43*(2), 114–124.

Solórzano, D., & Yosso, T. (2002). Critical race methodology: Counter-storytelling as an analytical framework for education research. *Qualitative Inquiry, 8*(1), 23–44.

Wenk, L., & Luschen, K. (In press). Multiple routes, alternative learning experiences: Developing analytic abilities, practical skills, creativity, and self-reflection at Hampshire College. In J. DeVitis (Ed.), *The college curriculum: A reader*. New York, NY: Peter Lang.

PART II

Bridging Diverse Community Knowledges Through Critical Storytelling

6

Engaging Co-Reflexive Critical Dialogues When Entering and Leaving the "Field": Toward Informing Collaborative Research Methods at the Color Line and Beyond

Sherick Hughes and Kate Willink

Echoing W. E. B. Du Bois one century before him, an acclaimed U.S. historian, the late John Hope Franklin (1993), admonished us about the legacy of racism in the twenty-first century and the problem of the color line. This chapter will discuss how researchers sharing one "field"[1] location can engage *co-reflexive*[2] *critical dialogue* as a collaborative method at the crucial moments of entering and leaving the "field." These moments can be particularly useful for diverse research teams, as we begin to anticipate and address issues emerging at the color line and beyond—issues that can be revealed in retrospect as hidden and silenced limitations of our data interpretations.

While pursuing doctoral degrees at the University of North Carolina at Chapel Hill (UNC), Hughes in Education and Willink in Communication and Cultural Studies, both of us had the opportunity to participate in the same Spencer Grant-funded project.[3] The project explored school desegregation history as experienced by local families of northeastern North Carolina.

Hughes entered the project as a self-identified "Black male local public schooled native ethnographer," while Willink entered the project as a self-identified "White female private-school educated Yankee," in the more traditional role of "going native."[4] In 2007, we began, quite haphazardly, a collaborative critical journey that would ultimately generate refreshing insights into our experiences of pursuing family histories as part of our ethnographic research. While brief, unplanned, and inconsistent e-mail correspondence began at that time, the first opportunity for us to reconnect in-depth was largely due to the 2010 American Educational Studies Association (AESA) and the 2010 American Educational Research Association (AERA) annual conference meetings. These events became our *kairos*, our opportune moments to expand our skills, challenge our taken-for-granted knowledge, and trouble our dispositions together. During these *kairos* moments, we began our most critical dialogues about the ethnographic research experiences that we had described in our dissertations and books. It was during these events that we began to find an approach to critical dialogue that would allow us the space to unveil our different positionalities and perspectives. We began to revisit and critique the years spent separately traversing the same small, northeastern, North Carolina counties of the Albemarle—an area of the country where such history remained largely isolated in oral history—to understand the past, present, and future of school desegregation. Although we graduated from UNC (Hughes in 2003 and Willink in 2005), our co-reflexive critical dialogues about the project after graduating from UNC are perhaps best described as "commencement exercises." We experienced the beginning and end of the project, both separately and collectively, as a commencement in essence, a beginning of remembering a series of episodes, encounters, and events that continue to promote critical dialogues between us.

These dialogues occur (a) through acts of remembering critical dialogues from the time when we were "entering" the "field" with a retrospective or backward gaze; (b) through the acts of emergent critical dialogues of our present with an intersubjective, dialogic-dialectic relational gaze; and (c) through individualized, new-self dialogues that seem to be moving us toward a more critically reflexive position, in the times where we may become complacent about what we are learning and unlearning about applying collaborative research methods within ethnographies.

In this chapter we perform a positioning and repositioning of ourselves—in relation to each other, our fieldwork, our research findings, and our past, present, and future selves. Accordingly, the central question of the chapter is not a prescriptive "how to" question, but instead we inquire into what we are learning from our critical dialogues and interpretations of our research at the intersection of raced, classed, gendered, and cultured color lines. In the spirit of cultural dialogue we ask the reader to engage in the same practices of patience, discomfort in learning and unlearning, challenging intellectual work, and grace that we are trying to do each time we revisit our work together. We follow Alexander and Warren (2002) and Willink and Suzette (2012) in the use of Conquergood's (1985) dialogic performance as a "compositional strategy" (p. 329) that serves our desire to achieve dialogue in, across, and through our differences and similarities. Through the type of critical dialogues that are supported by the work of Laubscher and Powell (2003), Milner (2003), and Taliaferro-Baszile (2006), we describe "oh no," and "aha" moments that began to enrich our understandings, not only of our livelihoods in qualitative research, but also of our lives as qualitative researchers, civil and human rights activists, interlocutors, and friends. Ultimately, we hope that our portrayal of our critical dialogues might highlight some of the useful differences, missteps, pitfalls, and promise that can comprise the complexity of "native ethnographers" collaborating with ethnographers "going native" in pursuit of rigorous, thoughtful, and credible qualitative research that can inform critically reflexive praxis when entering and leaving the "field."

Entering the "Field:" Co-Reflexive Critical Dialogues From Intimate Strangers

Sherick

> All you pretty pretenders, negligent vendors, aren't you precious inside, I have no need for anger with intimate strangers and I got nothing to hide. (From the song, "Reunion," by the Indigo Girls)

When it comes to going "home" to the coastal plains, Albemarle area of northeastern North Carolina, I am a hopeful Black man...most of the time. However, reentering the Albemarle after eight transformative educational years to pursue dissertation research as part of a larger, Spencer-Grant-funded ethnography project filled my mind with questions and oxymoronic phrases. "How do I reply to homophobic, sexist, racist, classist, and dogmatically self-righteous comments from participants (some of whom know my family intimately)?" I was being educated to fight for the civil and human rights and against the oppression of all of my students and their allies who experienced marginalization, irrespective of race, class, gender, and sexuality. The message stuck with me. To borrow the powerful words of Maya Angelou, the message of anti-oppression for all got "into my mind, my heart, my hair, my clothes, my shoes, my car"... and it literally engulfed me (Angelou, 2009, n. p.). Yet, most of my participants, and even some of my own family members, did not share the same transformative experiences of graduate school with me. Therefore, I began to feel uncomfortably comfortable each day that I awoke to begin anew, fulfilling the roles of insider/outsider, mainstream/homeboy, and intimate/stranger. The latter contradiction that I borrowed from the Indigo Girls' song, "Reunion," is perhaps most fitting and indicative of the person that I was/am becoming after leaving home to pursue higher education. Moreover, I know of no other Black male in the Albemarle who even knows who the Indigo Girls are, much less cites them among their favorite artists because of their lyrics, melodies, and harmonies.

I entered this project initially unaware that in some ways, I was becoming an island off the coast of the Albemarle of my birth—connected to the social ecology of the area and yet distinct from it. I feel like a unicorn when I go home sometimes. I sometimes feel like I have become a mythical creature to some of the local youth (including my family members), and it bothers me. The exceptionality narrative that centers the folklore about me as the always diligent and always pious child is pleasantly disturbing. As my fellow North Carolinian, Thomas Wolfe (1940), noted over seven decades ago, *You can't go home again*. I can and did, of course, physically go home again to pursue this project. I had a choice of projects to pursue, and my advisor did not strong-arm me into it. I am beginning to think that perhaps, my internal compass is always set for home, like a migratory bird that instinctively flies for the nesting ground of its birth. Yet, I did not and/or do not live there, and I am not part of the day-to-day changes. While folks may not have evolved in the same ways that I have, they have still evolved and adapted to the social climate and terrain.

My qualitative research design involved the common chain sampling technique. At the time of the interviews and observations of their home, my first, key informants, the Erskin family,[5] lived only seconds, by foot, down the road from my parents. The family was recommended to me by the Whitmores, arguably the most respected Black family of educators in Albemarle area K–12 schools. The Whitmore family lived beside my father's sister (my late Aunt Isabella), and the local press had recently published stories to acknowledge their contributions to school desegregation and equity in the Albemarle area. Mr. and Mrs. Whitmore each taught and administered K–12 schools for approximately 45 years, and they experienced school desegregation in at least three different counties of the five-county mainland plains region of the Albemarle. My mother was a mentee of the Whitmores. Aware that I was studying school desegregation with regard to K–12 public education, my mother saved newspaper clippings that ultimately would augment the work that I had done and documents I found during the months that I spent in the barred window basement of the building that houses the North Carolina State Archives.

It was the very first Erskin family informant that provided the narrative that would add clarity and life to the archival documents and newspaper clippings, and inspire the title of my book from the project, *Black Hands in the Biscuits Not in the Classrooms* (Hughes, 2006). Mrs. Dora Erskin's candid comments critiqued Whites who wanted her to work in their homes as an intimate stranger, the help, the person putting her hands in their food and in their children's mouths, and yet Mrs. Erskin had children who were deemed not worthy of attending school with non-Blacks. I interpreted the Erskin family's trusting treatment and rapport with me as indicative of their view of my renewed space in the school community as a native son, a homeboy with individual educational accomplishments for which they, other Black folks, and a few White folks in the community had struggled and hoped. Still, I entered the Erskin family home as I did all of the others, feeling the need to confirm that I had not gone too far in theoretical understanding to approach the real-life threats of marginalization and discrimination at home. I naturally and inadvertently slipped into "ya'll," "ain'," and then back to "talking proper," like the *emissarial*[6] Black man described by Grant and Breese (1997, p. 198), when talking with the Erskin family as well as the other families.

I am ashamed today as I remember, albeit on rare occasions, offering only awkward silence to exaggerated and misleading comments that blame the social ills of my informants' perceived worlds on "all of the ___ people," a blank that might be filled on one day with gay or lesbian, White, wealthy, college, Republicans; and on another day with Chinese, poor, Black, Mexican, and/or non-Christian. I began to be concerned about whether other native ethnographers of color also suffer through moments of remaining silenced in the "field," with the big picture of the burden of maintaining trust and access to entry points weighing heavily on the soul. As we shall discuss more in the text below, native ethnographers cannot leave the "field," because they tend to have lifelong ties to the locale; and alongside their families, native ethnographers of color are often the subaltern in the "field"—among the most vulnerable citizens. Ultimately, I decided to focus my portion of the project away from those misleading, exaggerated comments, toward understanding the role of pedagogy at home in Black families that largely survived and thrived in the wake of school segregation and desegregation. However, I continued to wonder whether other native ethnographers pursuing their "field" work would say that they adapted their language and actions for the situation (indicative of the emissarial approach), and whether they would describe their emissarial approach as relatively effortless and frequently useful.

The emissarial approach would become an asset and a liability, as my role as a graduate student shifted from "doctoral candidate/graduate assistant" to "doctoral candidate/supervisor of graduate assistants (GAs)" on the Spencer Foundation grant. In 2002, I was appointed to the latter role by the primary investigators (PI), George Noblit and Jim Leloudis, because our "field" location for this portion of the grant included my hometown and the four other counties of the northern plains of the Albemarle area of North Carolina. My role was multifaceted. I met with the PIs occasionally to brainstorm and ultimately select another graduate student who seemed capable of gaining the rapport necessary to obtain data thoughtfully, carefully, and credibly in the "field." I served as the key point person for briefing the team on what to anticipate with local weather, climate, ideology, political economy, and schooling.

My lived experiences of the "field" location, coupled with the critical race theory literature that I read in graduate school, sparked my initial concerns for the native and non-native ethnographers of school desegregation in that locale. Moreover, I wondered how race, class, and gender backgrounds might influence participant-researcher rapport and relations and the information that is generated from those transactions. I recalled old sayings from the Black community that produced me, "Whites in the North don't care how high you get as long as you don't get too close; Whites in the South don't care how close you get, as long as you don't get too high." The more I considered these lived experiences and graduate readings in critical race theory, the more I became adamant about the choice of GAs to gather data in the Albemarle area. My initial transactions about and with Kate supported and challenged my taken-for-granted knowledge about her abilities as a researcher in the Albemarle area "field."

As a native of the Albemarle, I felt confident that a 30-something, White female with a southern accent would be crucial to gathering data from the White families of the Albemarle. Black females, I felt, would gather the richest data from the Black families in the area. Noblit and Leloudis took my recommendations under advisement, and hired Kate for the role. My immediate concern about Kate Willink was that she was from the North and had no Southern accent (although her New York accent is quite subtle). I was disappointed initially, because Kate did not meet all of the characteristics that I had suggested to the PIs. However, Noblit assured me that "Kate will do fine, because, although she is not from the South, she is a great listener."

To Noblit, I replied, "Okay." I thought to myself, "great; but at some point she'll have to talk and her lack of a Southern drawl may limit our White informants' ability to trust her with their dirt on school desegregation...but, I know she'll get more out of them than I will." Noblit felt confident that when I met with Kate and began to correspond regularly with her, she likely would exceed my expectations for data collection. During our initial meeting, my job was to break the ice with Kate, build rapport with her, and brief her on the latest, relevant sociocultural, historical, and economic information for the Albemarle area. In subsequent meetings, I was to debrief with her and offer her advice that might inform her work on the project. To me, Kate and I initially felt like intimate strangers. We shared mentors and alma maters; however, Kate represented arguably the most protected group in the US, while I represented arguably the least protected group—distinctions that inform our lived experiences and interpretations of them. Despite this, and although it was initially unanticipated (at least by me), it has become clear to me that the more we communicated, the more Kate was informing and continues to inform me and my part of the project. Hopefully, it is at least as much as I have informed and continue to inform her and her part of the project.

Kate

For me, this project began one day during a conversation in Dr. George Noblit's office at the University of North Carolina at Chapel Hill. I was a second-year Communication Studies PhD student taking Dr. Noblit's Advanced Qualitative Methods class at the suggestion of my adviser, Dr. Della Pollock. Soon after class started, I sought George out as an informal mentor.

That afternoon, George mentioned a Spencer Foundation project, "Roads Not Taken: Education and Race in the Post-Brown South," that he was working on with historian Dr. Jim Leloudis. They were looking for a research assistant to conduct oral history interviews on school desegregation in Albemarle County from the perspective of the White community. "We were looking for a Southern belle, which you are not...But I think your ability to listen makes you a good choice," he said.

Conducting oral history interviews on school desegregations in a rural southern community was nowhere in my graduate school agenda. I had been contemplating interviewing the women in my spouse's family on the Navajo reservation, a familiar cultural milieu where I had spent the last ten years living. This opportunity, what Dwight Conquergood called, "an embarrassment of riches," came unexpectedly. And it frightened me, pushing me to the edges of my unknowing, and foregrounding my outsider status. Luckily, with the help of great advisers and the subsequent coaching by co-researcher and senior classman, Sherick Hughes, I accepted this amazing research opportunity. And it changed my life, my research agenda, and my White Northern liberal subjectivity.

For my entire childhood, I had spent holidays traveling from my home on the upper West Side of New York City to visit my grandparents and relatives in Georgia. I had an ambivalent relationship with "the South" (a.k.a. Augusta, Georgia). I was a New Yorker born and raised in the pre-*Sex in the City*, pre-Giuliani, Big Apple glory days, when *Time Magazine* ran a cover that called my home "the rotting apple." I always felt that my southern relatives thought they were better than their New York relatives, who lived in America's abject, dirty metropolis with all its social problems. And I, in turn, felt that they were snotty, Republican, racist debutantes. Unknowingly, I was falling into the trap of seeing what Jacquelyn Hall (2005) would call

> the trope of the South as the nation's "opposite other," an image that southernizes racism and shields from scrutiny both the economic dimensions of southern White supremacy and the institutionalized patterns of exploitation, segregation, and discrimination in other regions of the country. (p. 1244)

It is embarrassing to admit this narrow-minded, self-insulating, White liberal attitude now. Nonetheless, this is what I imagined of White southerners as I prepared to enter the field.

Looking back on the people I have come to know, and on my own place in and among multiple relationships of difference in this field research, I sometimes wonder how we managed to communicate. How was it that a White woman born and raised on the Upper West Side of Manhattan, who went to private school, ended up doing field research in a small, rural county in eastern North Carolina on public school desegregation? Somehow, the word *Yankee* is not adequate enough to capture the differences. To top it off, how does the fact that I am in an interethnic marriage (my husband's mother is Navajo) with two children who do not even resemble each other, play in a community where interethnic relationships, in this case Black and White, are still pretty unusual? When I contemplate these differences and I wonder why and how this research project worked, I return to Dr. Noblit's faith in the act of listening coupled with the goodwill and generosity of the people I interviewed and my extended Carolina network.

Although I did not know it at the time, I entered the field long before my first trip to the Albemarle region. My encounters with Sherick Hughes, an Albermarle native and advanced doctoral student, comprised my initial entry into the field. And to me it felt like a bumpy arrival. On our first meeting, which we had before a trip to the archives together, Sherick lectured me (well, honestly he probably told me gently, but at the time I was shocked by the news) that I should not use the term *African American* in the Albemarle region. He advised me to use only *White* and *Black*, which initially felt uncomfortable to me as a White, liberal Northerner. In Albemarle people only used the terms *Black* and *White*, Sherick informed me. Facing this advice made me uncomfortable. Later, Sherick told me that he went home to his spouse, Meghan, and said, "I don't think she believed me." At the time, Sherick was probably right. I did not believe him. I could not believe him. It offended my Yankee sensibilities.

Looking back now, I am clear that I did believe Sherick, but to believe him troubled me. Facing the material reality of the Black-White binary destabilized my understandings of race and myself as a progressive White person. As a liberal, White Northerner, I did not want to believe Sherick. Initially I thought, "I know the right words to use" (e.g., African American). I expected that my self-certainty of knowing the "right words" would serve as a pass to prove that I was not a racist. I felt Sherick respond to my resistance and performance of disbelief with frustration. I also know that he did not give up. You do not get to be a twenty-something Black man in the academy without the experience of explaining race and racism to a well-intentioned White, liberal Northerner. But I also know from our subsequent conversations and my conversations with his mother that Sherick grew up learning race beyond the brittle Black-White binary. He was simply offering me pragmatic and culturally sensitive advice on how to enter the field as an outsider ethnographer. But it was hard to hear past my White resistance.

In very different worlds and very different pedagogies, Sherick and I were both schooled by well-intentioned parents who wanted more from society, something beyond the Black-White binary. And they taught us to want more, too. I had not done the Mab Segrest (2002) work to investigate how Whiteness and White supremacy (Leonardo, 2004) in my family shaped my own life trajectory and my sense of self. In truth, I was saddened about the conditions I was about to face. Up until my research, it was easier to pretend that racism did not exist in my post-Jim Crow, post desegregation New York.

Looking back now, I recognize the costs of my unbearable Whiteness of being. Sociologist Howard Winant (1998) claimed, "race and racial identity, are not merely produced by racism, as neoconservatives (as well as some on the left) might claim. They are also means of self-representation, autonomous signification, and cultural (and thus social and political) practice" (p. 108). I know now that racism implicates and impacts all of us, and is embedded in our identities, whether privileged or marginalized. But at the time, I thought my Yankee status shielded me.

Mab Segrest (2002) pointed out, "exploitative relationships have cost us personally, familially, and socially" (p. 169). More directly, Segrest elaborated:

> What, then, is the cost to White people of racism?...
> Racism costs us intimacy.
> Racism costs us our affective lives.
> Racism costs us authenticity.
> Racism costs us our sense of connection to other humans and the natural world.
> (p. 171)

It took a long road to Albermarle and back and several years of deep listening for me to recognize these costs and the ways that they defined my life.

The next time I met Sherick, when we travelled to the archives in Raleigh, he told me, "In the North Whites don't care how high you get as long as you don't get too close. And in the South Whites don't care how close you get as long as you don't get too high." Again his words fractured my mask of Northern Whiteness. I knew what he said about the North was true. But I was not accustomed to the North and South being framed as equally, if differently, racist. Looking back, I see my conversations with Sherick, this original contact with the field, as critical to destabilizing my outsider, White, Yankee subjectivity. They were enough to potentiate and eventually necessitate other ways of understanding my positionality and entering the Albemarle relational network that Sherick opened for me. I am not sure I lived up to George's faith in my listening skills when I first interacted with Sherick. At the time, it had yet to dawn on me that I had already entered the field, even though I had yet to leave Chapel Hill.

From the beginning of this research, I have been marked as an outsider. In Albemarle, you do not have to be very far outside to be considered an outsider. For example, if you lived in South Mills (the northern part of Albemarle) and moved to Old Trap (in the southern part of the county), you will always be an outsider in Old Trap, even though you are from the same county and moved about fifteen miles down the road. I was an outsider most obviously in the beginning because of my accent (or lack of a southern accent) and my affiliation with the University of North Carolina at Chapel Hill. Then, when people found out I was born and raised in the Northeast, I became a Yankee outsider. I am an outsider because the only way I ever made it into this small community was on the grace of a few relationships.

Before heading to Albemarle for the first time, Sherick provided me with the names of Alex Leary and Fannie Lewis, the first two residents I visited. Also, before traveling to Albemarle, I visited with Professor Bland Simpson, longtime resident and writer of the Albemarle area and one of my committee members. He put me in contact with Don Pendergraft, Director of the Museum of the Albemarle in Elizabeth City, who prepared a long list of people for me to contact. The first person on the list was Billy Revelle, the first principal of the desegregated Marion Anderson High School.

I began my conversations based on relationships with the three people who were recommended to me, and they remain three of the touchstones for my research and my connections to the community. First I interviewed Mrs. Lewis, a Black cafeteria worker. This interview provided a comfortable starting place as well as a more informal introduction to Albemarle's African American community. Not only had Mrs. Lewis had six children who went through the Albemarle school system, but she had also worked as a bus driver and a cafeteria worker in the school for a number of years. Her willingness to share these experiences deepened my understanding of the subjective experience of desegregation for Albemarle's Black families. Next, I interviewed Mr. Leary, a local historian and former history teacher. He was one of the first Whites to teach at the still segregated Black school during the Freedom of Choice era. Recommended by Sherick, and viewed by the community as the local keeper of Albemarle's story and history, Mr. Leary seemed a natural starting point for gaining the context for understanding this place (particularly from a White perspective). Third, I interviewed Billy Revelle, a former White principal committed to economic and social justice, who worked as the first White principal of the all-Black Marion Anderson High School. He in turn connected me to many of my subsequent interviewees.

One of the differences between each of these individuals and me was our age. I believe our age difference proved beneficial to the interview process. I am about the age of their children. These former teachers and school workers could view me as a learner and themselves as teachers, particularly given that I was not from Albemarle and they could not assume that we shared any insider knowledge. The fact that I was the same age as their children set up what seemed to be a very natural relationship where, in many senses, they took care of me. While some researchers might find these power dynamics problematic, I think we all found them comfortable, which perhaps facilitated the ease with which they shared their stories, and fostered our ongoing relationships that allowed for more time and greater depth in the follow-up interviews. Everything needed to be taught and spelled out explicitly. Of course, the negative side of being an outsider is that people do not share other types of information, and you do not have the certain background that someone of that community would. What I learned in the process of the study is that the relationship between insider-outsider is multilayered, more complex than it may appear, and that either position has advantages and disadvantages.

I did get the sense that as a (sometimes) unaccompanied White woman, or even a woman who might be driving the roads of Albemarle or between Albemarle and Chapel Hill alone, Mr. and Mrs. Revelle and Mr. Leary felt the need to watch over me. I am pretty sure that if I were a man, they would not have had these same concerns. I am also not sure, and cannot know, whether they would have been so open with a male interviewer. Whether it is the southern (White) woman archetype that shaped in part their response to me, or the fact that I am generally unassuming and deferential in interviews, I do not know. I do know that when I interviewed a man or a woman who was substantially older than me, I generally received paternalistic or maternalistic treatment (with the potential for both negative and positive consequences) across races. However, given my generally privileged position as a White person in this community, and that I was an outsider, I gladly compromised some of my authority (in the positive and negative senses of the word) to be in relation with others and to know others better.

The last bump in the road in my initial intimate stranger relationship with Sherick came several months into my fieldwork. I met Sherick at the local co-op in Carrboro. We sat at a bench on a warm spring day catching up on the progress of my initial interviews. In passing I told Sherick a story I was told about the "integration" of a White Albemarle church with a deaf Black community member, and joked to Sherick about how the most segregated time in America is Sunday morning. I do not really remember how Sherick responded, but I remember how I felt. Sherick made it clear to me that his spiritual segregation was a source of pain and disappointment to him. And he did not consider it a laughing matter. Shortly after that, our meeting ended. A decade later and a bit further down my own spiritual journey I still feel ashamed about my display of insensitivity and callousness. Yet, when I broached this with Sherick recently he told me he did not even remember this exchange! Then he recalled that at that time he and Meghan (his spouse who is White) had been looking for an interethnic church with little success. My catty comment must have touched a nerve, he mused. But now that they were well ensconced in an interethnic faith community, this encounter felt like a distant memory. To me, it serves as a persistent reminder that an outsider positionality has many blind spots and insensitivities. And as a reminder about how little I understood when I entered into the field. And the dangers of what could happen when you lose what Maxine Green called your "wide-awake" sensitivity in fieldwork, play too fast and loose, and forget your outsider/learner/listener status. Even for intimate strangers intimacy must be earned.

Leaving the "Field"
Sherick

Native ethnographers may never be able to go home again to a time they remember, because times, persons, and places evolve. Yet, native ethnographers may never be able to leave (disengage with) home. While conducting research I was dismayed at the amount of time and painstaking energy that I was using to protect the anonymity of my key informants and other participants. I used pseudonyms for all persons, places, and pets; I refused to name the correct names of the counties that were at the center of my research. When I noticed that Kate, in the role of one "going native," could leave the setting, I felt feelings of joy and concern. I was concerned that if Kate did not have to worry about family, friends, and acquaintances in the Albemarle, then she would be less likely to work so painstakingly to protect their confidentiality and anonymity. I also began to worry about what she would do with our story (publicize it in the local newspaper and TV news, etc.?), and how she would interpret it (was it a backward state to her?).

Unlike Kate, I entered the families' homes, places of worship, and leisure spaces as a member of their family. As a native ethnographer, I was to some degree their child. My parents lived within 25 minutes of each of my key informants and participants, so I felt the pang to "get it right," to tell the story well and critically. I have six siblings, and four of them live in the Albemarle area. My mother and father have been married over 54 years, and have no plans of leaving the area. Therefore, my dissertation (now accessible to all) could have been quite embarrassing for my family, and could have led to issues for the little ones at school, such as bullying, verbal assaults, and physical altercations. The problem would have been less about showing my participants in an excellent versus a poor light, but more so about breaching the confidentiality clause and ethical agreements that can determine the degree to which any sensitive information is shared with the public. Another example from Larry Biggs further illustrates my point here. Long after the project, Mr. Biggs saw my mother at the grocery store and he said, "...Hughes, I really enjoyed that boy." Following my member-checking process, I asked all of the families, "what would you like for me to do with your story?" They replied, "share it with as many people as you can, 'graduate,' 'and get a good job,' and 'so people will know what's happening in our small towns' and so you will graduate." After all, I am their child, too.

Knowing the love for UNC among most of the Black family members of the Albemarle that I studied, I gave each family a framed certificate of appreciation at the end of the project, and each certificate was signed by the Dean of the School of Education at UNC. The love for UNC seems to stem from the fact that it was among the first historically White universities to admit Black students in the South. It was also among the first to admit Black athletes to play in the highly visible and most lucrative NCAA sports, basketball and football. The local Black families take some pride in counting Black male Hall of Fame inductees, Michael Jordan (UNC-Basketball), and Lawrence Taylor (UNC-Football) as members of the UNC Tar Heels family. Still, while some of their White counterparts boast of UNC students from their families, most Black families of the area have no one in their family who actually attended the university. Yet, they seem to love UNC for the same reasons that I do—for its promise and possibilities. It was recently voted in a key Black periodical as the #1 historically White university for Black students to attend and where they thrive. I hope the small certificates from UNC helped the families know how much I appreciated the role they allowed me to play in their families.

Indeed, unlike Kate, I can never leave the "field." When the Biggs family had a horrible home fire, I sent them $100 from the money I earned as a graduate student. I donated copies of the book version of the dissertation that emerged from their stories to a local, historically Black church that a few of the families attended. I was invited to speak on Men's Day at that same church. And while I am often reluctant to return to the Albemarle as the "speaker/teacher," because I feel that I have so much more to learn from the Black families, I did oblige, and the message was well-received, from the accounts I get from my parents. Occasionally, my parents send messages to me from one of the families, saying, "how's my boy?" Like most Black men, I abhor any reference to me as a "boy," because it conjures negative emotions of the Jim Crow folks who still cannot find themselves able to accept us as grown men. I learned from the families that this "boy" language from Whites is one of the main reasons why brothers began to say, "what's up, man," to each other in public—a greeting that has been co-opted by men and women nationwide. Still, I do not mind being referred to as "my boy" by the patriarchs of the Black families that allowed me to study their lives in the context of school desegregation in the Albemarle area. To me, coming from them, it is a term of endearment that I cherish. Indeed, I can never go "home" again, but as with other native ethnographers with family ties to the area who are pursuing academic research, I can never fully leave the "field." I would never want to do so, because it would mean leaving a part of myself, that part that makes me more resilient each time I revisit the pedagogy of struggle and hope of the Black families of the Albemarle. It is a blessing and a burden, a contradiction that Kate likely does not experience when reliving the project in her mind and heart as a researcher "going native."

Kate

While I do not share the same contradictions Sherick experiences, I have found leaving the field to be its own type of contradiction, what I might call "being inside out." But first I should say that, as a spouse of a Navajo man, I find the idea of "going native" at best fraught and problematic, and at worst colonizing. If I had a dime for every time someone told my spouse they were $1/32^{nd}$ Cherokee, or that they felt they were Native American in a past life, I would be a wealthy academic! So I never really aspired to go native. I often think more in terms of insider-outsider, but even then, there are too many gradations and permutations for that binary to be very illuminating.

What is clear to me now about leaving the field as an outsider, nonnative is that it is often a lonely road. I did not find out that Mr. Charlie, one of my cherished interviewees, had passed away until a year after he died. I could not go to the funeral, pay my respects, or mourn in community. I was out of synch with the rhythm of the community, its pains and joys. But then again, I was never really in synch with the community. I would blow in and out of town as my funding, family commitments, graduate school schedule, and pre-tenure path allowed. I remained an intimate stranger, even though I cherish these relationships forged in fleeting time.

In the field I experienced ethnographic oral history research as an embodied practice and process. More than focusing on native or nonnative categories, such fieldwork "privileges the processes of communication that constitute the 'doing' of ethnography: speaking, listening, and acting together" (Conquergood, 1991, p. 181). From this perspective, researchers become invested and implicated co-participants themselves, as well as co-creators and translators. Rather than speaking for others, my research emphasized speaking in concert with others to achieve dialogue in, across, and through our differences (Conquergood, 1985; Pelias, 1991; Spry, 2001). This ethnographic approach focused on research *with* community so that knowledge emerges from dialogic performance as different voices from various locations meet in sites of tension, disjuncture, and freedom, in the spirit of love and grace that a commitment to dialogue potentiates (Conquergood, 1985, p. 9). As a researcher, I aspired to co-performative witnessing: "what it means to be radically engaged and committed, body-to-body, in the field...a politics of the body deeply in action with Others"

(Conquergood, as cited in Madison, 2007, p. 826). In this construction, researchers become co-performers and co-subjects (Conquergood, 1985; Pollock, 2010)—what Pollock (2006) called "going into the social field at risk of going under" (p. 327).

And to be honest, there were times I went under. Listening to memories of pain and trauma and noting profound silences reverberates in your soul long after you leave the field. Perhaps that is what George meant when he said that I was a good listener. But such embodied listening has costs. And when you are an outsider, the reverberations are without precedent. It is not as though you grew up in the community and learned about a number of the issues over thirty years here and there. It is as though within a year or so of meeting twenty-five people and conducting a few hundred hours of fieldwork, you are listening to generations of trauma, integrating it into your own self and understanding of the world, and interpreting and analyzing it from a scholarly perspective. And I largely did it alone, in front of the glow of my laptop, while re-listening to numerous interviews on my iPod. This is all to say that co-performative witnessing is intensely intimate in the field, and sometimes very demanding and lonely once you have left.

Perhaps the article that ran in the Elizabeth City newspaper, the *Daily Advance*, before I returned to give a talk about my newly released book, *Bringing Desegregation Home: Memories of the Struggle Toward School Integration in Rural North Carolina* (Willink, 2009), best captures my contradictory experience:

> Author and professor Kate Willink is the ultimate Yankee: raised in New York City. Yet she readily admits that when she returns to the Albemarle region this weekend, it'll be like a homecoming. "Who would have ever thought that someone from Manhattan would feel a part of a small county in northeast North Carolina?" Willink said in a recent interview from her Denver, Colo. home…And while Willink's book is a brilliant retelling of a tumultuous time and how it affected a small, rural region, it is also clear that the time she spent here had a lasting effect on her and that the people of Camden County gave her something more than a story. "Part of it is their stories," said Willink. "To me it's an act of generosity, good will and a desire to teach and to pass on memories that were important to their lives. So I don't take it lightly when someone invites me into their lives."

Interpreting the Journey: Implications for Future Co-Reflexive Critical Dialogue Methods

Sherick and Kate

Three salient points on the art of learning co-reflexive critical dialogue are emerging, and they may provide useful implications for future critical collaborative research methods. First, we are learning the art of finding and cultivating compatible dyads. We must credit Dr. Noblit for "finding" us, and developing the opportunity for us to work as a dyad. He knew the common touchstones of our backgrounds that we did not, and he put us together with a sense that we would be compatible in the "field." We both have graduate degrees in Communication and Cultural Studies. We were both in interethnic marriages, and we both had a thirst for critical inquiry, equity, and justice that begins with critical self-reflexivity. We continue to learn from Dr. Noblit about finding and cultivating compatible research dyads on such projects.

Second, we are learning the art of collaborating by engaging critical dialogues at the color line and beyond toward cultivating:

1. Relationships with diverse, reputable border crossers as key brokers and mentors when pursuing critical research involving families (e.g., both Dr. Noblit and Sherick's mother, Maise Hughes, became key brokers and mentors for us as we pursued our research; and
2. Strategies that support validation, commitment, confidentiality, reasonableness, empathy, and peace when pursuing critical research (particularly when engaging critical dialogues, attempting to build relationships, and when in the act of interviewing).

Third, we are learning the art of collaborating in compatible, diverse dyads at the color line and beyond, including:

1. Learning to expect that your team member may be led to differing interpretations due to her or his lived experience, and to check in with your team member toward understanding the response biases of your team member and yourself;
2. Learning to anticipate that ultimately, together, your co-interpretation and co-translations will likely give a fuller picture of the phenomenon of interest;
3. Learning to embrace the potential development of long-term fictive kinships, and the development of ties with the families you study as well as the family of your research team partner (e.g., Sherick with the Erskin and Biggs families, and Kate with the Hughes family);
4. Learning to be open to being wrong, to changing, and to tolerating ambiguity; and
5. Learning to assess and address sensitivities and anxieties as a team by (a) assessing the sensitivity of an issue in a particular population separately before coming together to co-assign or assign participants

to particular interviewers accordingly; and (b) addressing known and anticipated anxieties of participants and researchers charged with discussing sensitive, primary, social identity issues (i.e., race, class, gender, sexuality, religion) with someone who does not share their primary social identities.

In closing, we are learning that people are not controlled by sensitive social issues and identities, but that our lives are informed by them—i.e., our perceptions, response biases, and willingness to participate and share sensitive information are informed by the social identities we embody. While we did not pre-plan to write a chapter on our experiences, perhaps this collaborative piece could broaden and enhance future critical dialogues among diverse research teams and the findings from their collaborative work, particularly at the analysis and synthesis stages.

Notes

1. Hughes applies quotation marks around the word "field" in the term "field work" to remind readers to be skeptical of using the term in order to limit purposeful and inadvertent marginalization. The quotation marks are also intended to remind readers that the term is part of an international dialogue, and thus, to remind readers to engage co-reflexive critical dialogues on the usage of the term.
2. The term *co-reflexive critical dialogue* is introduced here to describe the qualitative method we engaged initially and later named to make sense of and to make reference to our critical dialogic experiences at the color line and beyond. It names how we worked alone and in concert to question the taken-for-granted knowledge, lived experiences, and related selection biases that inform the lenses we use to see and interpret the "field." Like mathematical co-reflexivity, we are learning that if a is related to b then a may be equal to b ($a = b$), but if c is equal to d ($c = d$), it does not necessarily mean that c is related to d. Moreover, we are learning from and with our co-reflexive method that when entering and leaving the "field," co-reflexive critical dialogues are crucial to addressing crises of interpretation in our research, particularly as those crises are informed by researcher-participant experiences of race, class, and gender.
3. Hughes was involved in the project from 2001–2003, and Willink was involved in the project from 2002–2004, with our involvement overlapping in 2002 and 2003.
4. In contrast to "native ethnographers" who are pursuing cultural research through familiar and familial persons, places, and things that were problems and promise for their development from childhood to adulthood, the traditional ethnographer is one that is "going native," or going to study a culture in which they have little to no familiar and familial ties. Both the former and the latter forms of ethnographic research now have researchers like the authors of this chapter who are skeptical and critical of any research that further colonizes, or that has the potential to further marginalize, vulnerable groups in the "field."

5. Pseudonyms are used in place of actual names to support the participants' requests for confidentiality.
6. *Emissarial* African Americans are well-versed in the rules and norms of achievement of the dominant White culture in the US (Grant & Breese, 1997, p. 198). Moreover, Grant and Breese (1997) explained that emissarial folks of color know how to use the educational system to their advantage, although there may have been several painful racist incidents along the way.

References

Alexander, B. K., & Warren, J. T. (2002). The materiality of bodies: Critical reflections on pedagogy, politics and positionality. *Communication Quarterly, 50*(3–4), 328–343.

Angelou, Maya. "An Evening with Maya Angelou." [Student Entertainment Event]. College Park, MD. 29 Sept. 2009.

Conquergood, D. (1985). *Performing as a moral act: Ethical dimensions of the ethnography of performance.* Cambridge, MA: Harvard University Press.

———. (1991). Rethinking ethnography: Towards a critical cultural politics. *Communication Monographs, 58*, 179–194.

Franklin, J. H. (1993). *The color line: Legacy for the twenty-first century.* Columbia, MO: University of Missouri Press.

Grant, G. K., & Breese, J. R. (1997). Marginality theory and the African American student. *Sociology of Education, 70*(7), 192–205.

Hall, J. D. (2005). The long civil rights movement and the political uses of the past. *Journal of American History, 91*(4), 1233–1263.

Hughes, S. A. (2006). *Black hands in the biscuits not in the classrooms: Unveiling hope in a struggle for Brown's promise.* New York, NY: Peter Lang.

Laubscher, L., & Powell, S. (2003). Skinning the drum: Teaching about diversity as 'other.' *Harvard Educational Review, 73*(2), 203–224.

Leonardo, Z. (2004). The color of supremacy: Beyond the discourse of 'White privilege.' *Educational Philosophy and Theory, 36*(2), 137–152.

Madison, D. S. (2007). Co-performative witnessing. *Cultural Studies, 21*(6), 826–831.

Milner, H. R. III. (2003). Reflection, racial competence, and critical pedagogy: How do we prepare pre-service teachers to pose tough questions? *Race, Ethnicity and Education, 6*(2), 193–208.

Pelias, R. J. (1991). Empathy and the ethics of entitlement. *Theatre Research International, 16*(2), 142–152.

Pollock, D. (2006). Marking new directions in performance ethnography. *Text and Performance Quarterly, 26*(4), 325–329.

———. (2010) Doorjams and the promise of engaged scholarship. *Quarterly Journal of Speech, 96*(4), 462–468.

Segrest, M. (2002). *Born to belonging: Writings on spirit and justice.* New Brunswick, NJ: Rutgers University Press.

Spry, T. (2001). Performing autoethnography: An embodied methodological practice. *Qualitative Inquiry, 7*(6), 706–732.

Taliaferro-Baszile, D. (2006). Pedagogy born of struggle: From the notebook of a Black professor. In S. Hughes (Ed.), *What we still don't know about teaching race: How to talk about it in the classroom* (pp. 75–96). Lewiston, NY: Edwin Mellen Press.

Willink, K. G. (2009). *Bringing desegregation home: Memories of the struggle toward school integration in rural North Carolina*. New York, NY: Palgrave Macmillan.

———, & Suzette, J. (2012). Taking theories of cultural dialogue from the classroom to the street corner. *Cultural Studies—Critical Methodologies, 12*(3), 197–212.

Winant, H. (1998). Racial dualism at century's end. In W. Lubiano (Ed.), *The house that race built* (pp. 87–115). New York, NY: Vintage Press.

Wolfe, T. (1940). *You can't go home again*. New York, NY: Harper.

7

The Rose Creek Oral History Project: Elementary Cross-Grade Social Studies Curriculum in Review

DeeDee Mower

This chapter is an analysis and reflection of a two-year oral history project at Rose Creek, a suburban elementary school where I currently teach. Our school has about 1,000 students in grades K–6. In 2008, five teachers met together to see how we could utilize community knowledge in our classroom instruction. At the time, three of us were teaching third grade and two were teaching fifth grade. Third-grade social studies curriculum focuses on communities, and the fifth-grade curriculum has a focus on United States History. As teachers, our goal was to align with grade-level curricula, and we believed we could coordinate efforts to have students learn from each other and from community members in order to supplement their educational experience and increase student knowledge about historical events. While we decided to implement this oral history project as a pedagogical practice to tell detailed stories about historical events, we did not realize that the oral history project would also be a liberating pedagogical practice to make counterstories visible. This chapter will introduce the project, discuss teachers' goals to extend students' understanding of history through oral history practice and community knowledge building, and explore the tensions and possibilities for counterstorytelling within an elementary school history curriculum. I argue that creating a space for history allows teachers to engage in critical pedagogies by utilizing community knowledge to investigate how men, women, and children were involved in or directly affected by local, state, national, and world events.

The first year of the project was a powerful representation of the pedagogical possibilities afforded to us as teachers to engage students in critical thought and artful representations of power, prejudice, civil rights, conflicts, and civic participation. We received four thousand dollars in grants from Utah State History, Jordan Education Foundation, and the Charles Redd Center for Western Studies for tapes, recorders, and transcription services. We also received in-kind services and materials from the Utah Museum of Fine Arts. All of these resources combined to help us have a successful first year oral history project due to the number of interviews recorded and transcribed.

The second year of the project included three grade levels—third, fourth, and fifth—with the same teachers. The second year focused more narrowly on World War II, and specifically on the creation of camps for the incarceration of Japanese Americans.[1] One such camp was located in a small town just a hundred miles south of our school. Due to this project, students were able to have direct contact with people whose lived experiences illuminated the realities, effects, and outcomes of war and prejudice. This human connection to a world event, from their very own community, was powerful incentive for students to use higher-order thinking skills to try to understand the events. Rather than in a linear and dehumanizing approach, the project engaged them in conversation about the lives and experiences of the people they were witness to, and whose personal histories countered dominant narratives.

This chapter will provide an overview of the oral history project for both years in order to emphasize three key arguments. First, teaching history from multiple perspectives using oral histories is essential in developing a social justice and critical social studies curriculum. However, teachers must struggle to maintain these goals, particularly when we explore complex or unpopular aspects of history. Second, oral history gathering is a significant technique in helping students to develop critical thinking skills. Third, if a critical lens is not emphasized and maintained throughout the project, the curriculum pattern may revert to the production of dominant historical narratives that effectively keep children (and teachers) at a distance from the complexity of historical events. I will argue how educators' and narrators' efforts to "maintain childhood innocence" in our oral history project prevented students from participating in or listening to conflicts and emotionally intense events and stories. These efforts to keep children's innocence intact served to perpetuate social studies curricula and texts that eradicated multiple perspectives and the critical interrogation of historical events.

Teachers can use oral history projects as a way to craft critical historical stories, which demonstrate the complexities of social studies curriculum by filling in historical gaps and omissions. Teachers must be willing to leave their comfortable and familiar connections to the knowledge portrayed in texts, and allow a space for narrated local knowledges with which they are not familiar in order to provide students a more complete historical understanding.

Multiple Perspectives in Social Studies Curriculum

As teachers we have often heard the quote attributed to Winston Churchill that the victors write the history. It is apparent in our social studies textbooks that there is rarely room for multiple perspectives in regard to local, state, and United States history. History is revealed through our texts in a linear cause-and-effect fashion, giving the voice and perspective of mostly White participants. The complexities of human relationships are rarely publicized through the words on a textbook page, especially for children. By relying on these texts with their limited perspectives, educators perpetuate the knowledges they emphasize—knowledges that are in solidarity with White, middle-class experience and understanding. Historically, the research that informs the texts is infused with Western thought, and may be in conflict with other community understandings and beliefs. Dominant knowledges in texts portray a position of normalization and a priori foundational ideas, and create systems that cannot conceive other knowledges (Darder, Baltodano, & Torres, 2003; Freire, 1971; Giroux, 1981; McLaren & Lankshear, 1994; Sleeter & Cornbleth, 2011).

We wanted to develop pedagogical practices that disrupted or complicated the justified true beliefs or justified knowledges that were in the textbooks and likely incompatible with other knowledges, such as living knowledges. One way of thinking about these knowledges is from an indigenous perspective. Marie Battiste (2002), in reference to Indigenous epistemologies, purported that "knowledge is not secular" (p. 14). She went on to say that knowledge is not compartmentalized into different disciplines, that knowledge is a way "people envision themselves in relation to each other and to everything else…It is inherent in and connected to all of nature, to its creatures, and to human existence" (p. 14). She also stated that "knowledge is not what some possess and others do not" (p. 15). From this perspective, the teachers sought to include knowledges through oral histories that would show individual relationships to larger social events, as well as the connectedness of people. The teachers' allowance of oral histories into the curriculum showed their belief that educational practices should not define historical knowledge as a secular discipline detached from the experience of those who have lived or are living it. As teachers, we knew that oral histories would provide the supplemental resources to our social studies instruction, and possibly disrupt the cultural memory regurgitated in our texts, which was preventing an understanding of how the community and those in the state we live in had been impacted by national and world events.

Part of what the teachers learned for themselves and for their students through the oral history projects was that in our elementary teaching experiences we continually shield the students from harsh realities of history. We talk of conflict, but we distance the students from violence.[2] Michael Frisch (1990) expanded on this by saying that history in general is taught at a safe distance so we do not feel it. Frisch connected history with memory and described how myth and collective history combine to create a history that is a safe distance from the audience. Frisch provided examples of historical American names in texts, which overwhelmingly are political and military, and concluded that cultural imprinting has a function in society, a function of cultural symbolism, which creates a narrow collective cultural memory. This collective memory does not include critical thought, and produces "generations for whom a meaningful national history in even some of its richness and complexity is not an accessible resource" (p. 50). We recognized that our students were safely distanced from history through text, and that collectively, they came to understand history in a similar fashion to how we, as teachers, were taught history. In contrast, we now saw oral histories as a pedagogical practice we could use to understand recent historical events from first hand experiences and see how the communities around us were affected.

The First Year:
A Lesson in What Can and Cannot Be Said

The first year of our oral history project involved training teachers and students. A history professor from a local university came to our school and trained our students on how to obtain oral histories. The students practiced their new skill with each other and staff members. The original objective of the project was to have students collect oral histories, become more community oriented, and have alternative texts for literacy development and historical understanding. With the help of the curators from the Museum of Fine Arts, it became evident that our objectives needed to include more critical thought and activities, and move beyond efforts to gather and read oral histories in the same mundane and culturally dominant way as is presented in many history texts.

Preceding the oral history project, students engaged in art and literacy activities on civil rights. Students read short stories on Martin Luther King, Jr. and the Civil Rights Movement, and discussed what rights they had as students and citizens. Students created black and white art prints. The illustrations were their interpretations of those who have human rights and those who have been lacking in obtaining those rights. They also wrote poems to go with their art. A third-grade student wrote:

> Signs
> Signs everywhere for the Black
> Whatever happened to sugar and spice
> And everything nice?

Another third grader wrote:

> People are in a fog and trying to find their way to liberty.
> Finding their way home through the fog
> And they are trying to help other people get to liberty.

Students' creative work was displayed in the halls of the school. This allowed other students not involved in the art and literacy project to reflect upon their own understanding of civil rights by talking with their teachers and asking questions about the art representations prior to their gathering of oral histories.

As students began the oral history project, each grade level created a list of questions to ask of their narrators in an interview. Because of this particular art project, some fifth graders decided to include a question about civil rights in their oral history interview. They added the question, "What was the Civil Rights Movement like?" One local participant answered in a way that represented most of the participants in the project:

> Well fortunately being born and raised here in Utah we didn't have the contact with the civil rights that they had in the South. We didn't have a lot of black people that lived here. A few that we did have here were treated just pretty much like anybody else I think, about most the time. Because, we didn't feel the, we didn't have the problem that they had in the South during the civil rights movement.

This quote provides the general sentiment about race and civil rights offered by other oral histories we gathered. It suggests that our community was untouched by racial inequities, and hence the fights for civil rights that characterized the rest of the nation were not a localized issue.

It was through the gathering of another interview, when a narrator felt that something was inappropriate for children to hear, that I discovered that I might need to read between the lines and ask further questions about local race and civil rights issues in the community during the 1960s and 1970s. In their interviews, students had chosen to ask, "What city, state or world event had the most impact on you while you were growing up?" In one of these interviews, a student received an interesting response from the participant. The narrator answered, "Well, that's a good question. Well, let me think. I'm trying to think, now let's see, I'm not going to tell you *that* story," and then proceeded to talk about the local Christmas holiday celebrations when he was a child. The intriguing answer that stated he was not going to tell "*that*" story led me later to ask the narrator what he was alluding to. The narrator told me he did not want to have the story that came immediately to his mind go on record, nor did he want to tell it to the students. He then shared with me, off the taped interview, about how as a young boy in the late 1960s and early 1970s he remembered posters on telephone poles referring to "the Klan" and seeing hanging effigies at the cemetery. State and local history noted that the modern Klan rose in the 1970s as a reaction to various aspects of the civil rights movement (Gerlach, 1982; Bashore & Crump, 1994). This narrator's story suggested that Klan activity in the local city was a prominent part of this movement.

I realized that this narrator did not want to share this story with the students, but I also felt that even as we came to understand how the civil rights movement impacted other states and cities through history books, the local dynamics were an important aspect for the students and teachers to consider. However, voices from the state history texts and the oral histories concluded that civil rights activism, both positive and negative, was only happening outside of the local environment. But this submerged oral history demonstrated that people in the very city of our oral history project were affected by a growing national debate regarding race and civil rights, yet were not voicing their involvement or understandings of it. From the absence of discussion about racial conflict in this narrator's story, as well as in other participants' oral histories, there was a gap between what is known and what can be known. The local stories around civil rights were not to be illuminated, at least to children. Frisch (1990) reiterated why we do not narrow the gap between the known and unknown. He stated, "Audiences used to regarding their history from a safe distance often resist attempts at closing the gap, especially when that process collapses comfortable assumptions as well" (p. 23). So how do we capture embarrassing local information when it is purged from an interview and creates an uncomfortable feeling for the narrators?

Since, at the time, the information was offered to me, not to the students or other teachers, I felt it was my duty to research the information to find out if it was "true." I found information about the Klan's involvement in the city through the local library. I then wanted to include the question in interviews with other longtime residents of the community to hear their perspective of how it entered the community and was forced out. I quickly learned that when I approached other residents about the issue of the Klan, it was skirted away in the conversation, and I felt as if I were intruding where I ought not to go.

The new information about the Klan's influence in the city was an uncomfortable subject for all of us, and we, the teachers, colluded in hiding our community's involvement. We might have included this history if we had asked students to research current state and local civil rights issues. However, we limited our historical work and pedagogical choices, as we did not let our own questions, let alone those from the students, guide the curriculum. We all perpetuated the "border" (Anzaldúa, 1999) between the safe and distant, dominant textual narratives and the hidden, local racial narratives, allowing them both to remain unquestioned and unchallenged. This permitted us to keep the cultural ideals of the community intact and its history protected, concealing the past.

Some of the teachers were uncomfortable with the oral history projects that brought about intensity of thought and sometimes conflict, as with the example above. As teachers, we were not prepared to talk about civil rights issues at the local level. The knowledge of local involvement was an exposure we had not encountered before, because our personal narratives were similar to the many before us—that civil rights involvement was not an issue locally or in our state. Since most of the teachers were local residents, we were trying to understand the counternarrative ourselves, and shielded our own interpretations and understandings. We allowed the dominant discourse about civil rights as events outside of our community to remain intact.

The critical thinking and needed discussions about hard topics were unanticipated and unexplored this first year. It is obvious that teaching with a distance from historical events is much easier, but instead of avoiding challenging topics the next year, the teachers wanted to prepare for what they might encounter from the knowledges the oral histories would provide. As teachers, we felt that if we focused on a particular historical event, we might be able to help the students be critically prepared as well.

Oral History Gathering and Critical Thinking

The oral history project finished up the first year with 64 transcribed oral histories. The funds were utilized and project commitments to the donors completed. It seemed a great success. The state historical society took our compilation of tapes, CDs, and transcripts and archived them (The Rose Creek Oral Histories Collection, 2008, MssB 1907, Utah State Historical Society). We made duplicate copies for our PTA and the city's historical society as well. Students made posters and created a school display of the information they had gathered throughout the year.

There was no funding or in-kind support for a second year, but the same teachers were devoted to the importance of oral histories in our pedagogical practices. The participating teachers met again at the beginning of the following year and noted that several of the oral histories that were gathered the previous year had information about World War II. Since only a few of the students from the first year would be involved in this second-year project, we did not want to spend all of our time training the new students to gather histories and to transcribe them. Rather, we opted to focus on a specific historical event and conduct only a few oral history interviews. We chose the incarceration of Japanese Americans because of the significance to the participating grades' (now third, fourth, and fifth) social studies curriculum. By researching and asking questions of the existing histories, we hoped to develop a greater commitment to critical thinking skills and rely less on the culturally controlled knowledges that were presented in the oral histories the first year.

To prepare our students for gathering and thinking critically about a few oral histories in connection to the incarceration of Japanese Americans, the teachers wrote a scope and sequence for the year. We identified age-appropriate texts that would be important for familiarizing students with the various perspectives and interpretations of the incarceration. We also discussed ways to incorporate Japanese culture through art. Students chose origami creations to make, wrote in Chinese characters, painted water-colored cherry blossoms, and explored print making reflective of their understandings of war. Students also looked at art created by those interred in the camps. Students in third grade read *The Bracelet* (Uchida, 1996) and *So Far From the Sea* (Bunting, 1998). The students then created their own story or picture books from what they read, and discussed them with their fifth-grade buddies. Fourth graders read the novel, *Baseball Saved Us* (Mochizuki, 1995) and *The Children of Topaz* (Tunnell & Chilcoat, 1996), and wrote about the conflicting information. Fifth graders read *Journey to Topaz* (Uchida, 1988). The curriculum department at the district office donated two classroom sets of this book in order for us to proceed with this project.

Having been taught by teachers to use a critical lens to analyze traditional and age-appropriate texts, the students recognized that the World

War II event they were reading about was interesting, but not without questions. Students began asking questions of each other and of the text. They wanted to know if anyone was killed in the camp, and if so, why? They wanted to know why each family did not have their own house. They wanted to know what children did for fun. Although it was problematic to most of them that children their age had been under the watchful eye of someone with a gun, and they knew that there was something not fair about it, they still discussed the event as if this was a story and not something attached to who they were or where they lived.

When the teachers located the camps for the incarceration of Japanese Americans on a map, many students recognized the site of the camp that was closest to our geographical location. It was interesting to find out that several students had actually been to the place—Topaz, Utah. Many of the students reported that they visited to find topaz, the mineral, not knowing that an incarceration camp had been established there. Recently, there have been efforts to establish a museum in Topaz to reveal the history of the place. While this part of World War II history is not a significant part of our textbooks and has thus far been eradicated from the place, it is still vivid in personal memories.

A guest was willing to come and share her history with the students. She was a young child in the Topaz incarceration camp. She brought with her to class many pictures of her family, and art created by friends and family in the camp that depicted the surrounding mountains and landscape. She shared the following with us: "Living in Topaz, I thought our barracks were normal homes, but when I moved into a real home after leaving Topaz, I realized, 'This must be the houses most people live in and not in the barracks.'"

She also answered their questions about what they did for fun, and if everyone played baseball. She told them that they played with dolls, and that they celebrated holidays. She stated,

> In Topaz, we continued to have our annual Buddhist holiday, Obon, in the summers. We still continue to celebrate Obon festival every summer. I started dancing the Obon in Topaz. I am 66 years old and haven't missed any Obon festival since Topaz. Our family really gets into this with ordoi and taiko playing. As a family, this is our favorite holiday. This is the time to celebrate the rich legacy our loved ones passed on to us. This is not a sad occasion but a great joy.

This guest speaker alluded to the fact, in her narrative, that she did have one traumatic experience in the camp, but she was not yet ready to share that. She was a little emotional as she talked about her grandmother being sick and being left in front of the horse-stall makeshift housing in which the family had been forced to stay while being evacuated to Utah. Her grandmother was taken back to a hospital in California where she passed away a few weeks later of stomach cancer. In all other incidences she shared she tried to be positive and smiling. Since she largely avoided discussing conflict, similar to what happened in the first year of the oral history project, this narrator also may have left unsaid information that she felt was too painful for children. It became evident to us that many sources of information need to be included in discussions about historical events so that the "distancing" we create to protect ourselves and others can be exposed in meaningful ways in order to prevent similar, demeaning events from happening again.

Since the students had background knowledge through novels, they were able to hear her story as authentic, and it gave life to the things they had read. I observed the emotional attachment to the historical event they now had by the sensitive way they asked their questions about what her family had endured. The students asked about friends and how they played. They asked about school and what parents did. The guest ended by playing drums and talking about the cultural value of the drums, and then allowed the students a chance to play them.

The students were very attuned to all the guest speakers. This was clearly evident on a different afternoon when they sat quietly on the gymnasium floor for an hour as an elderly man read his prepared oral history to them. This guest was a Japanese American veteran, age 85, who fought with the volunteer Japanese American 522nd Field Artillery Battalion of the 442nd RCT (Regimental Combat Team) "which would later become the most decorated unit of their size and length of service in the history of the U.S. Army, also the unit to suffer the most casualties." He explained that he was sent to Germany to liberate prisoners "while [his] loved ones were back home in concentration camps." He came dressed in his military uniform, and brought several items that interested the students, including helmets from German soldiers. He shared his experience of coming to Utah for the first time on a dilapidated passenger coach train as part of the War Relocation mandate. He stated,

> The first 28 hours we had no heat, blankets, water or food so when we were abandoned from the all freight cars in Reno on a siding, the guard left and a man entered. Regardless of what would happen to us we complained about being cold, thirsty, and hungry. Then we got heat, water, and a baloney sandwich each and headed for Ogden where we were permitted to disembark for the first time.

This story had relevance for the students for several reasons. First, he was talking about coming to their state and listed places that were familiar to them. He then described what it was like to get out of an incarceration camp by volunteering to be in the military but still be under government surveillance. None of the other novels or texts portrayed someone leaving the camps—except to work on farms—by joining the military. There are no children's books on the Japanese American men that went to war to prove their patriotism to their county. His story particularly allowed for continued critical thinking by the students when he spoke about being in war and fighting for a country to which he was loyal despite the mistreatment he and his family endured. Through learning his story, what it meant to be loyal became a complex issue for students. The students had to grapple with the idea that being loyal to a country and being a citizen did not guarantee safety or freedom.

The third oral history provided a glimpse into the complexity of what it generally means to be free, safe, and protected. It became another way for students and adults alike to critically shape new understandings about the power of government over ownership of home and land. This third narrator allowed students to access his history through transcripts of the interview, but did not want to physically present his story to the group.

The third narrator's story was about being a young boy living with his family on an eighty-acre farm near Topaz, Utah. He remembered his father one day telling the family that the government would take over their land and outbuildings (barns, shed, etc.) or condemn the property if they would not sell. The family was paid $7,500 for their property. The family was forced to move to the nearby town of Delta, and his father had to drive 90 miles to Salt Lake City for part of the year to do carpentry work in order to provide for the family. Despite the changes to his family, this participant said that he believed that the incarceration of Japanese Americans at Topaz was necessary in order to "protect" the Japanese Americans. He stated, "Well, it was after World War II started and they were bringing all those people from the coast to get them out to save their lives. Some of them were citizens." He said that the town of Delta prospered because of the camp. Some of the Japanese Americans who were incarcerated there were able to work in Delta, and the cash they used to purchase any products was a boost to the local economy.

Despite what he felt were positive aspects of the camps, he recognized that there was some brutality connected to the incarceration of Japanese Americans. He remembered witnessing one man being killed by the guards. He said in his oral history,

> Well there was one fellow that I know of that tried to go through the fence and the guards hollered at him and he just kept going and they shot him and, uh, then the people said he was deaf and couldn't hear, so I guess you don't know what the guy was thinking, but that might have been one way of just ending it all.

This part of his story answered a question that the students had about anyone being killed, but implied a more harsh environment than in his previous statements. The students knew that the Japanese Americans were under armed guard while incarcerated at Topaz, and suspected that someone may have been killed, but their novels never mentioned it. Also, the students now had a story of someone like them, a White, middle-class citizen, who had been forced to surrender his property to demonstrate loyalty to the government. Not only did they see how they (as White middle-class students) might have been impacted by this historical event, this oral history also shed light on the complexity of the government to provide safety for all its citizens.

A local parent who helped gather this third oral history agreed with the narrator that the camp at Topaz was indeed created to ensure the safety of Japanese Americans. Only after she heard the Japanese American guests share their oral histories did she come to understand the complexity of the situation and how lives were indeed altered and misrepresented. Because of the multidimensional understandings from the three oral histories, and their connections to the incarceration of Japanese Americans, she could now engage with students and other adults about the prejudice and power associated with this historical event. In family and community gatherings, she reiterated what she had learned from the oral histories, and how her perception had changed. She explained that she was uncomfortable with the realization that the government had not been benevolent to the Japanese Americans, but that generations have protected the belief that the incarceration camps were in Japanese Americans' best interest. She spoke out because she wanted to end the perpetual illusion.

Helping students and adults understand why histories are shaped in particular ways is important. We came to understand the personal attachment to the war by the man whose family was forced to evacuate and leave their land and livelihood. However, we also understood that the way he (and others) spoke about the war and the incarceration of Japanese Americans had serious implications. Certainly, the government would want the support of local people when they placed a camp in a particular location. We can see how the government would want to communicate to people that the incarceration was for the benefit of the Japanese Americans so that the local population would accept the camp's existence. The persistence of narratives, almost 70 years later, that position incarceration camps for Japanese Americans as places designed for their safety, illuminates the strong hold that a passive attitude can have on the perpetuation of current viewpoints that dehumanize historical events. How people envision themselves in relation to others is contrived, and those in small communities were vulnerable to the discourse tactics that molded their understanding. As teachers, we wanted our students to consider what it would have meant to stand up for others. Bringing it to their life experience, we asked them to consider how their experiences at school allow them a chance to speak up about bullying and other forms of mistreatment. Still, after further reflection, it is clear to me that there was more we could have done to make this connection clearer.

It is invaluable for students to engage in gathering oral histories so that events of the past that seemingly have no relevance to present conditions become recognizable. In so doing, we might better understand our human connectedness and the barriers that keep us from making those connections. It is devastating to realize what could be lost once those voices are gone and their stories can no longer be told. This knowledge must motivate those who can still speak from personal experience to continually battle for an alternative outlook to the textbook story. Unfortunately, the prevalence of discourses of protection is one reason texts continue to avoid conflict and complexity. As a result, they perpetuate passivity and absence of emotional attachment to historical behavior, and position these events so far in the past that their effects on current events are no longer discernable.

Student Innocence and Teachers' Roles in Crafting Critical Understandings

The most unique thing about our oral history projects was that teachers learned information usually at the same time as the students. By this I mean that when we asked guests to come to our school or invited people for interviews, we did not know what was going to be said. We are accountable to give students the tools to think critically about what they are hearing, reading, and learning. The oral history projects presented above represent the importance of having a teaching plan that, regardless of teacher expertise on the event, allows for the powerful stories to illuminate and complicate the issue at hand and to cultivate in students a connection to the subject matter.

The first year of the oral history project reflects how easy it is to stifle those experiences that otherwise might enhance critical thinking and undermine dominant discourses. Because oral histories create a context where teachers are not always sure what will be told, they need to engage pedagogy that allows students to ask questions of the event and gain perspective on their inquiries, something they cannot do with traditional texts. In the above examples students asked questions that included violence, wanting to know if anyone was killed, how many people the war veteran killed, and about other types of violence about which they were interested. In a different way, they were impacted more when the Japanese American who fought in the war told them about when his troop was asked to launch an unexpected attack and break the German Gothic Line. To do so, the men had to climb Mount Fogarito that had a nearly 4,000-foot vertical precipice. They "climbed the mountain that was unclimbable, in combat gear…Men fell down [to their death] as they climbed the mountain and no man cried out as he fell, so as not to give away the position." Harrowing incidences of emotional abuse were told as well, such as being called names and being treated unfairly, also of having no privacy but continual surveillance. Students could relate emotionally to the harshness perpetrated in the Japanese American narrations because later they related experiences of when they had felt bullied, or when others thought they were untrustworthy.

Students and teachers often would shed tears when guests spoke of their experiences. However, there were also occasions when speakers tried to shelter the students from some forms of violence and harshness. The war veteran left out racially demeaning references, even though they were written in his narration. The woman showed resilience, rather than share the brutality of being forced to move and live under complete surveillance with few conveniences. The man who lived near the incarceration camp did not want to engage with the students in conversation. Yet, the narrators shared much more than the text or teachers could envision. Their narrations continue to be part of students' and teachers' memories, and continue to prompt our questions.

Following my participation in the oral history project, it is my belief that teachers should strongly consider using oral histories as a consistent practice in their teaching. Incorporating oral histories in a critical manner helps students reflect upon events that shape human experience and relationships. As students learn to appreciate the lived experiences of others, they can more fully understand the impact individuals have upon one another, and can analyze texts in ways that expose missing or deleted correlations. Creating opportunities for students to utilize many modes of personal history, from narrations to primary documents, in connection with secondary texts, creates greater understanding and a more intense need to analyze history through multiple perspectives. The knowledges we gained through these cross-age group projects were certainly the most memorable and the most valued pedagogical practices we have utilized.

Notes

1. The incarceration of Japanese Americans involved United States citizens and was not sanctioned under international law. The term *internment camp* is not used here because that refers to prisoners of war and selected enemy aliens. See Densho.org/Times at http://densho.org/learning/default.asp?path=times/Times.asp
2. We as teachers have observed that we allow less "rough" play on the playground, more so than in previous years. Field games often get banned because the students are "too rough and violent." These concepts may very well penetrate into our teaching pedagogy as well when we tend to pass over the violence in all of its forms—physical, spiritual, and emotional—in our discussions of historical events. It is sometimes evident that we "ban" violence in our telling of history.

Bibliography

Anzaldúa, G. (1999). *Borderlands: The new mestiza = La frontera* (2nd ed.). San Francisco, CA: Aunt Lute Books.

Apple, M. (1982). *Education and power*. Boston, MA: Routledge & Kegan Paul.

———. (2001). *Educating the 'right' way: Markets, standards, God, and inequality*. New York, NY: RoutledgeFalmer.

Bashore, M., & Crump, S. (1994). *Riverton: The story of a Utah country town*. Riverton Historical Society. Salt Lake City: Publishers Press.

Battiste, M. (2002). *Indigenous knowledge and pedagogy in First Nations education—A literature review with recommendations*. Ottawa, Ontario, Canada: Indian and Northern Affairs.

Bunting, E. (1998). *So far from the sea* (C. K. Soentpiet, Illus.). London, UK: Sandpiper.

Clegg, L. B., et al. (1992). Creating oral history projects for the social studies classroom. *Social Studies Review, 32*(1), 53–60.

Darder, A., Baltodano, M., & Torres, R. D. (2003). *The critical pedagogy reader*. New York, NY: RoutledgeFalmer.

Freire, P. (1971). *Pedagogy of the oppressed*. New York, NY: Herder & Herder.

Frisch, M. (1990). *A shared authority: Essays on the craft and meaning of oral and public history*. Albany, NY: State University of New York Press.

Gerlach, L. A. (1982). *Blazing crosses in Zion: The Ku Klux Klan in Utah*. Logan, UT: Utah State University Press.

Giroux, H. A. (1981). *Ideology, culture and the process of schooling*. Philadelphia, PA: Temple University Press.

Hickey, G. M. (1991). 'And then what happened, grandpa?' Oral history projects in the elementary classroom. *Social Education, 55*(4), 216–217.

McCormick, J. (1998). *The Utah adventure*. Salt Lake City, UT: Gibbs Smith.

McLaren, P., & Lankshear, C. (Eds.). (1994). *Politics of liberation: Paths from Freire*. London, UK: Routledge.

Mochizuki, K. (1995). *Baseball saved us* (D. Lee, Illus.). New York, NY: Lee & Low Books.

Sleeter, C. E., & Cornbleth, C. (Eds.). (2011). *Teaching with vision: Culturally responsive teaching in standards-based classrooms*. New York, NY: Teachers College Press.

Sommer, B., & Quinlan, M. (2002). *The oral history manual*. Walnut Creek, CA: Altamira Press.

Tunnell, M., & Chilcoat, G. (1996). *The children of Topaz: The story of a Japanese-American internment camp: Based on a classroom diary*. New York, NY: Holiday House.
Uchida, Y. (1988). *Journey to Topaz: A story of the Japanese-American evacuation*. Salt Lake City, UT: Publishers Book Services.
———. (1996). *The bracelet* (J. Yardley, Illus.). New York, NY: Putnam & Grosset Group.
Weeks, D. J. (2003). Historical inquiry: Charting journeys of learning. *NW Education*, *8*(4), 2–7.

8

Exploring (Dis)Connections Through Digital Storytelling: Toward Pedagogies of Critical Co-Learning

Kristen V. Luschen

"I am your friend," said the girl in front of me. She directed her declaration to Cristina,[1] the very quiet girl seated at the desk to my right. The classroom lights were dim and the next student's story had already begun to play. After four weeks and eight two-hour sessions working with their Hampshire College student partners, Mr. Covey's sixth-grade class at Liston Middle School viewed their completed digital stories collectively for the first time. All ten sixth graders and their four Hampshire college student partners watched excitedly, attentively, and with some nervousness, as their two-to-three minute videos played. Cristina's two-minute story revealed significant unhappiness. Her parents had separated, and she missed her father who lived in Puerto Rico; she wanted to return. She narrated that she had no brothers or sisters and few friends. The story left me with a sense of a young girl who felt very alone. At the moment her digital story concluded, and without missing a beat, the girl sitting in front of me turned around and declared her friendship to Cristina. She smiled, and said very simply, "I am your friend." To me, it was one among several important moments of connection that was engendered through the Educational Histories/Educational Hopes project (EHEH).

This chapter examines the possibilities and tensions involved in utilizing storytelling as a vehicle to develop critical consciousness about how institutional structures, policies, and relations of power impact students' experience of schooling. The students at the center of the project were 27 undergraduate students enrolled in my course, Schooling in a Multicultural Society (SMS)—a foundations course focused on education and power—and four middle-school classes at Liston Middle School. The digital storytelling project was embedded within the SMS class to complicate how educational inequality is sustained, as well as to invite SMS students to hear and understand multiple and sometimes conflicting perspectives, and to build connections across experiences and ideas. In discussing what she referred to as a "signature pedagogy for the new humanities," Benmayor (2008) argued for the importance of personal storytelling through the medium of digital storytelling:

> Digital storytelling is an assets-based pedagogy where students can bring their own cultural knowledge and experiences to the fore, including their skills and comfort with technology, to transform their thinking and empower themselves. The multiple creative languages of digital storytelling—writing, voice, image, and sound—encourage historically marginalized subjects, especially younger generations to inscribe emerging social and cultural identities and challenge lived cultural discourses in a new and exciting way. (p. 200)

As Benmayor identified, pedagogies that encourage the sharing and exploration of students' experiences and knowledge catalyze critical engagement and transformation.

Throughout this chapter I will provide an account of a course-based project involving digital storytelling and community-engaged learning in order to grasp whether, how, and for whom the process of reflecting on and sharing one's (hi)stories can be validating, transformative, and illuminate the power[2] of participating students to make change in their worlds. Further, beyond validation, what is the potential for digital storytelling and community-engaged learning to build connections across difference, and support multiple perspective taking, reflexivity, and informed action.

I begin this chapter by discussing the project context framing the creation of digital stories both by Hampshire undergraduate students and our middle-school partners at Liston Middle School. I address the ways in which the project facilitated critical exploration of educational inequality, and (dis)connection and visibility among Hampshire students and Liston students. I conclude by identifying the complexities and lessons learned about the possibilities for digital storytelling to facilitate critical consciousness and connections across communities of difference.

Project Context

The EHEH project was embedded in an undergraduate course I regularly teach on power, diversity, and multicultural education in American schooling. My goals in the SMS aspect of the digital storytelling project, Educational Histories/Educational Hopes, were that through the process and production of the media, students would critically examine their schooling histories, as well as share and ask questions about their classmates' schooling experiences.

The two groups of students—undergraduate and middle school—were seemingly very different, and these differences catalyzed inquiry into why the schisms and points of intersection across our experience existed. The enrollment in the SMS class was consistent with the predominately White student body of Hampshire College; about 20% of the students in the class were students of color. Students in the class hailed from urban, rural, and suburban areas. From their digital stories or personal interaction, I learned that some came from impoverished households and others from families with great wealth.

In contrast to the economic, geographic, and to a lesser extent, racial and ethnic diversity of students in SMS (though it was limited), Liston Middle School was much more homogeneous. It was designated as a "high poverty" school by the state, and in 2010, over ninety percent of the students enrolled at the school identified as Latin@. Nearly ninety percent of the students participated in the free or reduced lunch program. English was not the first language for nearly 70% of the students, and many of those students, nearly forty percent, were categorized under No Child Left Behind as "limited English proficient." In this school and in Massachusetts, this meant that the students were enrolled in classes taught in English with other students new to learning English. In contrast, approximately five Hampshire students were bilingual and four others had an introductory familiarity with Spanish from family interactions or courses while in high school or at Hampshire.

While in the midst of creating their own digital stories, Hampshire students partnered with sixth-, seventh-, or eighth-grade students in one of four classes to write, storyboard, and craft stories about themselves, their families, their hopes, and their struggles. Three of the classes were small, with between five and ten students in attendance for each workshop session. These classes were devoted to Spanish heritage speakers who had been assessed and categorized as "limited English proficient." The fourth class had an enrollment of 30 students who were either English dominant or "proficient" speakers and/or writers of English.

The Educational Histories/Educational Hopes Project

The project course began with Hampshire students—all twenty-seven—writing and crafting digital stories that shared with their classmates a story about themselves, their family, struggles, and hopes. As I will discuss later, Hampshire students' stories were drafted during February, the first month of the course. The collaborative project between Liston Middle School and the undergraduate students enrolled in the course kicked off during the first two weeks of March. In the latter half of March and through much of April, Hampshire students worked on producing their own digital stories and proposing, researching, and writing their individual research projects. In late April, Hampshire students returned to Liston for four more workshops that supported the completion and sharing of Liston students' digital stories.

The EHEH project was ambitious, given the time, level of commitment, and risk taking it required of students (both undergraduate and middle school), so the question of why we did it is important. As a scholar and teacher deeply influenced by critical pedagogy and feminist and critical race theory, I seek out ways for my students and me to question, understand, and transform political and social inequality in various forms. Over the past years I have built media-production assignments in my courses, because they help students to grapple with how knowledge-images-discourses are created. Professor and media educator Jason Ohler (2005) has written,

> Digital Stories provide powerful media literacy learning opportunities because students are involved in the creation and analysis of the media in which they are immersed. When students do the hard work of marrying story and technology to express themselves to others, they can see more clearly the persuasive nature of the electronic culture in which they live. (p. 47)

Production requires students to make choices about how they construct stories. In doing so they can transfer that experience to formulate questions about how the images, knowledge, and discourses they take for granted are formed.

To facilitate the development and sharing of stories and the critical examination of how narratives are constructed, in recent years I have introduced more assignments involving the use of digital media into my classes.[3] The assignments require that students reflect on their perspectives and, through the editing process, embody the knowledge that stories are constructed and partial narratives. As they encounter experiences similar to and different from their own, I wanted the Hampshire students to consider how they chose to represent themselves to others in the class, and what they did or did not share and why. In doing so, the project was intended to help them to learn and explore together with a willingness to ask questions of one another (and texts) and wonder aloud. Digital storytelling was a new medium for me, so when I initially considered its possibilities for teaching and learning in my class, I intended to facilitate only the undergraduate students' story production, as a way for them to become more familiar with each other, to build trust with each other, so that they could take intellectual risks in our learning environment.

Community-Engaged Connections

The Critical Studies of Childhood, Youth, and Learning Program (CYL) at Hampshire College has been involved in a partnership with Liston K–8 School for several years. Liston is a full-service community school that seeks to harness community resources and integrate them into the school in ways that support the academic achievement of all students. This work emerged from a community need-interest inventory, in which parents and community members identified a number of areas on which the school should focus its reform work. The CYL program is one of the programs focused on instructional partnerships, school culture, and college access. This sustainable structure intends to work against the "hit it and quit it" (Cushman, 1999) service learning projects that are university and service focused, rather than mutually beneficial projects that acknowledge community goals, knowledge, and expertise (Hansen, 2011).

As part of this broader initiative, the principal brought Mr. Covey and Mr. Matthews—two Social Studies teachers—and me together to develop course-based projects. The teachers wanted college students to engage in meaningful ways with their students as part of the school's efforts to build a college-going culture. The intent was that through formal and informal interactions, Liston students would gain an understanding of what it meant to go to college, and see themselves as future college students. On the Hampshire side, students would learn more about urban education, the impact of high-stakes education reform, and the experience of schooling from the perspective of Latin@ middle-school students who have been the targets of current efforts to "close the achievement gap."

After explaining my upcoming class, Mr. Covey and Mr. Matthews were strongly interested in Hampshire students supporting their sixth to eighth graders in crafting digital and audio stories about their educational hopes and experiences. Out of this discussion, The Educational Histories/Educational Hopes project was born. From the teachers' point of view, the project would encourage their students' engagement with Social Studies by anchoring discussions of history and perspective in their own experiences and family knowledges. I saw this as an opportunity for my college students to learn about the school and community from the perspectives of the middle-school students, and to gain a deeper understanding of the challenges and possibilities for schooling in under-resourced environments from their experience navigating the project and from listening to the students.

In SMS, though we critically read studies discussing educational reform and efforts to close the achievement gap between Black and Latin@ students and their White counterparts, I was concerned that students' perspectives would largely be absent from these accounts. Similar to Darcy Alexandra's (2008) sentiments when considering her digital story work with undocumented people in Ireland,

> I am therefore deeply curious to explore whether an analytically imaginative and creative practice of narrating multi-mediated tales, or digital stories, can play some role in defying the silencing of experience that occurs when our fragmentary, messy lives are reduced to information. (p. 101)

How might the development of digital stories through the EHEH project complicate my undergraduate students' notions of education, and catalyze their thinking about their educational histories in relation to others in the class and at Liston? How did the sharing of our experiences through digital stories work against our taken-for-granted notions of each other and schooling, and in particular, education in urban environments? In the end, I agreed to span the EHEH digital story project across the curriculum of both Hampshire and Liston middle-school students.

Crafting Critical Connections Within Hampshire SMS Class: Linking Together Community-Engaged Learning and Digital Storytelling

The digital story project was an ambitious undertaking in one semester. During the first month, SMS classes were divided between discussion of texts and work-shopping our developing story scripts. In many ways, the course remained a typical social foundations course, delving into American schooling through historical, sociological, and philosophical approaches. Hampshire students read educational theory and research examining the production, perpetuation, and intervention of educational inequality, particularly as it is organized around race and socioeconomic class. Discussions, written assignments, and independent research projects were intended to provoke and complement the themes emerging from students' digital stories.

While their retrospectives noted that students gained a great deal of critical insight into the educational system through the readings and discussion, the digital story project was the aspect of the course that most urged them to interrogate their prior knowledge and assumptions. One student wrote,

> The literature that we read was very enriching. Therefore, to be able to apply the knowledge that we learned, it was the best thing to me about this project...I appreciated this project because it did help me to examine my own assumptions. I have always *believed* that all students are unique, with distinct culture, dreams and behavior. However, working on this project has shed light on my hypocritical *behavio*r [emphasis added].

For this student, the mix of theory and experience helped her reflect on her own behavior, and as a future teacher, recognize that her interactions with students were not aligned with her desire to teach from an assets-oriented approach that acknowledged the potential of every child.

Learning within a critical framework—where educators "create the possibilities for the production or construction of knowledge"—is transformative (Freire, 2000, p. 30). In the process of sharing and building connections between texts (accumulated knowledge) and one's experiences, we become active agents in learning. Reflexivity involves a process by which we both question and reframe accumulated knowledge as well as our own experiences. Through critical readings, meaningful experiences, and careful reflection, many SMS students were transformed through the course and the EHEH digital story project. They were remade or re-formed as they taught and learned with the Liston students. However, as I will discuss throughout, transformative learning did not bar—indeed, it went hand in hand with—students' detailed analysis and critique of the complexities of the EHEH project. First, however, the next section will speak to the possibilities for forging connections across SMS students.

Sharing Experiences: Building Small (Group) Communities

Coming out of the framework of intergroup dialogue and critical pedagogy, I included the creation of digital stories in the SMS class with the guiding assumption that sharing personal narratives across positions of difference has the potential to support critical thinking, the interrogation of personal assumptions, and the capacity to explore issues from multiple perspectives (Lopez & Zúñiga, 2010; Nagda, Gurin, Sorensen, Gurin-Sands, & Osuna, 2009). I infuse aspects from these approaches into my Education Studies classes with the intention of creating an environment in which students take risks, learn from one another, question their assumptions, and come to understand how they are implicated and/or insinuated within relations of power, both marginality and privilege.

I began efforts to develop the sharing of experiences among students the first day of class with an introductory exercise. Each of us had a sheet of paper, and had to find someone who: has more siblings than you, went to a public school, is from Massachusetts, has a family member who is a teacher, saw a movie over the Winter break, or is an artist. We moved around the room introducing ourselves and inquiring about these fairly nonthreatening questions. While simple, the prompts provoked lively discussion, and cracked open the door among people who ranged in their familiarity with each other.

Over the next classes I facilitated a process by which SMS students shared more of their personal stories with classmates. I asked students to bring to class their responses to what I referred to as "story seeds." Mindful of possible discomfort with sharing their personal stories, the assignment explained that "in order to get to know one another a bit better and to begin to plant the seeds for our digital stories," they should respond to four prompts and be prepared to share two of their responses with their classmates in small groups. The prompts were:

1. Identify and explain your relationship with an adult who influenced your education,
2. Discuss an educational accomplishment,
3. Discuss a meaningful place related to your education, and
4. Discuss an ongoing practice in which you engage.

I also asked them to confine their answers to the arena of education and learning, but to remember that education does not only happen in schools. The students in each group took note of things that were compelling to them or that they wondered about the stories. I also encouraged them to ask questions that would help authors expand their descriptions, and articulate aspects of the story that were particularly meaningful to them. When I read the short narratives, I commented in the same manner.

At no point did I *require* that students explore and disclose emotionally difficult or traumatic relationships in their stories, though nearly all did. I believe that this was due to the kinds of questions students asked of one another, and the resources I used to model the creation of their work. In the first few weeks of the semester, we watched and listened to several stories created by ordinary people about their lives. We heard experiences recorded by youth, young adults, mothers and daughters, and people in long-term relationships on the Story Corps website, www.storycorps.org, and while those stories did not utilize images, students learned about the power of narrative and music together to convey a powerful story. In fact, all of the stories were emotionally compelling and spoke of difficulties or challenges of some sort. This was continued as we considered several digital stories on www.storiesforchange.com and www.storycenter.org and discussed why they did or did not engage us.

Through the readings and videos we watched, students ascertained that what made the stories compelling was the reflection on struggle. Given the context of the course, most stories focused on an educational tension that was present in their lives, why it was a struggle, and what they had done to address it. Students explored feeling isolated or not having a place they felt comfortable to learn. Some spoke about how learning disabilities or mental health problems affected their school lives and interests, about mentoring, about their families' sacrifices in order to become "educated," and some spoke of seeking out educational spaces where they could avoid harassment and low expectations. Some students spoke of the need for perfection, and of the difficulty of resisting family influences dictating their desires and shaping their identities.

Developing the digital stories was neither easy nor bereft of struggle. Staff from Hampshire's Advanced Media services held two production workshops, and they were available to meet with students throughout the process to provide any technical support necessary for creating the stories. Small-group work-shopping was an important element of the digital story project, and a meaningful shift occurred in this process during the month between the creation and production of SMS student draft digital stories. Through the first month of class, SMS students developed their narratives and shared their drafts in small, self-composed groups a few times. As a class, we generated the criteria for the kinds of feedback that would be helpful to them in strengthening their stories just before they submitted their first drafts. However, at the beginning of March, I formed workgroups of SMS students according to their schedules and availability, and assigned each team to a Liston middle-school classroom. Each team's responsibility was to work with the middle-school class and support them in developing their stories and producing their digital piece. With a few exceptions, the SMS student team worked together at Liston for the duration of the project, traveling to and from Liston together and facilitating story development workshops for the Liston students. Therefore, when it came time to comment on their own digital story drafts, SMS stories were reviewed by the SMS group members with whom they were paired to work at Liston. The change in capacity to cultivate relationships among the SMS students was subtle, but I believe that the working group structure that was important for working with students at Liston simultaneously created divisions in the SMS class culture. Students interacted a great deal with their assigned team members, but cultivating a SMS class learning community became more elusive.

Rather, the relationships formed at Liston were drawn back to Hampshire to support the production of their own digital stories. Students did not comment on this shift in their retrospectives, but I think it both strengthened the collaboration students experienced among the team of students working together at Liston, and it concretized the sharing of students' experiences and hence the conditions for connection with a small, defined group of students.

The goal of cultivating connections and reflection through digital stories shifted to witnessing when students shared their finalized digital stories. Because they had been work-shopped within small groups throughout the semester, digital stories were viewed by most of the SMS class for the first time during the screening in late April. Although each student understood the vulnerability, reflection, and the emotional work of crafting a story about oneself, students had very little to say to each other following the digital story screening.

In many ways, the screening became a practice session for how better to organize the large group screening of digital stories at Liston. Timing was certainly an element, as it tended to be throughout the project. Sharing twenty-seven stories in the SMS class and exploring connections across the stories and to our readings on power and educational inequality in two hours was not realistic, particularly given the time to transition between each student's story. While we commented and asked questions after the first few stories, time felt constrained, questions and comments ceased, and students began to trickle out of class for other commitments. What should have been an important moment of listening and learning from one another was, in my opinion, compromised. Throughout this project, learning experiences were abundant, and thanks to a wonderfully skilled teaching assistant, the screening at Liston went much more smoothly, and the student stories were firmly at the center of the experience.

Visibility, Voice, and Active Learning

I designed the EHEH project to bring students' experiences into the curriculum. A key aspect of this was my assumption that when students are connected to the curriculum, they are more likely to participate and engage in a learning community. In contrast to reading theory and research that positions education primarily as something one studies or reflects on through examples of other people's schooling, I wanted students to identify what they know from their own experiences, critically reflect on their positionality, and use their educational histories as important resources from which to engage and analyze education scholarship and institutions. Inviting student participation through sharing SMS students' writing, experiences, ideas, and reflections in the process of producing their own and Liston students' digital stories emphasized students' experiences as a vital resource through which to (re)consider educational research and theory.

The standardization of public education serves to further alienate or distance students from learning, because it does not emerge from or necessarily connect with students' lives and realities. This is particularly the case for students from historically marginalized groups. For these students, among other things, high-stakes testing and accountability efforts have resulted in the narrowing of the curriculum, the marginalization or elimination of spaces for art and personal creativity, and the ushering in of standardized curricula that may be uniformly deployed, irrespective of the cultures and knowledges of the student body or the teacher (Darling-Hammond, 2004; Nichols & Berliner, 2007). Here, the knowledges that children and families bring to the classroom are irrelevant, or, as in the case of the ban on Mexican American Studies in Arizona, considered harmful to students' learning and too radical in an age of increasingly conservative politics. While some students' family and community knowledges have been actively and increasingly eliminated or deemed irrelevant to learning in an era of standards and accountability, personal and/or digital storytelling provides a venue by which to make their experiences visible and utilize their knowledges as a vital component in the curriculum. For two Latin@ students in my course, this proved to be the case. One student wrote,[4]

> I have always found that sharing my story with my peers has been both scary and insightful. It is always interesting to see the reactions that my peers have, from the slightest facial expression to shifting on body language. For the people around me, the sharing of my story allows them to see a more personal side of me, a side that I had rarely shared before college. My peers get to know me better, and in some instances we become closer to one another, especially when we have things in common. For me, the experience lets me let out bottled up feelings. It gives me an opportunity to develop my story, and put more of myself into it.

Another student's retrospective read:

> The digital video project was the most challenging and engaging assignment for me. I am not an expert when it comes to technologies, therefore, I struggled a lot in the beginning to learn the different software...As challenging as it was, the video project was one of my favorite assignments. In addition to learning new techniques and gaining knowledge about different computer programs, I appreciated this assignment because it allowed me to express my ideas...putting in so much time did not seem like an obstacle because I was passionate about what I was doing because

it was my very own story. It was written, produced and organized all by me and that was a wonderful feeling.

Despite my efforts to cultivate trust and mutual sharing among the students, while encouraging them to examine their positionality and perspectives within relationships of power and privilege, asking historically marginalized students to share their experiences with historically privileged students was not unproblematic. For these students, it involved a great deal of bravery and willingness to be vulnerable, and it certainly was not always a comfortable process. One Latin@ student wrote about it this way:

> The digital story project was a difficult assignment for a few different reasons. I wasn't completely comfortable with sharing any of my stories. This made it difficult to find one I was okay with sharing and was still important. I also had trouble with the technological aspects which sometimes discouraged me from wanting to work on my story. The fact that I would be going to Liston made me more interested in developing my story and is a big reason why I put more effort into completing my story. It also gave me a way to think about my experiences as a first year at Hampshire and some of the struggles I had…Since my story is about where I am now, it was hard to take myself out of the situation and think about what my story really was about. After completing the project with the students at Liston, I would actually like to continue working on my story and add to it.

Clearly, for this student, sharing his or her experiences in the SMS class was complicated, and the transformative, empowering potential of crafting digital stories was questionable. However, paired with the community-engaged learning experience, the creation of this student's story became generative, thought provoking, and meaningful.

Another student—a first-generation, White, working-class student—also experienced the visibility afforded by the project in complex ways:

> The digital story project, both the personal and with the Liston school, was by far the most challenging aspect of this course. For my own project, it required that I talk about something that I'm not exactly comfortable with yet, it required me to look into my past and address that my road has not been as easy as many of the students that I come across at Hampshire. Yet, I'm glad I got to do it. I'm proud that I got to show my mother and that it received positive feedback. I think it was a general class consensus that it felt good to show something about yourself that was not necessarily obvious.

Interestingly, but perhaps not unexpectedly, students with considerable video production experience and most historically privileged students in the SMS class did not specifically address the meaning of sharing their own stories through a digital medium in their course retrospective. I did not ask a specific question about what the process meant to them, but it is curious to me which students addressed the challenges of "becoming visible" in a class of students predominately privileged in their racial and economic positionality. Other than briefly mentioning that the process was engaging and/or fun, or speaking at length about overcoming the technical challenges of the project, most historically privileged students spoke of the significance of the intersections of the course readings, their research project, and their time working with Liston students. I remain perplexed about this. From reading their retrospectives and seeing their digital stories, I am certain that historically privileged students in the class reflected on their positionality, though I remain uncertain about the extent to which they recognized the process of crafting their own digital stories as supporting this critical work.

Navigating Co-Learning Relationships Across Communities

Thus far, I have spoken to the possibilities and tensions involved in the process of crafting digital stories within the context of the SMS course. I have explored the potential for this methodology to support critical perspective taking, the integration of student experiences in the curriculum, and connections across students within a learning community. As the last sections addressed, SMS students learning in all these areas were significantly developed through the community-engaged learning project at Liston. Most students' retrospectives spoke at length about what they learned about education from the Liston students, from facilitating the project, and from spending time in an under-resourced urban school. SMS students conveyed how transformative the experience was for them, though they were equally critical when they believed that the project did not achieve the goals set out by the Liston teachers and me at the outset of the project. In this last section, I will briefly discuss the complexities of cultivating transformative learning for Liston Middle School students through digital storytelling. In particular, this section will explore the tensions involved in developing relationships between Liston and SMS students.

How to structure Liston and SMS students' engagements so that mutual learning could happen was an important consideration at the outset of the EHEH project. Mr. Covey, Mr. Matthews, and I initially considered positioning SMS students as tutors, but there were many drawbacks, most importantly, that this role would position Liston students as learning from the college students. They felt, and this was confirmed for me when a few Liston students spoke at an orientation for community partners, that college students frequently rotated in and out of students' lives. While our institutional relationship and my participation at the school would be sustained, I was aware that many SMS students likely would not continue working with Liston more than one semester. Therefore, we felt a time-specific project in which students shared their knowledges and created something together would create the conditions for meaningful interactions between the students. After explaining more about my upcoming class, Mr. Covey and Mr. Matthews were interested in SMS students supporting their sixth to eighth graders in crafting digital and audio stories about their educational hopes and experiences. From the teachers' point of view, the project would encourage their students' engagement with Social Studies by anchoring discussions of history and perspective in their own experiences. I saw this as an opportunity for my college students to learn about the school and community from the perspectives of the middle-school students, and to gain a deeper understanding of the challenges of schooling in under-resourced environments.

I often reminded SMS students that our responsibility at Liston was to help students share their personal stories, and to learn about schooling from their point of view. We were not there to begin lasting relationships, and I felt it would be disingenuous to suggest otherwise. This did not mean that we were to avoid being friendly, but that we should approach our experience at Liston as co-learners in a creative process and a specific project. The struggle around the nature of the relationships between SMS students and Liston students contributed to the most meaningful points of the project, as well as the missteps and tensions.

As co-learners, we felt it was important to get to know and develop reciprocal trust with Liston students. Through the workshops, Hampshire students facilitated numerous "get to know you" activities, and several shared their own digital story drafts. Through informal conversations, as well as in story-creation, students talked across their experiences of schools, family, friendships, and interests (e.g., movies, sports, etc). While generally not the case for SMS students, the Liston students also revealed more personal—sometimes joyful and at other times painful—aspects of their lives. In these moments, SMS students acted as witnesses to Liston students' feelings and experiences, and some wrote about their reactions and questions in their retrospective papers. By the end of the semester, Liston students, with the assistance of their Hampshire partners, created stories about the importance of and lessons learned from family members, about friends and teachers, about challenges they had overcome, about their favorite places or interests, or about dreams they harbored to become a police officer, model, or famous athlete. In between, the SMS and Liston students experienced many meaningful interactions, but our road to co-learning relationships was complicated.

Language differences and scheduling were two key arenas that influenced the development of co-learning relationships between the student communities. As I mentioned earlier, Mr. Covey and Mr. Matthews most wanted to integrate the digital story project into the classes for students who were more familiar with speaking and writing in Spanish. We all agreed that this could be a significant creative opportunity for students who did not have many chances to express their experiences and knowledges in an English-dominant institution. As such, SMS students encouraged Liston students to write, record, and represent their stories in Spanish, English, or Spanglish.

In some ways, relationships were easier to cultivate in the small class where there was one SMS student working with every two to three Liston students.[5] To design the best opportunity for a bilingual space that would support Spanish-dominant Liston students to effectively communicate their ideas, I assigned those SMS students who were fluent or had some grounding in Spanish to the small classes. In reality, while several stories were presented in Spanish, and Spanish was spoken between the Liston students and occasionally with a few of the bilingual SMS students, English was the dominant language of communication between the SMS and Liston students. In fact, when necessary, English-to-Spanish translation was often done by other Liston students in the class. In effect, Liston student relationships made it significantly more possible for communication—and relationships—to form between SMS and Liston students engaged in the EHEH project.

Scheduling around state- and federally mandated assessments and school vacations was another aspect that complicated the development of co-learner relationships. Due to school vacations and state assessments,[6] there was a five-week gap between when the project started at Liston in early March and when it resumed in late April. The chasm in the project schedule stalled developing relationships, and put additional pressure on the students to finish the stories before the SMS students' semester ended. For all of us, it was important that Liston students have a sense of closure to the project and be able to participate in the project screening the second week of May.[7]

Beyond the complexities of building meaningful co-learning relationships, the role of technology, its ownership, and its potential for supporting student expression was an area of tension among the SMS group. Quite simply, and not uncommon in an under-resourced school, the number of computers was limited, and those available were very slow and horribly outdated. Further, most students could not bring in photographs to be scanned for use in their stories. We included numerous digital photographs that SMS students took during the project of Liston students at the school, with their friends and teachers, and playing sports. However, given the nature of the stories, without pictures from home, we often needed to turn to found images on the Internet. This was complicated by school filters and extremely limited Internet access. Given the wealth of struggles with technology, we decided to use Hampshire student computers. This decision and time pressure to complete the digital stories before Hampshire students departed campus resulted in several cases in which the Hampshire student helped to create the digital story with the Liston student. That is, Hampshire students did the computer work while the middle-school student directed the editing and stylistic choices.

SMS retrospectives noted that for a few students, this decision was particularly grievous, and they felt that it worked against the project goals of listening to and supporting student voice. They felt that this bordered on another example of privileged college students "going into" an urban school and flaunting all of our fancy technology to which the Liston students would not have access to create stories again. I disagree, and am more aligned with Jason Ohler's (2005) advice to focus first and most strongly on the power of students' stories and writing before the power of technology (p. 45). If we could not do both thoroughly in the Liston component of the EHEH project, I was more committed to supporting Liston students in developing their stories, and in thinking critically about and sharing their experiences. While a few SMS students were uncomfortable with our demonstration of privilege, I think the more important point is how we used our privileges to support the expression of Liston students' stories. One SMS student said it in this way,

> (I) realized that one of the best tools you can give students was the element of choice. Allowing students to do things their way, within reason, opened up avenues of participation that would've otherwise been closed. I have realized that choice is something of a novelty in many schools, and sometimes being told you don't have to do things the same way as everyone else can be very empowering. I think that element of choice is what made their digital stories so beautifully unique and authentic. In the end, their stories reflected the parts of them that they wanted to share and at the same time it may have been a little more than they usually shared because they saw that their peers were also putting themselves out there.

The question remains, was EHEH a transformative learning experience for the Liston students? The truth is, I do not know, but I suspect it was for most. As Cruz & Giles (2000) and Boyle-Baise (2002) have noted, attempts to understand the impact on "the community" participating in community-service-learning projects often are overlooked and nonexistent. I also could have done a much better job at this. Admittedly, I took my cues from the teachers that the project was working well. They confirmed that students were very engaged and were always interested in attending the workshops. Students who they identified as having behavioral challenges demonstrated commitment to creating thoughtful stories, and revised and re-recorded their pieces several times. While this engagement and revision process could not be associated with every student, I witnessed it with many. A SMS student wrote,

> My work at Liston was definitely a highlight of my experience in this course. It was nice to learn along with the students as we worked on their stories. Working with a small group of my classmates was another bonus because we were able to bond and help each other through the project. I also enjoyed seeing the Liston students actually enjoy the process and get a chance to have their voices heard since it seemed likely they were often left silent especially considering the language barriers at Liston.

While it was not perfect, the EHEH project offered opportunities for historically marginalized students to see their knowledges as linked to the project of education, and provided them opportunities to express, reframe, and present their experiences in a creative manner. To me, this was a significant, though limited endeavor to build connections across communities...Liston and Hampshire, as well as Liston students' school and family knowledges.

Conclusion: Moving Forward, Thoughtfully

> We have explored how, by incorporating digital storytelling in the course, technologies can be used to "give voice" to individuals with disabilities and empower them to tell their stories. For our university-level students, the process of creating the stories as well as the sharing of the final product become key ways in which to learn and teach lessons about inclusion, advocacy, and accommodations for individuals with disabilities. The stories are transformative for the students who worked on the projects, the audiences, and the individual highlighted in the stories. (Skouge & Rao, 2009, p. 56)

As Benmayor (2005), Skouge and Rao (2009), and others in this volume have argued, digital storytelling is an important tool for supporting critical thinking and transformative learning. It supports an assets-oriented approach to teaching and learning that draws from students' experiences to analyze and revise our relationships to schooling in active and critical ways.

In this chapter, I have illuminated the complexities and tensions involved in employing this pedagogy to build connections across communities of learners, and to support the critical interrogation of power, privilege, and positionality within systems of educational inequality. The critical reflection fostered by and through the development of their digital stories alerted students to the complexity of experience that often is absent from images, reports, and studies portraying "urban education," "White college students," or "Latin@ youth." Through the process of storytelling and sharing their experiences, students gained glimpses into each other's worlds, and recognized and gained critical understanding of the overlaps and schisms across their lived experiences.

While the goals and practices of the EHEH project worked to create a transformative experience for most Hampshire and Liston students, there are many things I would change about the project. Perhaps the course would run for two semesters to allow more time to cultivate co-learning relationships and incorporate the more extensive use of technology by students at Liston. At Hampshire, I would integrate production into the class sessions more often. I would direct the writing assignments to have students write more frequently and reflectively across the semester to articulate connections between educational scholarship and their experiences as producers and co-learners in the EHEH project. At Liston, I would contain my enthusiasm, and confine the project to one or two classes so that students could work together one-to-one. I would structure opportunities for families to become participants early in the process. I also would encourage the Liston teachers to participate regularly in the workshops. We must work together to forge strong curricular connections between the digital storytelling project and the social studies curriculum (Ohler, 2005).

While there are multiple areas to support a more thoughtful, integrated digital story project for both the Hampshire and Liston students, the skeleton of the project was sturdy. The pedagogical strength of digital storytelling to develop bridges across communities of difference, cultivate critical consciousness, and engage learning communities is profound, and I am eager to move forward, thoughtfully.

Notes

1. The names of all individuals and K–12 schools used in this chapter are pseudonyms.
2. I use the phrase, "illuminate the power," rather than "empower," to suggest that students possess valuable knowledge and experiences—assets—to offer to their education. The notion of college participants "giving power" or "empowering" community participants suggests otherwise, and denies the exchange of knowledges characteristic of co-learning. I am indebted to the Family Access and Outreach Coordinator at the school as she was the first person I heard use the phrase "illuminate the power" as opposed to "empower."
3. I have been able to integrate digital media into my courses because of the generous and on-going support of the advanced media services staff at Hampshire College. My sincere thanks to John Gunther, John Bruner, Andrew Hart, Neil Young, and Matthew Newman for partnering with me around my course projects.
4. Please note there were so few students of color and White working-class students in the course, that to designate gender in this section may hint too closely at the identity of the student.

5. The SMS students in these groups remained relatively stable as well, whereas this was less the case in the large class, due to Hampshire College transportation issues.
6. Scheduling the project was complicated by the timing of MCAS, the annual high-stakes exams in Math and English Language Arts, and the MEPA, the Massachusetts English Proficiency Assessment given to all English Language Learners. In 2010, Liston's status under NCLB was "restructuring year 2" so preparing students to take the exams and making sure that they were available to do so was a great priority for staff, despite their support for the project.
7. Digital Stories that were completed by the final day Hampshire students visited Liston were screened within each student's class and at the evening project celebration. Parents became bystanders to and viewers of the project, rather than participants. This move also put additional pressure on all of us, because the audience for the project became parents—which the school appreciated, in terms of its outreach efforts to families. However, likely due to their lack of meaningful involvement in the project, the turnout of parents at the screening was rather dismal, with only one family attending the evening event.

References

Alexandra, D. (2008). Digital storytelling as transformative practice: Critical analysis and creative expression in the representation of migration in Ireland. *Journal of Media Practice, 9*(2), 101–112.

Benmayor, R. (2008). Digital storytelling as a signature pedagogy for the New Humanities. *Arts and Humanities in Higher Education, 7*(2), 188–204.

Boyle-Baise, M. (2002). Saying more: Qualitative research issues for multicultural service learning. *Qualitative Studies in Education, 15*(3), 317–331.

Cruz, N., & Giles, D. (2000). Where's the community in service-learning research? [Special issue]. *Michigan Journal of Community Service Learning, 7,* 28–34.

Cushman, E. (1999). The public intellectual, service learning, and activist research. *College English, 61*(3), 328–336.

Darling-Hammond, L. (2004). From 'separate but equal' to 'No Child Left Behind': The collision of the new standards and old inequalities. In D. Meier & G. Wood (Eds.), *Many children left behind* (pp. 3–32). Boston, MA: Beacon Press.

Freire, P. (2000). *Pedagogy of freedom: Ethics, democracy, and civic courage.* Lanham, MD: Rowman & Littlefield.

Hansen, M. (2011). 'O brave new world.' *Pedagogy, 11*(1), 177–197.

Lopez, G. E., & Zúñiga, X. (2010). Intergroup dialogue and democratic practice in higher education. *New Directions for Higher Education, 152,* 35–42.

Nagda, B. A., Gurin, P., Sorensen, N., Gurin-Sands, C., & Osuna, S. M. (2009). From separate corners to dialogue and action. *Race and Social Problems, 1*(1), 45–55.

Nichols, S. L., & Berliner, D. C. (2007). *Collateral damage: How high-stakes testing corrupts America's schools.* Cambridge, MA: Harvard Education Press.

Ohler, J. (2005). The world of digital storytelling. *Educational Leadership, 63*(4), 44–47.

Skouge, J. R., & Rao, K. (2009). Digital storytelling in teacher education: Creating transformations through narrative. *Educational Perspectives, 42*(1–2), 54–60.

PART III

Knowledge(s) of Resistance

9

Critical Storying: Power Through Survivance and Rhetorical Sovereignty

Sundy Watanabe

> The history of American Indian education can be summarized in three simple words: battle for power. (Lomawaima, 2000, p. 2)

Educators have long used and debated the way stories illustrate and theorize power as embedded and embodied in notions of educational difference and American Indian[1] students. Educational difference as it applies here is not about essentializing, i.e., all American Indian students learn "this" way. Nor is it focused on deficit, i.e., low test scores or underpreparedness. Rather, it is about acknowledging Native power despite the effects of colonization on American Indian history and despite the subsequent social, political, and educational marginalization of Native populations and knowledges. Difference, as I speak about it, alludes to American Indian tribal nations, communities, and peoples holding sovereignty, yet being set apart—placed as different—from the majoritarian U.S. nation-state.

As the introductory quote by Lomawaima (2000) suggests, American Indian education is a site of tension concerning which or whose stories hold, possess, and/or wield power, and how they do so. Brayboy (2005) attends to tension-filled battles for power in his explication of Tribal Critical Theory[2] (TribalCrit). TribalCrit is related to but different from other critical theories, in that, as Brayboy argues, stories are theories, not separate from them. Stories constitute legitimate sources of data and justifiable ways of coming to know and understand that data (Brayboy, Gough, Leonard, Roehl, & Solyom, 2011). Brayboy's notion of story as theory is not unusual; it is situated within a long tradition of Indigenous scholars. From Deloria (1970b), Warrior (1995), Weaver (1997), and Womack (1999) to Tyeeme Clark (2004), King (2003), and Archuleta (2006), theorizing with and through story has been standard practice. Vizenor, for instance, in an interview with Coltelli (1990) comments, "You can't understand the world without telling a story. There isn't any center to the world but a story" (p. 156).

Since my most recent work involves research with American Indian students in North American postsecondary contexts, it seems appropriate that I, too, story data to illustrate Native power in conflict with notions of difference. I approach this work influenced by theories/stories of sovereignty (Lomawaima, 2000; Lomawaima & McCarty, 2002). These stories are especially influential when exemplified through survivance (Powell, 2004; Stromberg, 2006; Vizenor, 1994) and rhetorical sovereignty (Lyons, 2000; Maughan, 2008), both of which I understand to be iterations of power and/or sovereignty. In this chapter, I offer two specific stories as examples. In the first, an American Indian graduate student and her non-Native mentor enact survivance as they struggle against the academic authority a non-Native instructor applies to a conventionalized writing assignment in the classroom. In the second, two American Indian graduate students wield rhetorical sovereignty in the form of a powerfully written document they used to counter public stereotyping in a residential dormitory activity. These are only two stories of many I could choose to illustrate Native power and how it is embodied through performative action. The stories are drawn from four years of research conducted at a large institution in the West. Through them, I argue that tensions arise because of discrepancies or discriminations concerning how power is present and strategically wielded and performed in academic contexts.

The organization of this chapter is (not surprisingly) framed around story. First, I tell the conventionalized academic story of literature review, including the theoretical and methodological frames tailored for use in this chapter. These frameworks include definitions and explanations of key concepts, as well as a brief outline of the methods or processes that follow as a result of these conceptual frames. Second, I tell the survivance and rhetorical sovereignty stories—the transcribed accounts of Native student experiences—along with interpretations and rivaling of those interpretations. I conclude with final remarks and a reflection written by one of the Native students, which, with permission, we have stylized in poetic stanza form. I expect readers will find these three stories familiar in some respects. They might also, however, find them destabilizing because they privilege Indigenous experience, which requires a willingness to know and understand from an Indigenous perspective.

When I theorize or story data in this chapter, then, I do so with the intention of coming to better know and understand specific tensions in

American Indian education, and to suggest that we might profitably extend the knowledge and understanding garnered here to other sites and situations. Indeed, one of the most basic tensions educators must attend to today is what it means for "diverse" populations—in this case Native students—to be present and to perform their educational pursuits within White-dominant higher education systems. An additional tension concerns what that pursuit demonstrates about differences, discrepancies, or discriminations related to the presence and performance of power.

The Theoretical, Methodological, and Methods-Process Story

Several concepts are crucial to understanding battles for power in American Indian education. The first, as suggested earlier, is an understanding of sovereignty. Sovereignty in educational contexts refers to the power or authority of Indigenous peoples to exercise self-governance and independence regarding the roles education plays in their lives and communities. It also refers to obligations the U.S. government has to American Indian nations, as a result of treaty agreements, to provide for their health, education, and welfare (No Child Left Behind, 2002). Sovereignty, as Lomawaima (2000) asserts, is thus "the bedrock upon which any and every discussion of Indian reality today must be built" (p. 3). Scott Lyons (2000) calls sovereignty "an ideal principle," suggesting that the ideal may not always be achieved, but indicating that through at least attempting to achieve it Native peoples can "see the paths to agency and power and community renewal" (p. 449). He emphasizes *rhetorical* sovereignty—through which Native peoples make actionable decisions regarding the goals, modes, styles, and languages of public and/or academic discourse—as the more achievable goal.

Attempts at sovereignty in educational contexts are undertaken with a firm sense of community responsibility and need (see Deloria, 2001; Medicine, 2001). Indigenous Studies scholarship often refers to this sense of community responsibility as self-determination (see Lipka, 2002; Reyhner, 1989). While acknowledging that not all agree on how the term is used or defined, I take self-determination to mirror rhetorical sovereignty, meaning Native communities' abilities to choose, despite external power differentials, collective courses of action that are in their own best interests—whether socially, politically, economically, or educationally—and to operationalize those choices for highest benefit.

Vine Deloria, Jr. (1970b) explains that the responsibility inherent in sovereignty "is oriented primarily toward the existence and continuance of a group" (p. 123). With this understanding, Jace Weaver's (1997) term, "communitist," becomes useful, in that it merges the ideas of community and activism to name a commitment to advocacy (Cox, 2006, p. 205). Sovereignty becomes communitist to the degree that it exhibits a "proactive commitment to Native community" (Stromberg, 2006, p. 7; see also Coffey & Tsosie, 2001, on "cultural" sovereignty). Sovereignty is therefore enacted or operationalized through self-determination. Those who criticize sovereignty fear what it allows American Indians to pursue: existence on their own terms, both within Indigenous communities and "in the presence of others" (Lyons, 2000, p. 457), including educators. Those who downplay the importance of sovereignty in educational venues obstruct and curtail Native "possibilities" and power (Lyons, 2000, p. 449; see also Powell, 2002).

Indigenous power is accrued through embodying and asserting sovereignty. Power in an Indigenous sense varies according to who possesses it and how it is used. It can be different in intensity and strength, and for Indigenous populations, it has balance or harmony as its primary purpose. Stoffle, Zedeño, and Halmo (2001) state that power does not reside in static positions, but in movement, in active presence. Medicine (2001), too, believes that power in Indigenous contexts involves movement, specifically adaptation, accommodation, revision, and change. Indeed, both adaptation and accommodation are imperative to increasing power. Adaptation is imperative because cultures, *all* cultures, "that do not [adapt] cannot survive" (Powell, 2004, p. 40). Accommodation is imperative because it facilitates the construction of necessary alliances across different rhetorical traditions, as in educators seeking to implement culturally inclusive pedagogies for the purpose of making school a more welcoming and productive environment for diverse student populations. In this respect, Medicine's stance aligns with Ladson-Billings's (1995) explication of culturally relevant pedagogy. Medicine (2001), however, provides the highly important caveat that Euro-Western academic culture must overtly adapt, revise, and change to be in harmony with American Indian ways, saying, "In constructing new pathways to culturally relevant curricula, the indigenous views need consideration" (p. 74). Such a stance does not deny the possibilities afforded by education in Euro-Western institutions, but seeks to place its influence within a relevant cultural context where Indigenous power is an integral part. This, in turn, affords broader understandings of Native historical and contemporary lives and epistemologies.

When acknowledged as a positive force, sovereignty exerts increased power and works toward self-determination through self-education. In educational settings, we see sovereignty via survivance and rhetorical sovereignty. I use survivance as Malea Powell (2004) does, and she follows

Vizenor's (1994) introduction of it in *Manifest Manners* as a combination of survival and resistance. But survivance should be understood as more than the potentially dangerous, precipitous act of (metaphorically) hanging on by the skin of your teeth, i.e., surviving, and more than the fixed state implied by the (also metaphorical) digging in of your heels, i.e., resisting. According to Powell's (2002) early archival research, survivance can be identified as action, including moves made both knowingly and not. Vizenor (Vizenor & Lee, 1999) calls them moves of "narrative chance" (p. 82), or "invention" (p. 85), or active "resistance" (Vizenor, 2008, p. 11) that perform "new stories of tribal courage" (Vizenor & Lee, 1999, p. 4). Survivance utilizes Native perspectives and includes actions performed within contested cultural spaces where Natives are at political and cultural disadvantage. Survivance in this sense describes a combination of Indigenous strategies applied for the purpose of countering colonization—the "surveillance and literature of dominance" (Vizenor & Lee, 1999, p. 5)—an idea that will become apparent and important as I move to story data. It will be seen to encompass more than happenstance or reactive response when it provides a catalytic shift into rhetorical sovereignty.

Rhetorical sovereignty goes beyond individual acts of survivance to an ambitious communitist endeavor. It means Natives having and exerting more deliberative "say" over Indigenous representation, doing, and being. It requires more infusion of Indigenous "reargument" and "countersentences" into legal and/or political spheres, and for the purposes of this chapter, it means recentering American Indian rhetoric in educational settings to teach, as Lyons (2000) suggested, the reasons behind treaties and agreements (p. 463), along with the consequences of the same. In rhetorical sovereignty, goals, modes, styles, and even languages (if we use a rhetorical sense of the term) work toward radically transforming representation (see also Maughan, 2008) in American Indian education. American Indians who practice rhetorical sovereignty more pronouncedly rely on a solid sense of self in relation to community and home. They boldly and deliberately work to increase participation within the academic domain, rather than accepting a victimized state.

Survivance and rhetorical sovereignty affect and are affected by educational praxis. Here, I define praxis as action "relating theory to practice in a specific context that challenges limiting situations" (Shor, 1996, p. 3). Praxis can also be defined as "critical reflection" upon such action (Moraes, 1996, p. 111). For the purposes of this chapter, praxis concerns, on the one hand, a teacher who does not fully practice the kind of strength-based support (Kanaʻiaupuni, 2004) that addresses Native-identified need, and, on the other hand, a group of residential students that do not initially honor Indigenous difference, but are pressed by Native students to do so. Praxis thus concerns not only classroom interactions, but also direct action concerning how, what, and why Native students learn in a university setting. Sovereignty and power are integrally connected to praxis, specifically to how presence (Vizenor, 1994, 1998) and performance (Claycomb, 2008; Cowell, 2002) are put into "play" (Gadamer, 1998) in the game of academic knowledge making.

In university settings, Euro-Western thought creates conventions, parameters, and architectures. These, in turn, determine how students and teachers move within their institutionalized boundaries. Since the terms of the game are already established, it does not create a very flexible space for students who approach with other governing traditions, and who try to push against its ivy-covered walls. As Gadamer (1998) reminds us, everything and everybody in the academy is "subject to the supreme criterion of 'right' [read Euro-Western] representation" (p. 118). Discriminations made in these environments tend to more highly value demonstrations of Euro-Western presence and performance, while ignoring or discrediting the presence and performance of others, particularly American Indians. Indeed, Euro-Western representations of Indigenous presence and performance rely heavily on stereotype, which makes interactions ripe for discriminations between "us" and "them."

When individual Native student performances do not fit the mold of "correct" being and doing, they are negatively labeled "deficient" and/or "resistant." Additionally, when Native student communities enact unexpected performances because they resist social and educational assimilation, they are often seen as having "failed." Not often are these experiences labeled as failures to recognize Native power or sovereignty concomitant with refusals to be governed or controlled. Nor does the academy typically encourage alternative performances, i.e., survivance and rhetorical sovereignty, as hybrid modes of thinking, doing, and being (see Deloria & Wildcat, 2001). This failure of the system makes it imperative to rediscover and recenter Indigenous ways of thinking, being, speaking, and writing in educational praxis. Recentering emphasizes that Native peoples know and understand their histories and lives best, and are in the most authoritative position to story them—(re)present and (re)interpret them—in educational settings.

To this end, I privilege Indigenous experience as I explicate and illustrate Native presence and performance in a particular educational setting. I tie critical ethnography (Carspecken, 1996; Madison, 2011, 2012; Noblit,

Flores, & Murillo, 2004; Thomas, 1993) to Critical Indigenous Research Methodologies or CIRM (Brayboy et al., 2011). Critical ethnography addresses "processes of unfairness or injustice within a particular lived domain" (Madison, 2011, p. 5). It investigates the "historical forces shaping societal patterns as well as the fundamental issues and dilemmas of policy, power, and dominance in institutions, including their role in reproducing and reinforcing inequities" (Marshall & Rossman, 2006, p. 6). Critical ethnography requires reflexivity, collaboration, and reciprocity (Brayboy & Deyhle, 2000). CIRM aligns with critical ethnography in that it rejects deficit or deprivation views. It then takes a step further to center Indigenous knowledges, cultures, and communities in practical and applicable ways, and to point toward better ways to account for and address contemporary educational realities while remaining cognizant of colonized histories (see also Smith, 2005). CIRM works to reconceptualize education from an Indigenous perspective (Deyhle & Swisher, 1997; Gilmore & Smith, 2005; Nicholls, 2009).

CIRM, furthermore, promotes deep listening. As its proponents assert, "We listen to our gut; we listen to our memories; and we listen to what the old mountains and the wily Coyotes care to share with us" (Brayboy et al., 2011, p. 440). Listening in CIRM is reminiscent of engaging Lyons's (2000) modes of rhetorical sovereignty, with its variety of goals, modes, styles, and languages. If we are to make praxis consistent with Indigenous rhetorics, in other words, we cannot solely rely on or listen to print texts and Euro-Western ways of knowing. Rather, we must also take into account and story the whole sensory world around us. Returning to Vizenor (Vizenor & Lee, 1999), we are reminded that "Stories are... not in the printed word, but in the sound of memories," and that "heard stories are visual, a performance of words in visual memories" (p. 140). To this end, deep listening is characteristic of critical storytelling. The stories themselves perform critical presence, but educators must also be aware of the histories behind them, truly hear them as embodied, and acknowledge them as epistemological.

One key aspect of CIRM, then, involves deep listening and drawing on respect, relationality, relevance, reciprocity, and responsibility as understood in an Indigenous sense (Barnhardt & Kawagley, 2005; Kirkness & Barnhardt, 2001). Responsibility, in terms of CIRM, leads us to ask questions differently, especially those concerning method. How, for instance, can teachers concretely facilitate CIRM in their praxis? Importantly, how can I—a non-Native teacher-researcher—utilize CIRM? I answer this question by looking at a combination of three methods, or more precisely, processes, by which to story and listen to interactional data. These methods or processes include Deloria's (1970a) concept of tangent points; Flower, Long, and Higgins's (2000) "learning to rival"; and Freeman's (2006, 2007) dialogic or practical hermeneutics. Each—separately and in combination—encourages openness, relationality, and self-reflexivity, thereby teaching me how to open my praxis to an Indigenous perspective.

Deloria (1970a) explains how it might be possible for Natives and non-Natives to engage their shared interests at intersecting tangent points. He maintains,

> Because tribal society is integrated toward a center and non-Indian society is oriented toward linear development, the process might be compared to describing a circle surrounded with tangent lines. The points at which the lines touch the circumference of the circle are the issues and ideas that can be shared by Indians and other groups. There are a great many points at which tangents occur, and they may be considered as windows through which Indians and non-Indians can glimpse each other. Once this structural device is used and understood, non-Indians, using a tribal point of view, can better understand themselves and their relationship to Indian people. (p. 12)

The responsibility is to find those tangential points of shared interest, the points where concerns of non-Native instructors intersect with those of Native students. These points can then be used as structural devices to facilitate greater understanding, respect, and relatedness. This way, educators fulfill their responsibility or accountability to students, to the local context, and to the larger world around them—to all their relations.

Flower, Long, and Higgins (2000) describe learning to rival as a process of becoming more relational and more accountable. Learning to rival involves "talking across difference" or "intercultural inquiry" (p. 40), and it is one way to bring multiple scripts and stakeholders into dialogic exchange for the purposes of larger community benefit. Freeman's (2006) dialogic or practical hermeneutics also provides a space for dialogue, for "substantial, critical, and reflective" engagement (p. 83) through interpretation and (re)interpretation. This type of engagement is "essential to building and/or maintaining the… deliberative capacities of communities" (p. 83). According to Freeman, all community members become more fully present as they story and deliberate data, as they perform interpretations of excerpted interview scripts. Since the goal of this chapter is to identify, explain and/or interpret, and understand how Native students deliberately enact difference through survivance and rhetorical sovereignty in the presence of others, Freeman's ideas become especially salient. Storied interpretation creates an opportunity to examine and interrogate textual and rhetorical dialogue and data content from students' lived experiences, while acknowledging that multiple perspectives are needed to increase understandings and allow for shift or change in praxis. Storied interpretation leads to recognizing the power inherent in American Indian student communities, and nudges toward greater understanding in Euro-Western educational communities.

For convenience, I call this combination of intersecting dialogue and storied interpretation *rivaling*. Rivaling, as I design it, comprises an iterative cyclical process by which Native students and those of us who work with them in the classroom confront disparate stories and interpret them for greater understanding. It is a method reminiscent of Vizenor's "socioacupuncture" (Vizenor & Lee, 1999, p. 82) in that it is intended to release and/or redirect the energy involved in storying conflictual lived experience toward healing. Through rivaling, stories move toward, between, and among students and educators. The rivaling process helps those who participate in its practice learn to confront, hear, and understand different knowledges, peoples, and communities. It asserts that we cannot "turn our backs and walk away from the story that we do not like or believe" (Cox, 2006, p. 135). Rather, it is a process of deliberately confronting hard things. Rivaling provides a catalytic energy that, in turn, propels more actionable praxis.

Rivaling Strategic Survivance: Mary's Story

> In situations of domination, the appropriation of literacy may involve strategic *avoidance of writing*, as well as *strategic uses of written language*. (Rockwell, 2005, p. 6)

To help us understand how CIRM, survivance, sovereignty, and rivaling work together as socioaccupuncture, I story interactions between Mary,[3] Lisa, and an instructor. Understanding this story is crucial to re-visioning Native performance within contested cultural spaces. In this excerpt, writing mentor, Lisa, rivals an experience she and her Native mentee, Mary, shared. To give some background, Lisa's heritage is Anglo-American. At the time of the experience, she was a highly accomplished graduate research assistant in an American Indian teacher education program. She has since received her doctorate. Mary is Navajo. She is a (grand)mother and a teacher at a reservation school within her community. She is generally soft-spoken, very determined, and well-respected by those who know her. At the time of the experience presented here, Mary was completing her master's degree, and has since received it. Lisa originally rivaled the story with me in person, and this is the story I now textually rival here. My hope is that as I retell and reinterpret, readers will bring their own collaborative reflexivity to bear on the story, a willing perspective that allows them to understand not only from their own lived experience, but also from an Indigenous perspective.

As the story goes, Mary was assigned to write a review of a journal article for one of her master's classes, an assignment with which most teachers and students are familiar. Mary completed the assignment, but when she turned it in she received a negative assessment. When the professor asked her—more than once—to rewrite it, Mary came to Lisa for help. Lisa describes the situation this way:

> The teacher wanted her to rewrite it and rewrite it. And she was willing, but the crux of the matter, as I saw it, was that she read the article, she didn't particularly like the article or value the article, and she had something to say about the issue that was not talked about in the article. And so she wrote about what she saw as the central issues of the topic and did not talk about the article that she was reviewing.

Given her extensive background with academic writing, Lisa understood that Mary's approach to the assignment might present a problem for her instructor. Her first thought was to teach the academic convention, thinking that Mary did not understand the genre, that she did not understand how to create an article review in the right format. Lisa says:

> I think in the beginning, she didn't know, at least at one level, what was expected of her in terms of a review. She certainly recognized how to engage with the article. But in terms of formal details of what a review looked like, in that setting, I don't think she knew.

However, according to Lisa, Mary "was a very capable student," and so it only took "one conversation" to clear that [misconception] up." That one conversation, Lisa says, demonstrated that Mary understood the format. She was just not willing to change her stance or her *way* of writing about "what she saw as central issues of the topic."

What Mary wrote instead, was "a subtle critique," highlighting what was absent from the article. In doing so, "she pointed out the failures of the article, at least in terms of reaching her as an audience member." She performed critical scholarship. Because of the discrepancy between what the teacher wanted and what Mary was willing to do, Lisa "ended up" "sort of mediating that conflict," although, as she states, "I had a person that I thoroughly thought was right and one that I thought should hush up!" And still, because it was not in proper review form, the professor would not accept it. Lisa's attempt to mediate the tension met with little success. "The professor wanted her to do a correct bibliographic citing of the article and provide a summary of the article, and [Mary] was tenacious in her unwillingness to do that." Lisa concludes by asserting that Mary knew what was expected, but what was expected was in contradiction with what she thought was valuable and practically useful knowledge. It was an "inauthentic" assignment, and the "format wasn't useful," so Mary resisted.

Hearing Mary's experience through Lisa's interpretation may needle a little, considering our investment in things like writing literature reviews, "proper" bibliographic citations, and article summaries. We might ask why, if she knew and understood what was expected, could she not just do what the professor wanted? From Lisa's rivaling of the situation, we know that Mary felt the performative weight of enacting an impractical and inauthentic academic convention, so she resisted. We could interpret her resistance as failure, as her professor did, but we could also interpret her resistance as successful survivance. Mary's survivance was enacted as she put in her time and jumped through the hoops. She deliberately gave the impression that she was playing the role of student "correctly." She rewrote and rewrote, as many times as the instructor demanded, but she refused to be intimidated or to write in a way that was not relevant to her experience and that she did not choose. Her choice was to neither submit to assignment expectations nor to the force of instructor and academic constraints. She resisted a genre that was not practically useful to her as a special educator in an Indian-serving school, a genre that did not address an issue or topic she felt was important to her community. She chose instead to respond to the imperative of her home community and the community where she knew she would eventually work. As she enacted survivance, she understood that she was playing a game with risk. She took that risk for the serious possibility of a future "re-creation" (Gadamer, 1998, p. 119) wherein Indigenous concerns might be shifted from the margins of academic thought and become more centrally positioned.

We could interpret the actions of those who survive by agreeing to "play the game" as undermining their integrity and denying themselves (Gadamer, 1998). But we could also say that students in situations like that described by Mary's mentor above actually hold onto "continuity" for themselves and "only withhold it from those before whom [they are] acting" (p. 111). They disguise themselves in order to give the impression that they are playing the game "correctly." In Mary's case, she demonstrated an ability to maintain continuity with herself and play the game strategically. Referring back to Rockwell's introductory quote, in this situation of domination, Mary made Indigenous presence more visible as she performed survivance. She performed survivance or "strategic uses of written language," in a way that allowed her to both survive (pass) the course and resist assimilating its values. She rewrote as many times as the instructor demanded, but refused to shed her personal, academic, and cultural integrity to write in a way she did not choose, that was not practically useful, and that did not address an issue or topic she felt was important. Mary's response counters master narratives concerning how academic literacy is typically accomplished in the classroom, and emphasizes a more respectful listening to Indigenous worldviews. It highlights survivance, or those actions "performed for the purpose of countering colonization, a history of surveillance and [a] literature of dominance" (Vizenor, 2008, p. 5). Survivance, as we see in Mary's experience, comprises both survival and resistance. It involves "narrative chance," and performs "new stories of tribal courage" (Vizenor, 2008, p. 4). Native stories of survivance work within the small fissures or cracks of history to ensure future individual survival and possibility. Mary, in fact, "never did write a review the professor accepted," but she did achieve the goal of a master's degree in education. Survivance allowed Mary to maintain her integrity even when unequal power relations were present.

Rivaling Rhetorical Sovereignty: Connie and Dana's Story

Rhetorical sovereignty requires above all the presence of an Indian voice, speaking or writing in an ongoing context of colonization and setting at least some of the terms of debate (Lyons, 2000, p. 462).

I have previously discussed how an instructor attempted to wield colonizing power, and how Mary resisted that imposition through strategic survivance. A second story presents an enactment of rhetorical sovereignty by Connie and Dana, two Native students who were completing master's degrees at the same time as Mary. Connie and Dana were roommates in a residential hall when the incident occurred. They encountered a sign that advertised an upcoming dormitory event the organizers called "Cowboys and Indians." Upon discovering the advertisement, the two students immediately composed and sent a letter of complaint to the residential staff and to administrators responsible for maintaining a welcoming campus environment. Their letter was addressed "To Whom It May Concern," and the students included their tribal affiliations in their signatures. The letter reads as follows:

> We would like to bring your attention to an activity happening within one of [Western University's] dormitories that we find to be offensive, derogatory, and racist. There is a sign posted at the Heritage Center front desk advertising an activity called Cowboys and Indians. When asked what Cowboys and Indians was the individual at the front desk said it was an activity occurring in one of the residents' halls. Therefore, we are not sure what exactly this activity entails. We can only assume that this is a game where the players are divided into two groups, thus creating opponents out of the Cowboys and Indians.

> While Cowboys and Indians, like Cops and Robbers, is a children's game played across the country that some adults may have fond memories of playing, we can assure you that as Indigenous individuals residing on this campus it is not a game that we would enjoy playing, nor would we want our fellow students playing. After all, there would never be any activities allowed on any university across the country called Nazis and Jews, Border Patrol and Wetbacks, Masters and Darkies, or even Mormons and Catholics. So the question is this: why would the term Cowboys and Indians be any less offensive, especially at a school where their mascot bears the name of an Indigenous group of people?
>
> It is our hope that the housing and residents staff received some type of cultural sensitivity training as part of their annual orientation. However, it appears that this training may have missed a section on stereotypes and how they are the most covert form of racism that exists today. We hope the lack of this information is an oversight that will be quickly remedied.
>
> If you wish to contact us to discuss this concern any further please feel free to contact us at 000-0000.

The letter outlines succinctly, clearly, and persuasively the students' objections to the proposed "game," and calls for a quick remedy to the situation. In drawing comparisons, it performs socioacupuncture in the extreme. It makes readers acknowledge multiple oppressions in such direct language that we wince. The anger that is apparent in the language perhaps crosses a line that should not be crossed. However, by naming oppressions using overtly derogatory terms that often float in the sludge of public discourse, the students' audience was forced to confront a widespread complicity in continuing racism. Thus, drawing on widely recognized representations and symbolic relationships they clearly understood, the students performed a practical and valuable service for their immediate Native community. As a result, the advertisement was quickly pulled, and the activity cancelled. If rhetorical sovereignty means various peoples' and communities' abilities to not only decide how their decisions will be put into play but also the goals and purposes they hope to achieve through acting upon those decisions in public and academic settings, then we can see how Connie and Dana's action in writing the letter fits that description. Just as in historical contexts, this recent example demonstrates that it is possible to enact rhetorical sovereignty to exert self- and community-determined power even under less-than-favorable circumstances.

Concluding Thoughts

Exploring stories of difference means confronting conflict. However, few feel comfortable doing so, especially in the company of others. Many would rather ignore, avoid, or gloss over conflicting ideas. Yet, this is precisely why they need to be studied. In this regard, a quote from Linda Flower (2003) becomes salient. She observes a dialogic "paradox" when she states that

> the things dividing us that are hardest to share—the deep roots of history, the racially shaped experience, and the repertoire of interpretive strategies we use to make sense of that experience—may also be the ones we need most to communicate. (p. 55)

If educators are to live up to rhetorics of American Indian educational support, they must confront absence-presence and performance face-to-face. If, in doing so, they sometimes feel needled or stung to the core of their social consciousness, that is to be expected. If experienced at the right time, it can "heal and liberate" (Vizenor & Lee, 1999, p. 82).

I argue that now is the time to experience socioaccupuncture in theory, methodology, and method, and to critically story toward healing and liberatory change. As the literature and examples presented indicate, the purpose of focusing on iterations of sovereignty in this chapter—i.e., survivance and rhetorical sovereignty—is to increasingly rival and resist Euro-Western impositions of authority that conflict with Native power. This is necessary because while Native peoples certainly have the necessary power (knowledges, histories, and experiences) to determine and direct their own educational paths, university systems too often applaud and glorify "Western societies as the highest form of human organization, and promote the emulation of North American culture to the next generation of citizens (and to Indigenous students as well unless there is some critical intervention)" (Alfred, 2004, p. 96; see also Barnhardt, 2002 for a similar argument). Educational scholarship must work to change the power dynamics of this situation. More specifically, educational instructors would do well to change the power dynamics in their classroom praxis, releasing their sense of colonizing control and deficit thinking in favor of employing respectful relationality, a deep awareness of students' lived experiences—both personal and historical—and a deep listening in interactional moments to what students story as practical and relevant to their immediate schooled experience, including its influence on their communities' futures. They would do well, in other words, if they were to take student knowledges seriously, and understand that the work of increasing knowledge is a reciprocal process. Instructors can, if they will, take responsibility for increasing such respect, relationality, relevance, and reciprocity within and without the classroom context. They can learn to see attempts at survivance and rhetorical sovereignty not as "failures," but as laudable successes.

Dana's Reflection[4]

I feel alone in the world. So far away from what I love and value, in a world that doesn't value what I know and see as wisdom and knowledge. For the first time different, and to not have that difference valued or even have someone want to explore it.

I haven't read the classics. I haven't read the great philosophers. I've come to my knowledge in a different way, in a way that I think Mom and Dad and Grandma and Grandpa would be proud of me. I've observed and I've watched.

I've lived. I've thought about hozhoo and about the beauty that exists in the harmony we create between ourselves and the majesty that exists around us. I think of Grandma lying unconscious on her deathbed. I remember vividly her hands. It's overwhelming to me

to think of those hands, which I often watched. They were old and wrinkled and had stains from charcoal or dye. I remember watching them as they wove rugs, masterpieces in their creation. I watched her hands sit patiently on her lap while she slept.

They held beauty and wisdom. The things that she had done with her hands, the work that created her wisdom. My own hands are so far from emulating what I saw and valued. Knowledge is not in me; neither is it in this setting, or this institution. It's not valued

or respected. I cry because it's ignored. I cry because it's looked past. They see only Western knowledge, not even stopping to look at what's within my world—more here than they can possibly imagine or contemplate—the complexity, the depth of its existence. They see one

way of thinking and don't see there exists another way, my way. The beauty is not valued or seen or known or understood. Wisdom that Mom and Dad and Grandma and Grandpa hold, it's not acknowledged. There's beauty here, within me and within my mind, within

my people and my culture. There's beauty in hozhoo, a peace and calm and wisdom that exists, untapped and unvalued. It's more than personal. It's me and my people and my loved ones that are trodden down.

Notes

1. While noting the debates surrounding naming terminology concerning First Nations people of North America—i.e., some may take exception to the terms used here or use others—I have chosen to use *American Indian*, *Native*, and *Indigenous*, following current Indigenous Studies scholarship. These terms are used interchangeably, with *Indigenous* specifically referring to North American Indian populations in this context.
2. Tribal Critical Theory challenges discriminatory practices through activism and privileges stories as data. It pays explicit attention to American Indian issues, including liminal legal and/or political status, i.e., sovereignty and colonization.
3. All names have been changed to protect anonymity.
4. This piece is a co-creation, a poem created by me, with Dana's permission, from Dana's original prose reflection.

References

Alfred, T. (2004). Warrior scholarship: Seeing the university as a ground of contention. In D. Mihesuah & A. C. Wilson (Eds.), *Indigenizing the academy* (pp. 88–99). Lincoln, NE: University of Nebraska Press.

Archuleta, E. (2006). 'I give you back': Indigenous women writing to survive. *Sail, 18*(4), 88–114.

Barnhardt, R. (2002). Domestication of the ivory tower: Institutional adaptation to cultural distance. *Anthropology and Education Quarterly, 33*(2), 238–249.

———, & Kawagley, A. O. (2005). Indigenous knowledge systems and Alaska Native ways of knowing. *Anthropology and Education Quarterly, 36*(1), 8–23.

Brayboy, B. M. (2005). Transformational resistance and social justice: American Indians in Ivy League universities. *Anthropology and Education Quarterly, 36*(3), 193–211.

———, & Deyhle, D. (2000). Insider-outsider: Researchers in American Indian communities. *Theory Into Practice, 39*(3), 163–169.

———, Gough, H. R., Leonard, B., Roehl, R. F., & Solyom, J. A. (2011). Reclaiming scholarship: Critical Indigenous research methodologies. In. S. D. Lapan, M. T. Quartaroli, & F. J. Riemer (Eds.), *Qualitative research: An introduction to methods and designs* (pp. 423–450). San Francisco, CA: Jossey-Bass.

Carspecken, P. (1996). What is critical qualitative research? In P. Carspecken, *Critical ethnography in educational research: A theoretical and practical guide* (pp. 1–22). New York, NY: Routledge & Kegan Paul.

Claycomb, R. (2008). Performance studies and composition. *Enculturation, 6*(1), 19–26. Retrieved from http://enculturation.gmu.edu/6.1/claycomb

Coffey, W., & Tsosie, R. (2001). Rethinking the tribal sovereignty doctrine: Cultural sovereignty and the collective future of Indian nations. *Stanford Law and Policy Review, 12*(2), 191–222.

Coltelli, L. (1990). *Winged words: American Indian writers speak.* Lincoln, NE: University of Nebraska Press.

Cowell, A. (2002). Bilingual curriculum among the Northern Arapaho. *American Indian Quarterly, 26*(1), 24–44.

Cox, J. H. (2006). *Muting White noise: Native American and European American novel traditions.* Norman, OK: University of Oklahoma Press.

Deloria, V. Jr. (1970a). Introduction. In V. Deloria, Jr., *We talk, you listen: New tribes, new turf* (pp. 9–18). New York, NY: Macmillan.

———. (1970b). Power, sovereignty, and freedom. In V. Deloria, Jr., *We talk, you listen: New tribes, new turf* (pp. 114–137). New York, NY: Macmillan.

———. (2001). Knowing and understanding. In V. Deloria, Jr., & D. Wildcat, *Power and place: Indian education in America* (pp. 41–46). Golden, CO: Fulcrum Resources.

———. Jr., & Wildcat, D. (2001). *Power and place: Indian education in America.* Golden, CO: Fulcrum Resources.

Deyhle, D., & Swisher, K. G. (1997). Research in American Indian and Alaska Native education: From assimilation to self-determination. *Review of Research in Education, 22*(1), 113–194.

Flower, L. (2003). Talking across difference: Intercultural rhetoric and the search for situated knowledge. *College Composition and Communication, 55*(1), 38–68.

———, Long, E., & Higgins, L. (2000). *Learning to rival.* Mahwah, NJ: Lawrence Erlbaum.

Freeman, M. (2006). Nurturing dialogic hermeneutics and the deliberative capacities of communities in focus groups. *Qualitative Inquiry, 12*(1), 81–95.

———. (2007). Performing the event of understanding in hermeneutic conversations with narrative texts. *Qualitative Inquiry, 13*(7), 925–944.

Gadamer, H-G. (1998). *Truth and method* (2nd ed.). New York, NY: Continuum.

Gilmore, P., & Smith, D. (2005). Seizing academic power: Indigenous subaltern voices, metaliteracy, and counternarratives in higher education. In T. McCarty (Ed.), *Language, literacy, and power in schooling* (pp. 67–88). Mahwah, NJ: Lawrence Erlbaum.

Kana'iaupuni, S. M. (2004). Ka'akālai Kū Kanaka: A call for strength-based approaches from a native Hawaiian perspective. *Educational Researcher,* (December), 26–32.

King, T. (2003). *The truth about stories: A Native narrative.* Minneapolis, MN: University of Minnesota Press.

Kirkness, V. J., & Barnhardt, R. (2001). First Nations and higher education: The four R's—respect, relevance, reciprocity, responsibility. In R. Hayoe & J. Pan (Eds.), *Knowledge across cultures: A contribution to dialogue among civilizations.* Retrieved from http://www.ankn.uaf.edu/IEW/winhec/FourRs2ndEd.html

Ladson-Billings, G. (1995). Toward a theory of culturally relevant pedagogy. *American Educational Research Journal, 32*(3), 465–491.

Lipka, J. (2002, January). *Schooling for self-determination: Research on the effects of including Native language and culture in the schools. Eric Indian Education Research Digest.* (ED459989).

Lomawaima, K. T. (2000). Tribal sovereigns: Reframing research in American Indian education. *Harvard Educational Review, 70*(1), 1–21. Retrieved from http://sfxhosted.exlibrisgroup.com.ezproxy.lib.utah.edu/uutah/

———, & McCarty, T. L. (2002). When tribal sovereignty challenges democracy: American Indian education and the democratic ideal. *American Educational Research Journal, 39*(2), 279–305.

Lyons, S. (2000). Rhetorical sovereignty: What do American Indians want from writing? *College Composition and Communication, 51*(3), 447–468.

Madison, D. S. (2011). *Critical ethnography: Method, ethics, and performance* (2nd ed.). Thousand Oaks, CA: Sage.

Marshall, C., & Rossman, G. (2006). *Designing qualitative research.* London, UK: Sage.

Maughan, E. (2008). *Working rhetorical sovereignty in challenging rhetorical situations* (Unpublished doctoral dissertation). University of Utah, Salt Lake City, UT.

Medicine, B. (2001). My elders tell me. In B. Medicine, & S-E. Jacobs (Eds.), *Learning to be an anthropologist and remaining 'Native': Selected writings* (pp. 73–82). Chicago, IL: University of Illinois Press.

Moraes, M. (1996). *Bilingual education: A dialogue with the Bakhtin Circle.* Albany, NY: State University of New York Press.

Nicholls, R. (2009). Research and Indigenous participation: Critical reflexive methods. *International Journal of Social Research Methodology, 12*(2), 117–126.

Noblit, G. W., Flores, S. Y., & Murillo, E. G. (2004). *Postcritical ethnography: Reinscribing critique.* Cresskill, NJ: Hampton Press.

No Child Left Behind Act. (2002). Public Law 107–110, Jan. 8, 2002. 115 Stat. 1425, No Child Left Behind Act of 2001. Retrieved from http://www2.ed.gov/policy/elsec/guid/states/index.html

Powell, M. (2002). Rhetorics of survivance: How American Indians use writing. *College Composition and Communication, 53*(3), 396–434.

———. (2004). Down by the river or how Susan La Flesche Picotte can teach us about alliance as a practice of survivance. *College Composition and Communication, 67*(1), 38–60.

Reyhner, J. (1989). *Changes in American Indian education: A historical retrospective for educators in the United States. ERIC Digest.* (ED314228).

Rockwell, E. (2005). Indigenous accounts of dealing with writing. In T. McCarty (Ed.), *Language, literacy, and power in schooling* (pp. 5–27). Mahwah, NJ: Lawrence Erlbaum.

Shor, I. (1996). *When students have power: Negotiating authority in a critical pedagogy.* Chicago, IL: University of Chicago Press.

Smith, L. T. (2005). Building a research agenda for Indigenous epistemologies and education. *Education Quarterly, 36*(1), 93–95.

Stoffle, R. W., Zedeño, M. N., & Halmo, D. B. (2001). American Indian worldviews I: 'Power' and its connection to people, places, and resources. In R. W. Stoffle, M. N. Zedeño, & D. B. Halmo (Eds.), *American Indians and the Nevada test site: A model of research and consultation* (pp. 58–76). Washington, DC: U.S. Government Printing Office.

Stromberg, E. (2006). Rhetoric and American Indians: An introduction. In E. Stromberg (Ed.), *American Indian rhetorics of survivance: Word medicine, word magic* (pp. 1–12). Pittsburgh, PA: University of Pittsburgh Press.

Thomas, J. (1993). *Doing critical ethnography.* Newbury Park, CA: Sage.

Tyeeme Clark, D. A. (2004). Not the end of the stories, not the end of the songs: Visualizing, signifying, counter-colonizing. In D. A. Mihusuah & A. C. Wilson (Eds.), *Indigenizing the academy: Transforming scholarship and empowering communities* (pp. 218–232). Lincoln, NE: University of Nebraska Press.

Vizenor, G. (1994). *Manifest manners—Narratives on postindian survivance.* Lincoln, NE: University of Nebraska Press.

———. (1998). Fugitive poses. In G. Vizenor, *Fugitive poses: Native American Indian scenes of absence and presence* (pp. 145–166). Lincoln, NE: University of Nebraska Press.

———. (Ed.). (2008). *Survivance: Narratives of Native presence.* Lincoln, NE: University of Nebraska Press.

———, & Lee, A. R. (1999). *Postindian conversations.* Lincoln, NE: University of Nebraska Press.

Warrior, R. A. (1995). *Tribal secrets: Recovering American Indian intellectual traditions.* Minneapolis, MN: University of Minnesota Press.

Weaver, J. (1997). *That the people might live: Native American literatures and Native American community.* New York, NY: Oxford University Press.

Womack, C. S. (1999). *Red on red—Native American literary separatism.* Minneapolis, MN: University of Minnesota Press.

10

The Politics and Poetics of Oral History in Qualitative Research: This One's for Nikki Giovanni

Hilton Kelly

Not long ago, I had the once-in-a-lifetime opportunity of having Nikki Giovanni—world renowned poet, commentator, activist, and educator—dedicate a reading of "Nikki Rosa" to me. My college's English department had invited her to evaluate the creative work (poetry and fiction) of our talented students, and to give a public reading of her own work. I dashed to the airport with a colleague in the department to pick up our esteemed guest, who had arrived earlier than expected and who had been waiting for more than an hour. Let me just say that Nikki Giovanni was not very happy when I greeted her alone in the airport. Besides the fact that she had been waiting for quite a long time, Giovanni apparently had expected to be picked up by my colleague with whom she had been corresponding all day. "Dr. Giovanni!" I shouted with excitement when I saw her. "Yeeesss, and who are you?" she answered with the worry and grimace of someone being stalked. After some explanation, she demanded to know: "Where is the person that I have been calling for over an hour?" and "Why have a cell phone if you are not going to answer it?"

The beginning of the ride back to campus was tense—very tense. Cautiously, I attempted to break the tension and her silence by formally introducing myself, albeit in a rambling manner: "I work in the Education department but I was trained as a sociologist—a historical sociologist actually; I love your poem, 'Nikki Rosa.' So much so, I always find a way to *use* it in all of my classes." Immediately, it seemed to me, the idea that I "use" her work captured her attention. As I recited the opening stanzas of my favorite Nikki Giovanni poem, the tension began to break:

Nikki Rosa

Childhood remembrances are always a drag
if you're Black
you always remember things like living in Woodlawn
with no inside toilet
and if you become famous or something
they never talk about how happy you were to have
your mother
all to yourself and
how good the water felt when you got your bath
from one of those
big tubs that folk in Chicago barbeque in
and somehow when you talk about home
it never gets across how much you
understood their feelings
as the whole family attended meetings about Hollydale
and even though you remember
your biographers never understand
your father's pain as he sells his stock
and another dream goes . . .[1]

We had a memorable and engaging conversation about the politics and the poetics of the poem, and about other childhood memories that would be hard to understand unless you grew up a Black girl or a Black boy on the Black side of the tracks. Born in Knoxville, Tennessee, and reared in Lincoln Heights (an all-Black suburb of Cincinnati, Ohio), Giovanni attended all-Black elementary, grammar, and high schools, including Fisk University's Basic College program, and later graduated from Fisk University (Fowler, 2001).

One "childhood remembrance" that we discussed intensely dealt with "segregated schooling," especially the quality and character of legally segregated schools for Blacks. In the car ride back to campus, Nikki Giovanni reminded me of something about segregated schooling that even I had forgotten, despite the fact that I had collected, analyzed, and published a book on Black teachers' collective remembering of legally segregated schools for Blacks. At some point in our conversation, I made a statement, looking to her for validation as someone famous who attended all-Black schools in the South: "You attended all-Black Fisk University for both high school and college; you turned out well and you had an all-Black faculty." Quickly and candidly, Ms. Giovanni corrected me: "Fisk did not have an all-Black faculty. The faculty was integrated, although the student body was not." While I had forgotten for a moment this important distinction between the faculties at historically Black colleges and universities and all-Black public schools, the lesson learned proved to be more important than I realized at the time. More than a clarification of fact, I argue, Giovanni possessed a particular kind of knowledge (or knowing) that makes oral history important in qualitative research. Whether through forgotten details in interviews with key informants, or through untapped primary sources in archives, oral historical methods can add value to qualitative inquiry.[2]

In this chapter, I aim to think through the place of oral history methods in qualitative research. After a discussion of my larger study on Black teachers who taught in legally segregated schools for Blacks, I draw upon examples from this research to show how oral history in qualitative research can unearth subjugated knowledge as a critical intervention for progressive social change to occur.[3] Dividing my analysis into two parts, the first demonstrates the ways in which dominant narratives are often disrupted in oral history interviewing, which opens up possibilities to challenge the world-taken-for-granted. The second part shows how the poetics of using oral history methodology in qualitative research can lead to a reinterpretation of feelings, emotions, and (sociological) imagination. Ultimately, however, this manuscript is for Nikki Giovanni, whose poetry has had everything to do with my early understanding of the power of counternarratives to challenge dominant discourses about Black life and culture.

Memories of Segregated Schooling: Using Oral History Methods in Qualitative Research

In a qualitative study entitled *Race, Remembering, and Jim Crow's Teachers*, I set out to use oral history to examine both how and what former teachers remembered about working in segregated schools for Blacks in the coastal plain of North Carolina during the Jim Crow years (Kelly, 2010).[4] To summarize briefly, participants in my study—individually and collectively— drew upon hidden transcripts to recall "good" memories of their all-Black schools before and after the 1954 federal mandate to desegregate schools in the South. The hidden transcript, a sociological construct borrowed from James Scott (1990), consists of latent oral or written reports of the social world created in the all-Black school that is not a part of the public record and memory of legally segregated schools for Blacks. As I have argued in the larger study, hidden transcripts mediated how former teachers remembered legally segregated schools. Participants revealed pedagogical responses and initiatives to the politics of race and racism that critiqued White racism and advanced the acquisition of skills, knowledge, and credentials. In addition to well-documented educational barriers, participants remembered undocumented, unknown, and unacknowledged ways in which they prepared poor and working-class Black youth for a dual labor market and for a world beyond a segregated Black society.

As part of the legacy of Jim Crow's teachers, participants in my study used schools as spaces of constant possibility and contestation. Considering the social, political, and economic predicament in which teachers worked in the coastal plain of North Carolina, the public transcript of "inherently inferior" all-Black schools did not tell the whole story of teaching and learning within segregated classrooms and schools. As Scott (1990) duly noted, "every subordinate group creates, out of its ordeal, a hidden transcript that represents a critique of power spoken behind the back of the dominant" (p. xii). The primary purpose of the study was to establish the quality and character of teachers and teaching in legally segregated schools for Blacks by listening to their voices of collective remembering, and to uncover hidden transcripts made public decades after the power structure had changed and powerful people were no longer living. Moreover, the study documented "offstage gestures and practices that confirm, contradict, or inflect what appears in the public transcript" (Scott, 1990, p. 4).

In this chapter, however, the question remains: What was the place of oral history in the design, analysis, and writing of my qualitative study? The study drew upon oral history interviews, archival research, and secondary historical materials. I conducted semi-structured interviews with 44 former classroom teachers who taught in all-Black schools in three counties (Edgecombe, Nash, and Wilson) in the coastal plain region of North Carolina.[5] I interviewed 14 males and 30 females, with an age range from 59 to 85. Only a few of the voices of collective remembering are provided here. All participants were asked open-ended questions, such as: "What do you remember about teaching in all-Black schools before integration?" "In the school(s) where you taught, what do you remember about the quality of education children received?" "What are your best and worst memories of teaching in all-Black schools before integration?" In a conversational manner, participants answered questions about how they remembered their work before school integration.

Retrospective accounts alone proved to be insufficient to make the claim that there may be hidden transcripts that trouble how our society remembers the all-Black public school during the Jim Crow years. To be sure, the accounts from the teachers I interviewed had been influenced by the days, months, and years since the 1954 Brown decision (Leavy, 2011; Ritchie, 2003; see also, Shircliffe, 2001, 2006). I had known that Schwartz and Schuman (2005) suggested the use of survey research in collective memory studies as a traditional methodology that could, in my case, allow a comparison of what these teachers might have thought in earlier decades to what they believe now. Other than a published study of North Carolina Black principals in the early 1970s by Frederick A. Rodgers (1975), however, I had found no surveys in which Black teachers were asked to give their opinions of Black schools and education in the Age of Jim Crow. In addition to oral history interviews and the Rodgers survey, I turned to archival materials to confirm and disconfirm stories that participants told. When I write that I used "oral history" interviews, I mean that I sought to ask informants only about past events with a goal to bracket as much of the present as I could. I retrieved most of the archival data for my analysis from archives and special collections housed at historically Black colleges and universities and the North Carolina Collection at the University of North Carolina at Chapel Hill (North Carolina State Department).

For instance, the archival research provided additional information about teaching in all-Black schools before integration. Like Nikki Giovanni's reminder of a time long past in which the Black social world (at least at Black colleges and universities) was not as segregated as the dominant narrative suggests, I searched for documents that could tell me something about how Jim Crow education and society worked. Fourteen participants attended Fayetteville State Teachers College (FSTC), one of three all-Black "teachers colleges" in North Carolina during the Age of Jim Crow. Fayetteville State University (originally State Normal School) was the first normal school for Blacks in North Carolina. Until 1960, the only major the school offered was education (Smith, 2003). The other two teachers' colleges were Winston-Salem State Teachers' College and Elizabeth City State Teachers College; teachers from these institutions and others were represented in my sample. From these college archival resources, then, I could know something about the curriculum that teachers in my study experienced. In addition, the North Carolina Collection provided multiple volumes of newspaper clippings about "Afro-American Teachers" and "Afro-American Education," which I searched from the mid-1940s (when some participants began teacher preparation) to 1975 (when all schools had been desegregated or closed). This archival source holds over a quarter of a million printed items documenting the history and literature of North Carolina and its people. There are numerous editions of "State School Facts" that compare White, Indian, and Negro students, faculties, and buildings throughout the Jim Crow years. Later, I will show how these archival sources supported my research tremendously. More importantly, however, the archives possessed a treasure trove of "hidden transcripts" that challenged a dominant narrative about legally segregated schools for Blacks.

Secondary sources also complemented the archival data, which I used to lay out a textually mediated memory of segregated schools for Blacks (Wertsch, 2000). While some of the sources that I used constructed a history of Southern Black schools before integration as backwards and inferior (e.g., Frazier, 1957; Tyack & Cuban, 1995), others sought to reconstruct a collective memory and history of segregated schools as good and positive environments for the education of Black youth—despite the lack of financial resources and White supremacy (e.g., Foster, 1997; Walker, 1996). While individual and collective remembering is "always subject to the nostalgic interpretation of experience," as Beauboeuf-Lafontant (1999) explained, the "points of convergence in these separate investigations of Black segregated schools are many and they suggest in a compelling manner that African Americans are recalling aspects of their history that warrant the attention of educational researchers" (p. 710).

The Politics of Oral History in Qualitative Research

And though you're poor it isn't poverty that
concerns you
and though they fought a lot
it isn't your father's drinking that makes any difference
but only that everybody is together and you
and your sister have happy birthdays and very good
Christmases

Oral history, in its most basic definition, is "a method of collecting narratives from individuals for the purpose of research" (Leavy, 2011, p. 4). Giovanni, however, tapped into what ought to be the main purpose or function of oral history in qualitative research: To unearth subjugated knowledge. Here I use "subjugated knowledge" in the Foucauldian sense, which acknowledges that the ways of thinking, knowing, and doing among Blacks and other ethnic minorities have been devalued, neglected, or overlooked within the dominant apparatus of power and/or knowledge (Foucault, 1980). Readers of the poem learn a lesson about the ways in which researchers, in this case qualitative researchers, have walked into Black communities with pen and pad, and walked out with theories of pathology and "cycle of poverty." Giovanni offers a counternarrative to what some scholars have called the "Negro Problem." Stirring up a conflict in remembering, she challenges the dominant narratives about her life as a "poor Black girl." Giovanni's words and perspective become subjugated knowledge filled with wisdom and possibilities for critical intervention and progressive social change.[6] In essence, the poem and the author demand that the reader see things differently, which is, arguably, essential to any kind of social change (see also, Janesick, 2007).

Similarly, in my book-length qualitative study, oral history interviews unearthed knowledge about how southern Blacks lived their lives under state-sponsored racism. Contrary to popular belief, southern White people did not control every aspect of Black life and culture during the Jim Crow years. Overwhelmingly, participants reported that White superintendents in charge of all-Black schools were "totally absent" in their daily operations and management, which, ironically, provided space for Black students, teachers, and communities to prosper. With some research and luck, I found a pioneering study conducted by Frederick A. Rodgers which was published in 1975 as a book, *The Black High School and Its Community*. This was a timely and significant study because, less than five years after school integration, Rodgers surveyed principals, superintendents, teachers and special staff, students, parents, and community leaders. Rodgers also collected state data that schools reported to the North Carolina Department of Public Instruction (NCDPI) each year. What is important here is that Rodgers (1975) gave a qualitative report of the "professional contact" between the Black principal, the White superintendent, and the White community:

> The Black principal often had no real idea what was going on at the White schools... Often when the superintendent met with the Black principal, he met with him alone, and the principal would have no idea what White principals were being told by the central office. These meetings were rare, and rarer still were visits to the schools from anyone in the central office. Quite frequently the [all-White] central office was not even aware that Black schools had yearbooks, and they cared little about what was included in programs of instruction. Said one principal: "As long as we prepared you to dig a straight ditch and cook a good meal, and you didn't blow up the building... that was all they were concerned about." (Rodgers, 1975, p. 54)

One of the teachers that I interviewed, Maureen Brown, confirmed,

> Coming from an all-black school, an all-black situation, or an all-black setting—over here and over there. I never even thought about over there because I was concentrating on this over here—which [was] all-black. And, I would hear of Coon and Fike (former all-White schools in Wilson County, North Carolina), but that was just the scope of it. I knew that I didn't belong there, so it didn't bother me. (Kelly, 2010, p. 30)

Similarly, Athalene Emory remembered,

> We didn't know what was going on in the white community—we had our students. I guess what we were doing was trying to say okay when you graduate from here you are going to be in a bigger society and you need to be able to fit into it and you are going to have to compete. (Kelly, 2010, p. 30)

As subjugated knowledge, the oral history narratives of Maureen Brown and Athalene Emory challenge the world-taken-for-granted, or, in this case, the idea that Whites controlled every aspect of Black life in the Jim Crow South. Consequently, I searched for new language that might explain what oral history interviewing had uncovered. In the study, I employed the term, *benign neglect*, denoting an attitude or policy of noninterference, which may have a more beneficial effect than assuming responsibility. Rather than thinking about the term as something negative, however, I learned through oral history interviews that benign neglect actually provided an opportunity for former Black teachers and administrators to develop and to prosper away from the gaze of White educational authorities. My point here is that new understandings led to new language to talk about past social relations and relationships that had been hidden or forgotten. And with new understandings and new language, people and groups can begin to imagine certain oppressive situations and spaces differently.

Nevertheless, it should be clearly understood that the spatial realities of Jim Crow did present moments of "contact" between Blacks and Whites outside of the schoolhouse gates. Since Frederick Rodgers's (1975) study interviewed White principals just a few years after schools were integrated, he was able to document that "the White principals did not seem to know much about what was happening in the Black schools, in spite of the fact that they often said that they enjoyed a good relationship with the Black administrators" (p. 56). While participants in my study also stated that they did not know much about the all-White school and its community, some informants did recall concrete incidents of a "bad relationship" with Whites in public spaces. Recounting an incident that she believed would always be implanted in her memory, for example, Mildred Hines remarked:

> I will never forget how we would come out to the road to catch the bus. [White children] would see us coming and form a line, so that we would have to jump into the ditch to get to the bus. I remember I had a little raincoat and a hat that my mama bought me. And, I remember very well that [a white boy] saw me and [he] jumped in mud so that it would get all over my coat. I cried. But there was a white girl on the bus—my mama ironed for them—she was so mad that she reported it when she got to school. I remember those kinds of things. (Kelly, 2010, p. 31)

Another example came from Gloria Burks, who also described incidents of violence in the street on the way home from school:

> When they came up from Kenan Street and hit Broad Street, we were coming along Broad Street to come home too... They would say nigger and that's it! And you would come home many days being scraped up—that is why I learned to fight. (Kelly, 2010, p. 31)

Both Hines and Burks spoke about the violent interactions away from the all-Black school in White public spaces. Remember also that Hines spoke about the "White girl on the bus" who reported her White male classmate when she arrived at school. (The girl must have felt sympathy for the ironing woman's child, as Hines had never interacted with the girl before the incident.) Clearly, these accounts point to mostly "bad relationships" between the races, but even positive accounts, like the "good relationships" that the White administrators reported in the Rodgers study, are complicated by unequal power relations.

In legally segregated schools for Blacks, after studying good triangulated data, I concluded that Whites were indeed "present" through the politics of race and racism. In a biographical account of her mother, who was a pioneering Black female psychoanalyst and medical doctor, sociologist Sarah Lawrence-Lightfoot (1995) articulated what it meant to always be in the presence of Whiteness, even when White people were not physically around:

> Like many cities and towns in the Deep South, the residential segregation did not appear to be clearly drawn. That is, neighborhoods were often inhabited by both Blacks and Whites, the races living side by side. But this apparent color mixture was misleading. It did not reflect integration or easy relationships across color lines. It reflected the fact that the southern psyche had so fully incorporated the caste system between races that there was no need for geographic boundaries. The map of segregation resided in the minds of Blacks and Whites, and there was no need to draw it on the land. (p. 48)

The power of White people to totally control what occurred in the all-Black public school should not be overemphasized, however. Recall that the dominant narrative about legally segregated schools for Blacks claimed that White people controlled everyday life in schools; benign neglect, however, allowed Black teachers and administrators the space to prepare, to create, and to build.

Historical evidence that supports the idea that Blacks were active, not passive, in their own liberation can be useful. When qualitative researchers use oral history to unearth subjugated knowledge as a critical intervention for progressive social change, then we begin to have a fuller picture of how people really lived (and live) their lives. More than collecting narratives for the purpose of research, oral history methods in qualitative research give us the possibility to challenge dominant narratives with sources that complement in-depth interviewing. In the end, while some Black administrators and teachers may have functioned well with the daily physical absence of White authorities, the social, psychological presence of Whiteness had been woven into the social fabric of the Jim Crow South.

The Poetics of Oral History in Qualitative Research

Black love is Black wealth and they'll
probably talk about my hard childhood
and never understand that
all the while I was quite happy

Like Giovanni's words, Black teachers' oral history narratives challenge what is easily accessible and publicly known about "segregation," but they cannot be separated from emotion and imagination.[7] My sociological training compels me to listen to voices of collective remembering with a great deal of suspicion, in the name of objectivity and of rigor. Moreover, I have been trained to focus on collecting good data (stories with thick description) that I can later retell in light of theories from the field. In my study, for example, I faced a dilemma in which Black teachers I interviewed reported passionately and proudly that "Black teachers were more qualified than the White teachers" before school integration in the state of North Carolina. While I could not ignore this "unexpected story" that nearly all participants reported, and while I knew that my colleagues would certainly dismiss such subjugated knowledge as false memory, I had to find a way to express their sentiments and to satisfy other sociologists and qualitative researchers (Cary, 1999). Thus, I used oral history methods as a way to "triangulate" or to check the "hard to believe" stories that my participants told with sincerity. In order to be considered an objective and rigorous qualitative researcher, I could not rely solely on what participants told me about their personal experiences and personal troubles (Polkinghorne, 2007). Emotional subjugated knowledge would not stand; I needed stronger evidence to support their claim.

Rather than simply reporting that "Black teachers were more qualified than White teachers," I employed what C. Wright Mills (1959) called the "sociological imagination." In this way, I could serve two masters, so to speak: link the personal and cultural experiences of my participants to the larger public and structural issues that my colleagues *understood*. In addition, the task required that I be systematic by paying close attention to elements of narrative poetics, such as narration, point of view, and irony. For example, in their history of public school reform, educational researchers, David Tyack and Larry Cuban (1995), gave a rather negative impression of the quality of Black schools, in general, and an even worse one of Black teachers. Sketching the dominant narrative about inferior legally segregated schools for Blacks, Tyack and Cuban wrote:

> In 1940 about two out of three blacks lived in rural areas, overwhelmingly in the South. Racial oppression compounded inequalities created by the poverty of the region. Disenfranchised blacks had to make do with the starvation diet of school funds that white officials allocated to the segregated 'colored' schools. Blacks constituted over a quarter of the public school students but received only 12 percent of revenues. *Half of the black teachers had gone no further than high school, compared with 7 percent of white teachers* [emphasis added]. They often lacked the most basic aids to learning—textbooks, slates, and chalk, or desks—and frequently had very large classes when the children were not needed for farm labor. (1995, p. 23)

When you consider the italicized sentence about the scholastic training of Black teachers and their working conditions before integration, it is no wonder why Black teachers have been remembered as unqualified or underqualified compared to their White counterparts. The dominant or official narrative supports a particular memory of legally segregated schools and their teachers. Close examination of Tyack and Cuban's (1995) footnotes reveals that this quotation was made in reference to a single East Texas school before the 1940s from a "visitor" to the school (p. 151). While this assessment may have been true for this one school in East Texas, it probably was not true of all segregated schools for Blacks in East Texas or throughout the state.

Again, the former teachers I interviewed had a different point of view; they reported that Black teachers in North Carolina were certified across the board. This was a consistent message in my interviews that participants discussed enthusiastically. As a qualitative researcher, however, I could not take what participants said at face value. There was a politics of remembering that I had learned in qualitative research classes, in which participants could not be trusted to tell the truth. Participants stood accused of romanticizing events or only remembering the good—especially when it benefited them and their communities (Dougherty, 1999; Shircliffe, 2001).

My study, however, supported an ever growing number of counter-narratives by researchers in history and education of "the good all-Black school" and "exemplary Black teachers" before school integration, including North Carolina's Black public schools and teachers (see Cecelski, 1994;

McCullough-Garrett, 1993; Noblit & Dempsey, 1996; Philipsen, 1999; Randolph, 2004; Shircliffe, 2006; Walker, 1996). It was hard to ignore the irony in what I heard throughout interviews: that not only were Black teachers qualified, but that they were overqualified. For example, Alton Bobbitt remembered:

> We had a survey of teacher certification and the superintendent came over to Frederick Douglass [School] and said, 'I should not be over here talking about certification because the principal has a masters degree, there are 42 people on this faculty and out of that 42, there are 17 masters degrees here,' and everything else was A certificates... This was in 1964. And, he said I should not even be over here. I should go back to Elm City High School (the white school) where we have people with nonstandard certification, B certificates, C certificates, and no degrees. But they were still teaching. (Kelly, 2010, p. 33)

Contrary to popular belief, Bobbitt claimed that Black teachers were overqualified on the Black side of town in comparison to White teachers. Adding some support, Elmer Cummings, a former teacher, counselor, and principal, recalled:

> At that time, we did not have a shortage of black teachers. In fact we were over supplied with black teachers. We had a surplus of black teachers because that was the only thing that most of us could go into. They went on and got their masters, doctorates, and things like that. The supply of white teachers wasn't that great, so they were hiring teachers with B certificates. (Kelly, 2010, p. 33)

If Tyack and Cuban were correct, then my teachers' memories and impressions must be incorrect. Using my sociological imagination, and bracketing the emotions attached to the subjugated knowledge that my participants told me, I used the Rodgers study and my own exploration of state data to explore the matter further. I chose to look for data that would give me a sense of teacher training and preparation in North Carolina during the time in which the teachers I interviewed would have been teaching. The oldest person I interviewed started to teach in 1942.

In North Carolina, the Rodgers study found that "by 1947–48 the quality of teacher training and preparation for Blacks and Whites was reversed from what it had been in 1924–25. In fact, from 1941 to 1948, the number of White teachers teaching on non-standard certificates rose from 1022 to 2909, while the number of Black teachers holding 'A' standard certificates went from 5806 to 6240" (p. 32). Following Rodgers's lead, I searched the archives at the North Carolina Collection on the campus of the University of North Carolina at Chapel Hill for data from the North Carolina State Department of Public Instruction (NCDPI). As I explored further the Tyack and Cuban thesis that Black teachers were not as qualified as White teachers, I found that in 1939–1940, North Carolina teachers had a total index of training of 776.4, with White and Black teachers having a separate score of 785.7 and 752.6, respectively (North Carolina State Department, 1941). For both Blacks and Whites, the number of teachers with "4 years college" training increased tremendously from 1929–30 to 1939–40. The NCDPI reported that there were 47 White teachers and 182 Negro teachers in the state of North Carolina having no college training (North Carolina State Department, 1941). In addition, the 1939–1940 data showed that 88.8 % of White teachers and 67.8% of Black teachers were college graduates.

Between 1937–1939, there were 203 Black public high schools and 743 White public high schools in North Carolina, while there were 2,174 Black public elementary schools and 1,884 White elementary schools (North Carolina State Department, 1941). The percentage gap between the number of college graduates for Blacks and Whites, I argue, can be partially explained by the smaller number of Black high schools prior to the mid-1930s (Anderson, 1988; Perkins, 1989; Rodgers, 1975). Since high school departments were just beginning to become commonplace in rural Black communities in North Carolina, it makes sense that there were fewer Black teachers who had college-level preparation to teach in the public schools. The majority of Black teachers would have taught in primary and grammar schools, where low levels of scholastic training were expected (Anderson, 1988; Rodgers, 1975). Once more public high schools opened and the college degree was a requirement for elementary teachers, then the percentage gap in scholastic training became smaller over time.

Interpretations of percentage gaps in scholastic training (which were smaller than the exaggerations read in history texts) have been used as evidence of Black inferiority. I view the percentage gaps as evidence of racism and discrimination in the building and funding of Black high schools. And these gaps offer little to no insight about the quality of the teachers themselves. James Anderson (1988) concluded that "the development of teacher training programs for Black students in the South evolved at a slower pace, in large part because southern White school authorities were unwilling to enforce equally high standards for Black schools" (p. 113). However, Walker (2001) documented that, by the 1940s, "the professional preparation of African American teachers began to increase noticeably, and in some cases surpassed that of Whites" (p. 765). Likewise, Rodgers found that "teacher preparation continued to improve until by 1949–50 it surpassed that of White teachers" (p. 32). Rodgers (1975) reasoned,

> As the country became involved in World War II, White teachers found more profitable jobs in areas other than teaching. This did not hold true for Black teachers. As a result of this, White teachers left their profession in great numbers, and by 1948 there were sixty times more nonstandard certificate holders among White teachers than in 1937. (p. 32)

After all of this archival mining, I found one newspaper clipping that verified what participants had conveyed in both facial and bodily expressions at the time of their interviews. The North Carolina Civil Rights Advisory Committee reported in the *Durham Morning Herald* on October 2, 1960 that Negro teacher salaries were higher than White teacher salaries, even though "the average Negro income [was] approximately one-half the average white" ("Afro-American Teachers"). According to Rodgers (1975), "Salaries also reflected [the] difference in training, since the law passed in 1944 equalized salary schedules. Black teachers' salaries were 103 percent those of white teachers in 1950–51 as opposed to 73 percent of Whites' salaries in 1940" (p. 32). According to the Advisory Committee, "one of the reasons for the difference has been that more Negro teachers hold higher certificates, more Negro teachers remain in their teaching jobs for longer periods of time, thus building up longevity pay" ("Afro-American Teachers"). As early as 1960, the hidden transcript had been revealed in the local Durham newspaper, yet neglected until recently. "Public" records in the archives confirmed what participants expressed in oral history interviews many decades later. When you consider the few employment options that Black teachers had, due to the politics of race and racism in Jim Crow North Carolina, the likelihood of a surplus of Black teachers seems plausible. All things being equal, Black principals, or the White superintendent in some areas, could almost handpick the best applicants. In my study, it might be important to note, all of the participants had college degrees when they started teaching, and all met the standards for teacher certification that applied to them.

Conclusion

While theoretical discussions of "subjugated knowledge" are not new in academic discourses, and have existed for as long as the publication of Giovanni's "Nikki Rosa," qualitative research designed intentionally to use oral history methods to unearth subjugated knowledge is recent history (Lincoln, 2010). One of the best examples has been in the area of educational research on segregated schooling with scholars from anthropology, education, history, and sociology. In the foreword to *Race, Remembering, and Jim Crow's Teachers*, George Noblit explained the emergence of these historical qualitative studies: "The official story is literally a whitewash of experience. It is not only a story from the point of view of Whites—it is also written over the stories of people of color. Color and indeed variety are obliterated in the process. By valorizing the stories of everyday people, oral history has become a way to reveal the accounts suppressed both by white supremacy and the norms of academic scholarship. Through oral history, African Americans have given themselves a voice that had been denied them by speaking of the lives they have lived. What is inspiring is that these stories are not only accounts of the White racism that so shapes their lives. These oral histories are so much more—accounts of struggle, of perseverance, of invention and creativity, of the power of their humanity. Such histories have obviously much to teach our nation, if we are willing to learn (Noblit, 2010, p. xiii). What remains to be seen, however, is the degree to which socially constructed rules and models of conventional qualitative research will be broken or rewritten to allow more critical approaches to become normalized within oral history and qualitative research (Lincoln, 2010). At best, we see the emergence of whole new areas of qualitative research marked as "critical," to distinguish it from conventional qualitative research (Denzin & Lincoln, 2000).

Within the discipline of history, oral historians have had their challenges as well. As Donald Ritchie (2003) observed: "Some social historians have accused oral historians of swallowing whole the stories that informants tell them. They argue that a truer 'people's history' must be based on statistical analysis and other objective data rather than on subjective individual testimony" (p. 27). In essence, some historians believe that the politics and poetics of oral history interviewing have gotten in the way of "good old-fashioned historical research." Ritchie and others have not taken such criticism lightly, however. They, who drink deeply from the cup of qualitative methodology, continually question the ways in which traditional histories privilege the archive without acknowledging the omissions, deletions, and silences—not to mention competing narration, point of view, and irony—in their work. Ultimately, the archive and its users have a way of privileging the elite or dominant narratives in society in the same way that historical qualitative researchers are accused of privileging the voices of collective remembering among subjugated peoples.

In the end, I have demonstrated that oral history methods can be used in qualitative research to unearth subjugated knowledge (see also, Janesick, 2007). More importantly, I think that such efforts are essential steps toward creating critical interventions for progressive social change. As the old saying goes, "truth crushed to earth shall rise again stronger than ever." The truth that Nikki Giovanni and I uncover (poem and prose) is intended to disrupt or to challenge the world-taken-for-granted and to introduce new understandings and language. As another "new frontier" in qualitative research methodology, oral history is essentially a traditional research method that can be used in nontraditional, qualitative ways (Eisner, 1997). At least, this is what I learned from Nikki Giovanni—a world renowned poet, commentator, activist, and educator.

Notes

1. Unless otherwise stated, words from the poem were taken from Giovanni (1970).
2. Oral history includes an array of methods, such as interviewing, archival mining, and surveying, which can be used in combination to create a historical narrative. Throughout this chapter, when I am arguing for the strengths of oral history in qualitative research, I am referring to an array of methods used in combination, not just interviews. I thank one of the editors of this volume, Kristen Luschen, for helping me to articulate this important point.
3. Sociologist Patricia Leavy first pointed out that feminist researchers have highlighted the importance of oral history in revealing "women's subjugated knowledges." According to Leavy (2011), "In the recent decades, feminist researchers have highlighted the possibilities of oral history in the social sciences. As a result, some mistakenly categorize oral history as a 'feminist method'" (p. 4). In addition, Valerie Janesick (2007) made a similar point about oral history as a social justice project: "feminist oral history offers a means to document and interpret women's stories to advance a social justice agenda. Doubtless there are many more examples for others to find, use and write about" (p. 119). Here I expand the notion that oral history in qualitative research and in the social sciences can unearth subjugated knowledge(s) for other oppressed groups as well.
4. The term *Jim Crow* originated around 1830 when Thomas Rice—a White man in Black face—mimicked Black people as part of a performance entitled "Jump Jim Crow." (For a detailed discussion, see C. Vann Woodward's 1955 classic, *The Strange Career of Jim Crow*). Over time, state-sponsored legal segregation and discrimination began to be referred to as Jim Crow laws and practices, such as "quadruple public bathrooms, special trains and tramways, separate restaurants and hotels, double waiting rooms, [and] colored coded drinking fountains" (Lewis, 1993, p. 270).
5. For a detailed discussion of the methodology that supports my research on Black teachers in legally segregated schools for Blacks, see the appendix to *Race, Remembering, and Jim Crow's Teachers* (Kelly, 2010).
6. My analysis here does not extend beyond acknowledging that "critical interventions" are necessary for progressive social change to occur. While I do not prescribe a pill for progressive social change, the examples that I offer can raise consciousness and provide new angles of vision.
7. According to Donald E. Polkinghorne (2007), "experienced meaning is not simply a surface phenomenon; it permeates through the body and psyche of participants" (p. 481). Knowledge that we gain from oral history interviewing, subjugated or otherwise,

represents "experienced meaning" that has emotional aspects that are often overlooked. See Polkinghorne (2007).

References

'*Afro-American teachers*' [Newspaper clippings]. North Carolina Collection. Louis Round Wilson Library, University of North Carolina at Chapel Hill, NC.
Anderson, J. (1988). *The education of Blacks in the South, 1860–1935*. Chapel Hill, NC: University of North Carolina Press.
Beauboeuf-Lafontant, T. (1999). A movement against and beyond boundaries: 'Politically relevant teaching' among African American teachers. *Teachers College Record, 100*(4), 702–723.
Cary, L. (1999). Unexpected stories: Life history and the limits of representation. *Qualitative Inquiry, 5*(3), 411–427.
Cecelski, D. (1994). *Along freedom road: Hyde County, North Carolina and the fate of Black schools in the South*. Chapel Hill, NC: University of North Carolina Press.
Denzin, N. K., & Lincoln, Y. S. (2000). *The Sage handbook of qualitative research* (3rd ed.). New York, NY: Sage.
Dougherty, J. (1999). From anecdote to analysis: Oral interviews and new scholarship in educational history. *Journal of American History, 86*(2), 712–723.
Eisner, E. W. (1997). The new frontier in qualitative research methodology. *Qualitative Inquiry, 3*(3), 259–273.
Foster, M. (1997). *Black teachers on teaching*. New York, NY: New Press.
Foucault, M. (1980). *Power/knowledge: Selected interviews and other writings, 1972–1977* (C. Gordon, Ed. & Trans.). New York, NY: Pantheon Books.
Fowler, V. C. (2001). Giovanni, Nikki. In W. L. Andrews, F. S. Foster, & T. Harris (Eds.), *The concise Oxford companion to African-American literature* (pp. 167–169). New York, NY: Oxford University Press.
Frazier, E. F. (1957). *Black bourgeoisie*. Glencoe, IL: Free Press.
Giovanni, N. (1970). *Black feeling, Black talk/Black judgment*. New York, NY: William Morrow.
Janesick, V. J. (2007). Oral history as a social justice project: Issues for the qualitative researcher. *Qualitative Report, 12*(1), 111–121. Retrieved from http://www.nova.edu/ssss/QR/QR 12–1/janesick.pdf (no longer accessible).
Kelly, H. (2010). *Race, remembering, and Jim Crow's teachers*. New York, NY: Routledge.
Lawrence-Lightfoot, S. (1995). *Balm in Gilead: Journey of a healer*. New York, NY: Penguin Books.
Leavy, P. (2011). *Oral history: Understanding qualitative research*. New York, NY: Oxford University Press.
Lewis, D. L. (1993). *W. E. B. Du Bois: Biography of a race, 1868–1919*. New York, NY: Henry Holt.
Lincoln, Y. (2010). 'What a long, strange trip it's been . . .': Twenty-five years of qualitative and new paradigm research. *Qualitative Inquiry, 16*(1), 3–9.
McCullough-Garrett, A. (1993). Reclaiming the African American vision for teaching: Toward an educational conversation. *Journal of Negro Education, 62*(4), 433–440.
Mills, C. W. (1959). *The sociological imagination*. New York, NY: Oxford University Press.
Noblit, G. (2010). Foreword. In H. Kelly, *Race, remembering, and Jim Crow's teachers* (xiii–xvi). New York, NY: Routledge.

Noblit, G., & Dempsey, V. (1996). *The social construction of virtue: The moral life of schools.* Albany, NY: State University of New York Press.

North Carolina State Department of Public Instruction. (1941, July). *North Carolina State school facts.* North Carolina Collection. Louis Round Wilson Library, University of North Carolina at Chapel Hill, NC.

Perkins, L. (1989). The history of Blacks in teaching. In D. Warren (Ed.), *American teachers: History of a profession at work* (pp. 344–367). New York, NY: Macmillan.

Philipsen, M. (1999). *Values-spoken and values-lived: Race and the cultural consequences of a school closing.* Cresskill, NJ: Hampton Press.

Polkinghorne, D. E. (2007). Validity issues in narrative research. *Qualitative Inquiry, 13*(4), 471–486.

Randolph, A. W. (2004). The memories of an all-Black northern urban school: Good memories of leadership, teachers, and the curriculum. *Urban Education, 39*(6), 596–620.

Ritchie, D. (2003). *Doing oral history: A practical guide* (2nd ed.). New York, NY: Oxford University Press.

Rodgers, F. A. (1975). *The Black high school and its community.* Lexington, MA: Lexington Books.

Schwartz, B., & Schuman, H. (2005). History, commemoration, and belief: Abraham Lincoln in American memory, 1945–2001. *American Sociological Review, 70*(2), 183–203.

Scott, J. (1990). *Domination and the arts of resistance: Hidden transcripts.* New Haven, CT: Yale University Press.

Shircliffe, B. (2001). We got the best of that world: A case for the study of nostalgia in the oral history of school segregation. *Oral History Review, 28*(2), 59–84.

———. (2006). *The best of that world: Historically Black high schools and the crisis of desegregation in a southern metropolis.* Creskill, NJ: Hampton Press.

Smith, J. C. (2003). *Black firsts: 4,000 ground-breaking and pioneering historical events* (2nd ed.). Detroit, MI: Visible Ink Press.

Tyack, D., & Cuban, L. (1995). *Tinkering toward utopia: A century of public school reform.* Cambridge, MA: Harvard University Press.

Walker, V. (1996). *Their highest potential: An African American school community in the segregated South.* Chapel Hill, NC: University of North Carolina Press.

———. (2001). African American teaching in the South: 1940–1960. *American Educational Research Journal, 38*(4), 751–779.

Wertsch, J. (2000). Narratives as cultural tools in sociocultural analysis: Official history in Soviet and post-Soviet Russia. *Ethos, 28*(4), 511–533.

Woodward, C. V. (1955). *The strange career of Jim Crow.* New York, NY: Oxford University Press.

11

"Some of Us Got Heard More Than Others": Studying Brown Through Oral History and Critical Race Theory

James H. Adams and Natalie G. Adams

In a recent graduate-level class about the persistence of institutional racism in schools, an African American female student offered Bell's (2004) interest-convergence theory as the explanation about the passage of *Brown v. Board of Education* and its subsequent failure. In brief, the theory suggests that "the interests of blacks in achieving racial equality will be accommodated only when that interest converges with the interests of whites in policy-making positions" (Bell, 2004, p. 69). Bell argued that at the height of the Cold War, with the United States trying to position itself as a superpower and a model for the superiority of democracy over communism, *Brown* was passed primarily because it served the international interests of the US, and helped remedy the image problem the United States was encountering as people worldwide witnessed the atrocities committed against African Americans on our own soil. As the African American student presented this very compelling argument about the macro forces leading to the passage of *Brown* in 1954, the only White male student in the class became visibly agitated. When she finished, the male student exploded:

> I think Thurgood Marshall and hundreds of other African Americans in the South who gave their lives for the cause of desegregation would be appalled at what you're suggesting. It totally negates the hard work people did in the field to make this happen. Sometimes theory can be total bullshit in the way it erases the hard work teachers do day in and day out to make change happen.

While we are not ready to discount the power of theory in general or the value of critical race theory (CRT) in particular, we are sensitive to the frustration that many of our students, particularly K–12 teachers and administrators, express about the danger of theory to negate the hard work of social justice in the everyday, and often mundane doing of school. This sensitivity comes not only from our own background as former middle-school and high school public school teachers, but also from our work over the last two years collecting oral histories of teachers, administrators, students, and parents involved in the court-enforced desegregation of public schools in Mississippi from 1967–1971. We understand, as did Janesick (2007) and French and Swain (2006), that oral history provides a rich medium not only for retelling important historical events from the perspective of those marginalized in traditional accounts of history, but also for highlighting how ordinary people can work for social justice within the constraints of their own lives as raced, classed, and gendered beings. However, allowing stories to stand alone without any critical interrogation of the raced, classed, and gendered assumptions embedded in them can be problematic.

In this chapter we present excerpts from the oral histories of four educators working in Mississippi public schools when *Brown* was finally enforced in the late 1960s. Some historical context is needed to understand the stories of these educators. Long known for its opposition to Black suffrage (e.g., in 1954 only 4% of Black Mississippians could vote), Mississippi was also the last state to comply even minimally with *Brown v. Board of Education*, and the fiercest in its maneuvering to resist moving to a unitary, integrated school system. The members of the Mississippi legislature used every political and legal weapon they could to delay the implementation of *Brown*, including an amendment that would abolish public schools if the Supreme Court ruled favorably in *Brown*, the allocation of public funds for private, segregated White academies, and the adoption of "freedom of choice" policies in the 1960s (Bolton, 2005). The landmark 1969 decision *Alexander v. Holmes* finally closed every loophole previously used to circumvent *Brown* in Mississippi. The Court made crystal clear the timeline for enforcing *Brown*: "Under explicit holdings of this Court the obligation of every school district is to terminate dual school systems at once and to operate now and hereafter only unitary schools." Nine months later, every school district in Mississippi was desegregated. In many cases, school districts were ordered to be totally integrated by January 1970—two months after the ruling.

This is the historical context framing the educational narratives of Mrs. Lilly Davis and Drs. Fenton Peters, Clyde Muse, and Tom Dulin. When desegregation was enforced, Mrs. Davis was a teacher, Dr. Peters was the principal of the segregated Black[1] high school, and Drs. Muse and Dulin were superintendents. All were born and reared in Mississippi during the era of segregation and Jim Crow. All are now in their 70s or 80s, and continue to reside in the towns and cities they helped integrate. Davis and Peters are Black; Muse and Dulin are White. In the next section, we present their stories with a brief analysis. We then end by highlighting how these oral histories can provide a framework for examining the recursive relationship between theory, policy, educational practice, and history.

"We Got Desegregation But...": Black Educators, Power, and the Disappointment of *Brown*

Lilly Davis

Lilly Davis has lived in Marks, Mississippi for most of her life. In 1947 she was the valedictorian and one of three students who comprised the first Black graduating class in Quitman County. She graduated from Rust College (Holly Springs, Mississippi) in 1957 with her undergraduate degree. In 1972 she received her master's degree from The University of Mississippi. Mrs. Davis has dedicated her life to public education, first as a teacher, then as an assistant principal, and now as a school board member. The first story below describes the role Mrs. Davis played in the early attempts at desegregation efforts in her school district. The second story provides a glimpse into what would have been a common experience for all teachers during this time period—the annual classroom Christmas party. The final story reflects Mrs. Davis's thoughts about desegregation now that she serves as a school board member in the public school system described in the first story—a school system that is now 99% Black.

> **Story #1: "I didn't want to go."** [In 1969] I was asked to go into the all-White school here in Marks. And I did not want to go. But I was told that I had to go; they gave me some choices. If I did not go, they would send my children over there [to the White school] and that I would not have a job in Quitman County. And knowing as I did know—this I'm going to say it just like it is—these White people would do anything they wanted to do and you had to accept it. So I said, "I will go because I don't want my children to go." My children hadn't ever worked around White people in their lives. They only had been used to Black people and I didn't want my children to go over there. So I had to go by force, and I was asked from the superintendent why I did not want to go. I was very blunt. I said, "you White people are vicious, you believe in killing black folks; that's why I don't want to go."

Story #2: The lonely Christmas party. So coming up for the Christmas party the parents came and met and they decided on how they were going to have the party. And I was not included. I was just somebody sitting there. I was not included. I wasn't asked anything. I was just a nobody over there. I just sat there. Sometimes there are things in life we have to accept. We can't do nothing about it but accept them because I know that things are going to get better.

Story #3: The failures of Brown. Integration didn't do what it was supposed to do. We still don't have equal opportunities. We still don't have the type of schools that we need. We still don't have the buildings that we need. You take for instance here in Quitman County, we have one gym and we have three schools, only one gym. And it's still not where we should be. You know, Black folks are not worried about trying to socialize with White people. We want a quality education for our children. That's all we want. And we want them to have the same chance and the same opportunity that other children have. We should have made more progress than what we have made but we haven't. And I think it's going to take many years to come before we reach that point where we should be as far as educating all the children. It is still a system that really, to me, really doesn't want you to achieve, really don't want Blacks to achieve.

Fenton Peters

Fenton Peters is a 75-year-old Black man who was born, reared, and lived most of his life in Starkville, Mississippi. He earned his undergraduate degree from Rust College and received both his master's and doctoral degrees from Mississippi State University. Dr. Peters was the principal of Henderson High, the Black high school in Starkville, when court-ordered desegregation occurred. The first story describes his role in the decision-making process for how desegregation would take place in the Starkville schools. In the second story, he shows how notions of the racial inferiority of Blacks were reproduced during the desegregation process. In the final story, he relates his ambivalence about the success of the desegregation efforts that he supported 50 years ago.

Story #1: Being at the table but not really heard. In my mind they took none of our recommendations. When I say "us," I mean Black people at that time. Took very few recommendations from us. Most of them came from the White community, and so my feeling is if it had not been court ordered it probably would not have happened 'til this very day. There is another thing I would like to say with regard to that. That is the "powers that be" at that time felt that having someone to say that you had to do it gave them a scapegoat for somebody to lean on and say, "they made me do it," and that's how it got done. I was part of the process but it was not left entirely up to me. The rules and what not came down from on high. All of the strategies and what not came from the superintendent's office and, of course, he and his assistants, the central office staff and the school board, I think devised and contrived a major plan and process about what was going to happen and what way we were going to do it. Now, we had an administrative council that was in on it as well, and of course it was all the administrators and what not there surrounding the superintendent and we came up with some things there that we felt, as professionals, if we did that it would probably go best or work better as opposed to that way and that is how we came up with it. Of course, as I said, everyone had their input. I don't know if everybody got heard. Some people got heard a little more than what others did.

Story #2: The Black intellectual inferiority myth. I want to mention another racial thing—a tool of elimination that was a racial thing—the inferiority of Black people compared to White. We [all teachers] had to resign and reapply for our jobs, meeting the new criteria that had been set forth by the school board and superintendent, and it was to make a certain score on the GRE, a score that we had been charged to meet. Turned out the lawyers who helped to handle our cases found out the score that the school district prescribed, only about, I believe I am right, only about 5% of Blacks scored that score so it became very evident what it was for to start with. Well, we went ahead. You had to do that or else you had to enroll in a graduate school and get at least a master's degree in a certain length of time, and of course, couple all of those things together and it weeded out about 50% of the Black teachers. That left no doubt in our minds what was going on. That was a tool that was used to purge us, and that specter still hangs over Starkville schools right now.

Story #3: The failure of Brown, Part 2. I thought that the only way we were going to get a fair shake was to get in there with them, and I believe that desegregation was the answer but…and the old cliché is that they gave us desegregation, but they gave it to us on their terms so it didn't turn out. Those of us who were preaching desegregation at the time did not get it as we thought it was going to be. First place, we lost our schools. In terms of prestige, we lost our schools. Starkville High school became THE high school. Henderson, for us, was THE high school.

Black educators in the South occupied a tenuous position as middle-class Blacks with respectable jobs, employment security, and at least some degree of financial security. Speaking out against segregated schools cost many their jobs, particularly in the late 1950s and early 1960s (Bolton, 2005). Yet, by the mid- to late 1960s, with the court-enforcement of desegregation, the White power structure sought the cooperation of Black educators in implementing a peaceful transition to desegregate schools. How that "cooperation" was approached varied greatly, as reflected in the stories of Dr. Peters and Mrs. Davis. Mrs. Davis's cooperation was coerced, with threats to her livelihood and her children. Dr. Peters was ostensibly more involved in the decisions around the implementation of desegregation in his school district. He was invited to the "table," but his voice wielded no power or authority, and he was no more trusting of the White power structure ("the powers that be") than was Davis. In cooperating with the superintendent and school board, they were being asked to place great trust in an institution that had treated them as inferior for a hundred years, and their cooperation did not translate into having a voice in decision-making about desegregation.

As teachers in the segregated, poorly funded schools in Mississippi in the 1950s and 1960s, Mrs. Davis and Dr. Peters believed that *Brown* offered the only hope for them and their children to ever have a chance at equality of educational opportunity. They, like most Black Southerners, knew desegregation would come at a cost, but they felt it was imperative in disproving the myth of Black intellectual inferiority, which was at the heart of White supremacy and the oppression of Blacks in the South. Fifty years after *Brown*, they are sorely disappointed in its failure to achieve equality of educational opportunity, and the unforeseen costs to the Black community. They understand, as do critical race scholars, that Brown failed to "dismantle the structures that had produced and supported school segregation in the first place" (Dixson & Rousseau, 2005, p. 20). Thus, 50 years after Mrs. Davis was forced to be part of the dismantling of segregated schools, her school district is once again segregated and short on resources.

"Deep Down We're All the Same": White Educators Enforcing the "Law of the Land"

Dr. Clyde Muse

Dr. Clyde Muse was born in 1929 in a small town in Mississippi. He earned a bachelor's degree from Delta State (Cleveland, MS), and a master's and doctorate from Mississippi State University. He began his teaching career as a teacher and a coach, then moved into being a principal and superintendent of several school districts in Mississippi. Today, at 83 years old, he serves as the President of Hinds Community College. The first story relates Dr. Muse's experience in New Orleans when the Fifth Circuit Court of Appeals rendered its decision that Mississippi could no longer delay desegregation. The second story conveys his belief that "Southern values" trump race, class, and gender differences, and are responsible for the success of desegregation. In the last story, he relates why it was important for him to send his own children to the newly integrated public schools.

> **Story #1: Pleading for time.** The day after I was sworn in as the Hinds County superintendent—Hinds County at that time was the second largest school district in the state of Mississippi—17 different schools, 132 school bus routes—well I wound up going with the attorney, the next day to the Fifth Circuit Court of Appeals. There were 32 school districts that were going to be affected by this order. Stacked in front

of the court was pleadings and stuff this high from all over the different school districts represented there. But I never shall forget. They came in with the black robes and all of the pledges of allegiance and other pomp and circumstance of the Fifth Circuit going into session. And the chief judge called order and he said, "Let's get on with this damn school case. I'm tired of it." That woke this "lil ole country boy" up. Finally, I said to Bob [one of the attorneys defending the school districts], "Bob, can I speak to the court?" And he asked the judge would he allow me to speak and he said he would. And I just began to say as a school person, please give me at least the second semester so that students, teachers, parents, and everybody can make decisions. And anyway it's just not educationally sound to do that. Well he said, "Well, Dr. Muse, we think you can do it with school people like yourself. It can be done." So I sat down.

Story #2: Weathering integration and the success of Brown. I am convinced as of 'til this very day that every parent wants the same thing for their children, Black, White, green, yellow, purple, whatever. They want their child to be in an environment that's safe, and they want their children to get good teaching and to be treated fairly. True, you got Black and White families that could care less about what happens to their children. Got it more today than you had in '69, '70, '71. But basically all your basic core people in the South have a strong faith in God. They're fine Christian people. Yes, there's differences in people but what you look at in terms of core values is there. And we in the South weathered that storm. We have more desegregation in the South now than these big cities that were looking down their noses at us like Boston, Chicago, and they have so many problems they don't know how to handle it. But what we've got in a small community, we got people that know each other. They see each other on the streets. In many occasions, they've played with them growing up, you know, that type of thing. So you don't have the kind of, I guess, animosities and fears and prejudices that you have in other settings.

Story #3: Sending my own children to public schools. When I went to Meridian, my little 10th-grade daughter, pretty little blonde-headed girl, she went to Harris which was the 10th-grade school. I got a call one night from a fellow. He said, "Do you know what's going on down at Harris?" I said, "Well, I hope I do." He said, "Well all the Black boys down there are pinching the White girls on their buttocks and on their breasts." I said, "I tell you what I'm going to do. I'm going to go in there and ask my daughter (she goes to school down there) is that happening." He said, "Wait a minute. You have a daughter down there in the school?" I said, "I sure do." He said, "Well, hell, just forget I called." So it came in handy to have a junior high child, and a high school child, and an elementary child, but I wasn't fearful for myself or for my children. I never gave a thought to sending my children to private school. Why, if the schools are not good enough for my own children and I'm superintendent of the schools, boy, that sends a big message to a lot of people, Black and White. So if I was going to be superintendent of schools, my children were going to be in those schools.

Dr. Tom Dulin

Dr. Tom Dulin was also born and reared in Mississippi. He has an undergraduate degree in engineering, four master's degrees (mathematics, physics, guidance counseling, and educational administration), and a PhD in Administration and Supervision—all from Mississippi State University. He began his career teaching mathematics and physics, and like Dr. Muse, moved up to principal, assistant superintendent, and then superintendent. In the first story, he discusses how he and other White educators were committed to moving desegregation efforts forward, even in the face of violence. The second story reveals his frustration with White civil rights attorneys from the North who championed integration in the South but did not live by those same principles in their personal lives. The final story relates how his school district was able to negotiate with the federal government for more time to desegregate, in return for voluntarily agreeing to desegregate their schools.

> **Story #1: Violence against White educators.** Many of the White people were not wanting integration, and it was a rather difficult time. In fact, I had crosses burned in my front yard and FBI surveillance for about 3 months. I had some teachers, though, who were real strong, and incidentally—I found this sort of interesting—the strongest teachers I had were the women. They were more willing to help me with different situations than were my men teachers. I had two women who were especially supportive of what was going on, what we were trying to do. They knew it was the law of the land and most people should have known, but everybody didn't seem to know it. So they got threats, death threats, bomb threats, bomb and dynamite caps put around their cars, as I did mine. It was just a difficult time. This was even before partial integration took place, and one of the men in a group stood up in front of several hundred people in there with a pistol and pointed right at me and said if I did not take care of his child—if anything happened to his child—he would kill me right there. I mean in front of all those people, so it was pretty heated and intense.
>
> **Story #2: Hypocrisy of outsiders.** You know, I spent a lot of time on the witness stand, and this one lawyer, he just asked me all kinds of questions to all kinds of stuff. Finally I asked the judge, "Will you let me ask him something?" He said, "It's rather unusual, but I am going to let you ask him." So I asked him, "Do your children go to the public schools?" And he was from Chicago or somewhere, and he didn't want to answer and the judge said, "Yes, you are going to answer. He's been answering your questions, so now you answer his." And his children did not even go to the public schools. He had his children in a private school, and he was down here doing what he was doing, but he was not even living by his own principles, and you would have thought by listening to him that he was deep into desegregation, and he was not even a part of an integrated system where he lived. We had a good bit of that kind of stuff. People making us do things but they weren't doing it themselves.

Story #3: Begging for integration. We had a conference call and we were pleading with them to let us integrate the school system partially, and then do it wholly at the beginning of the school year, so we would have time to prepare our people, and we spent a great deal of time telling them that we think we can get some Black people to come. We will work at it and we will try to swap teachers. White teachers go to the Black schools and Black teachers come to the White schools. Just give us a little time to get our community ready. Just don't throw it on them all at once because they would leave. We were afraid they would leave, and I believe they would have. It was an interesting eight hours. I had those tapes, and I hid them because during the process of negotiating with them we were actually begging them to let us integrate the school system, which was a strange tune for Mississippi at that time. We were going against the grain, probably the only school in the state of Mississippi that actually begged the government to let us integrate. It worked, though, because they did let us.

Muse and Dulin would consider themselves progressive pragmatists who were passionately committed to public schools and to the rights of Blacks to equal education under the law. Both of them were targets of White violence because of their leadership in the desegregation process. In their roles as superintendents, they enacted some progressive policies that helped alleviate some of the tensions around race and schooling in their districts. Dulin adopted what would have been considered at that time a radical policy that said that every teacher, administrator, and school board member in his district **must** send their children to the public schools. If they enrolled them in the private, White academy, they lost their job or their seat on the board. Unlike many White educators, Muse refused to send his children to the private, segregated school. Rather than fight desegregation or have it be court-enforced, as was typical in most Mississippi school districts, Dulin and his school board voluntarily agreed to desegregate their schools. They knew that what they were asking was so unusual that they hid the tape recordings of their discussions for fear of what Whites would do if they discovered their role in working cooperatively with the federal government to enact desegregated schools.

Like many White Southerners of this era, they had a general distrust of "outsiders," particularly White Northern civil rights advocates, whom they saw as hypocrites sent to the South to stir up trouble while retreating to their own personal enclaves of segregationist living. Perhaps unsurprisingly, their evaluation of the success of *Brown* 50 years later contrasts with that of Peters and Davis. Muse and Dulin tell a liberal story of progress. Yes, things were unequal 50 years ago; yes, we had to fight a lot of uphill battles and everything did not always run smoothly, but in the end, *Brown* achieved its goal of equality, and they are proud of their role in desegregating Mississippi schools. As Muse notes, "we weathered the storm in the South" with the result being that more Blacks and Whites go to school together in the South than anywhere else in the country. He espouses a color-blind explanation of its success by emphasizing the commonalities that all Mississippians share because of their Southern sense of community ties and Christian beliefs. It does not matter if one is "Black, White, green, yellow, purple," we all share a common goal for our children. While Dulin's declarations about the success of *Brown* are not as profuse as Muse's, he, too, subscribes to the belief that the public schools in Mississippi are infinitely better off today than they were 50 years ago.

Can a Story Stand Alone?: Interrogating Oral Histories Through Critical Race Theory

In explaining the importance of oral history in capturing the nuances and complexities of larger historical movements, Quantz (1985) noted: "Attention to the larger forces of history provide a framework for understanding, but without a depiction of the finer detail of the participants' subjective realities, we fail to fully understand the dynamics of history" (p. 441). Our oral historians' experiences of angst, ambivalence, and hope as they made difficult choices during a difficult time cannot be easily captured by macro-only theoretical explanations, such as interest-convergence theory. Further, the juxtaposition of the oral histories of Black and White educators reveals the significantly different ways in which people living in the same communities interpret the same set of historical circumstances. The stories of Peters and Davis illuminate how Black educators devoted much of their professional lives to the hope that *Brown* would make a difference in the lives of Black students and teachers. Sometimes they had to make compromises in the hopes that "things will get better." Similarly, as leaders of their school districts, Muse and Dulin were left with the arduous task of implementing a desegregation plan with little help from the judges, politicians, attorneys, and policy makers at the forefront of the desegregation debate. How do we keep all the children safe? How will teachers be assigned? What schools will be closed? How will students be assigned to classes? Will community members and parents have their voices heard? How will bus routes be determined? Do we have enough textbooks and desks? These are the kinds of mundane questions Dulin and Muse had to answer. The oral histories of these four educators resonate with our teachers, because they reveal how larger social and historical movements were made possible by the day-to-day action of ordinary people working within extraordinary circumstances.

However, as seductive as oral histories are, a danger exists in allowing stories to stand as "truths" that cannot be questioned because they "belong" to someone and reflect someone's own subjective reality. Indeed, several scholars (Dixson & Rousseau, 2005; Ladson-Billings, 2005; Sleeter, 2008) have argued for critical race scholars to move beyond simply telling counternarratives to a more sophisticated analysis of how other tenets of CRT operate in society. Thus, when we use these oral histories of educators in our classes, we look to CRT for the interpretive tools to foster critical conversations about racism in the United States. One of the central tenets of critical race theory is that "racism is endemic to American life [and] that racism has contributed to all contemporary manifestations of group advantage and disadvantage" (Dixson & Rousseau, 2005, p. 8). Thus we ask our students: "What do these stories reveal about the endemic nature of racism?" Our students soon propose that Peters and Davis are, indeed, critical race theorists, although this academic terminology is not one they would use to describe themselves. Both Peters and Davis express skepticism about the supposed objectivity, color blindness, and neutrality of the desegregation efforts in their district. They knew these plans were implemented to maintain a social order in which Whites held social, economic, and cultural power. Peters poignantly speaks of the "tools of elimination" for "purging" the majority of Black teachers from the school system, and the impact of such actions on the lives of Black teachers today. Davis questions the myth of equal educational opportunity by citing specific examples of how Black children in the re-segregated schools in her town do not receive the services or resources that public education promises. Blatant acts of racism may be harder to name in 2012, but the subtleties of how racism plays out in the everyday lives of Black children is as destructive to Black children today as it was 50 years ago. "It is still a system that really, to me...don't want Blacks to achieve," Mrs. Davis astutely notes.

Likewise the oral histories of Muse and Dulin warrant a critical interpretation of the ways in which Whiteness as property (Harris, 1993) operates. This is explicitly reflected in their retelling of their role in the desegregation court proceedings. When they asked to address the court, they assumed that the White judges would not question their competence, intelligence, or verbal skills. Such is the privilege of Whiteness. Both were granted the opportunity to voice their concerns in a formal court of law. This basic right to be included is a fundamental characteristic of citizenship, and one long denied to Black Southerners like Davis and Peters. Harris (1993) noted that a key characteristic of White privilege is "the legal legitimation of expectations of power and control that enshrine the status quo as a neutral baseline, while masking the maintenance of white privilege and domination" (p. 1715). Dulin and Muse both were passionate in their commitment to having a strong public school system in Mississippi. They reference this commitment as driving everything they did during the desegregation process. But a critical analysis of their stories uncovers how their actions were first and foremost about making sure that White children's lives and education would not be disrupted by the inclusion of Black students. They believed that the public schools were only as strong as the White students who attended them. They feared that the demise of public schools would be a mass exodus of White students from them, as apparent when Dulin says, "We were afraid they would leave, and I believe they would have." White is the unstated antecedent for "they." The Other (i.e., the Black children) has no reference. They are negated by their absence. Muse's and Dulin's efforts to assure that Whites would continue to have the best of the public schools was framed within a discourse of progressive, democratic, equal education while "masking the maintenance of white privilege and domination" (Harris, 1993, p. 1715). This is the power of White privilege.

Employing critical race theory to interpret oral histories offers a way to talk about how White privilege and power is accomplished not through racist acts of violence, but through subtle but intractable exclusionary relations of power (Bonilla-Silva, Lewis, & Embrick, 2004; Scheurich & Young, 1997). Muse and Dulin talk about being allies with Blacks to help bring about change that would make equality of educational opportunity a reality for the thousands of Black children in Mississippi. They had great faith that progress could be made by adhering to the "law of the land" (i.e., *Brown*), and they believed that they acted in the best interests of all their constituents, both Black and White. Reading their oral histories, one certainly gets the sense that they were good, well-intentioned men, who regarded themselves as social progressives during their time period. This reading of their work is important, because it demonstrates how good, well-meaning, left-leaning, social-justice-advocating Whites can be implicated in racism. Like the White teacher so disdainful of theory in our opening discussion, most of the students in our education classes are White, and many of them are passionate about social justice. They see themselves on the "right" side of the discussion about race, class, gender, and sexual identity, yet class discussions about White privilege often leave our White students feeling angry, defensive, or hopeless—all of which can be debilitating if one sees himself or herself as an agent of social change. The oral histories of all four of these educators can open a pedagogical space for interrogating systemic and institutional racism AND opening up a discussion about how Whites can be allies with people of color in working for social justice. Doing so requires "connect[ing] whiteness with the language of possibility that provides a space for white students to imagine how whiteness as an ideology and social location can be progressively appropriated as part of a broader politics of social reform (Giroux, 1997, p. 384). After reading the oral histories of Black and White educators, we ask our students to create a readers' theater performance in which Muse, Dulin, Peters, and Davis interact with each other in the context of a civil but pointed conversation about desegregation then and re-segregation now.

Dixson and Rousseau (2005) argued that for critical race theory to be effective in transforming unjust institutions, it must move beyond simply telling stories. Similarly, oral histories have been critiqued for their over-reliance on letting the stories speak for themselves, without critical interrogation of what is being said (Sangster, 1994). Bell (2003) contended that stories serve as a "bridge between individual experience and systemic social patterns. Thus, their analysis can be a potential tool for developing a more critical consciousness about social relations in our society (Bell, 2003, p. 4). Davis, Peters, Muse, and Dulin were all working within a larger historical, social, and cultural context; their thoughts and actions during this time were produced, in part, by the complex convergence of race, class, gender, geography, and religious beliefs. Neither heroes nor villains, they were, as we all are, multidimensional people with flaws and redemptive human traits. Reading their stories through the lens of critical race theory can provide what both of our students in the opening scenario wanted: **confirmation** for theories that attempt to explain the pervasiveness of everyday racism, and **affirmation** for the important work that ordinary people, working within the constraints of their own lives, do to enact social change.

Notes

1. All of the oral historians in our larger study use the term *Black* rather than *African American* to talk about racial identity. Thus, we use *Black* in this chapter to reflect the language of our participants.

References

Bell, D. (2004). *Silent covenants: Brown v. Board of Education and the unfulfilled hopes for racial reform.* New York, NY: Oxford University Press.

Bell, L. (2003). Telling tales: What stories can teach us about racism. *Race, Ethnicity and Education, 6*(1), 3–28.

Bolton, C. (2005). *The hardest deal of all: The battle over school integration in Mississippi, 1870–1980.* Jackson, MS: University Press of Mississippi.

Bonilla-Silva, E., Lewis, A., & Embrick, D. (2004). 'I did not get that job because of a Black man . . .': The story lines and testimonies of color-blind racism. *Sociological Forum, 19*(4), 555–581.

Dixson, A., & Rousseau, C. (2005). And we are still not saved: Critical race theory in education ten years later. *Race, Ethnicity and Education, 8*(1), 7–27.

French, S., & Swain, J. (2006). Telling stories for a politics of hope. *Disability & Society, 21*(5), 383–396.

Giroux, H. (1997). White squall: Resistance and the pedagogy of Whiteness. *Cultural Studies, 11*(3), 376–389.

Harris, C. (1993). Whiteness as property. *Harvard Law Review, 106*(8), 1707–1791.

Janesick, V. (2007). Oral history as a social justice project: Issues for the qualitative researcher. *Qualitative Report, 12*(1), 111–121.

Ladson-Billings, G. (2005). Is the team all right? Diversity and teacher education. *Journal of Teacher Education, 56*(2), 229–234.

Quantz, R. (1985). The complex visions of female teachers and the failure of unionization in the 1930s: An oral history. *History of Education Quarterly, 25*(4), 439–458.

Sangster, J. (1994). Telling our stories: Feminist debates and the use of oral history. *Women's History Review, 3*(1), 5–28.

Scheurich, J., & Young, M. (1997). Coloring epistemologies: Are our research epistemologies racially biased? *Educational Researcher, 26*(4), 4–16.

Sleeter, C. (2008). Critical family history, identity, and historical memory. *Educational Studies, 43*(2), 114–124.

12

Mojarra Linguistic Syndrome, Evading Capture by the Tongue: Heritage Speakers of Spanish and Their Stigma

J. Luis Loya-García

The following study took place at Saint Mary's College, Notre Dame, Indiana, a women's college where I worked as a Fellow for the Center for Women's Intercultural Leadership (CWIL) and taught Spanish to heritage language learners. My class consisted of seven Latina students[1]: four of them identified themselves as Mexicanas, Latinas, and Hispanas; one as Tejana and Latina; one as Anglo with Nicaraguan roots; and one as Anglo raised by a Mexican babysitter. My responsibility as a CWIL Fellow was to teach in the Department of Modern Languages and to do research. This study intended to reflect on the teaching strategies targeted to heritage speakers of Spanish, as explained below, and to contribute to the dialogue concerning the cultural, social, academic, linguistic, and individual needs of students with Hispanic cultural and/or familial ties. I wanted to better understand the needs that heritage language learners of Spanish have in the classroom and at Saint Mary's College specifically. My objective was to improve the organization and structure of my classes.

In this chapter, I used my students' assignments as the primary source of my written analysis. I believe that heritage speakers of Spanish arrive in the classroom with *sabiduría del hogar* or knowledge of the home; that is, Hispanic students practice what scholars such as Judith Flores Carmona and Dolores Delgado Bernal (2012) identified as "pedagogies of the home," where members of the family and the community transmit knowledge through the practice of oral histories in the form of *cadenas* or chains. The duration of subject participation took place during the second half of the Fall semester 2011, where I gave an assignment with ten questions. During this period, students answered questions and submitted them to me at the end of the semester. There were oral presentations where students reflected on their written project; most of the information provided in this study comes from my students' written assignments. All the information and data collected for this project followed the Institutional Review Board's (IRB) guidelines and approval as established by Saint Mary's College. Any information obtained in connection with this study that can be identified with the student will remain confidential. I used a pseudonym instead of the student's name so that no one will be identified or identifiable. The participant's name was altered when making reference to her work. I did the same for family members, friends, and/or other people mentioned.

Defining a Heritage Speaker

Lewelling and Peyton (1999) identified three categories of heritage speakers. The first category consists of third- or fourth-generation, US-born Hispanic students who are "receptive bilinguals" In other words, English is their dominant language; they understand "almost all spoken Spanish, but they have limited speaking skills in Spanish and do not read or write it." The second category consists of first- or second-generation bilingual students; they have different levels of proficiency in Spanish and English: "In most cases, these students have received their education in English and have developed few if any literacy skills in Spanish" (p. 3). The third category consists of recent immigrants; Spanish is their dominant language. They have diverse levels of English proficiency, and their formal education in Spanish varies.

In "Knowledge of Tense-Aspect and Mood in Spanish Heritage Speakers," Silvia Montrul (2009) argued that heritage speakers of Spanish

> have been shown to display erosion and loss of the tense-aspect and mood system in oral production. In particular, while they retain the preterit–imperfect difference in the past, the meanings and forms are often confused. Subjunctive morphology, on the other hand, is even more affected. (p. 239)

In this study, I argue that cultural linguistics is a potent tool to empower Latina/o students in Spanish classes designed for heritage speakers. I use "pedagogies of the home," oral histories, cultural linguistics, and the archeology of words to illustrate the linguistic dislocation, in English and Spanish, that Latina students suffer due to their direct or indirect ties with indigenous, non-Western views of the world and the many cross-pollinations among their cultures of origin and the Anglo language and culture. I also propose an assignment based on cultural linguistics that can be used as a semester project; the questions in this assignment are not based on ideas of "deficit" or "remedial" language approaches. They are designed to help the student practice self-reflection about her identity, her language, and her culture. I treat my students and their oral narratives as valid and legitimate sources of theory; this essay is a tribute to their tongue. I select key words to describe the particular conceptions of time and space that people of Mexican, Mexican American, Texan, and Nicaraguan origins use; this particularity influences the direct or indirect perception of reality (as mediated by language) of Latina/o students. I argue that heritage speakers of Spanish suffer a linguistic manifestation of the *Síndrome de la Mojarra* (Loya-García, 2011), which is the feeling that some type of freedom depends on the ability to evade linguistic capture; in other words, getting caught in English and/or Spanish because of the way one speaks.

El Síndrome de la Mojarra

El Síndrome de la Mojarra is the condition of feeling persecuted, believing that freedom depends on the ability to evade capture. This condition is particular of the *mojarra*. I use the term *mojarra* to identify a person who crossed the U.S. border as a *mojada/o* (an undocumented immigrant), swimming a river, navigating the ocean, and/or negotiating any other aboveground or underground surface. Indeed, I use the term, *mojarra*, instead of *mojada/o* to emphasize the stigma of the undocumented immigrant, one who might have to swim like a fish in order to survive. Lila Downs (2001), in her song "El Bracero Fracasado," described the *mojarra* condition in the following lyrics:

> I arrived in Santa Ana with bleeding feet
> My sandals worn down quickly,
> My hat and shirt, I lost in the rush around,
> Because some White guys wanted to catch me. (My translation)

In her song, Lila Downs tells the story of a *bracero fracasado*, an unsuccessful border-crosser who crossed the border and lived, evading capture. Lila Downs, in this song, portrays the *mojarra* condition well; her lyrics are an expression of *Mojarra Aesthetics*. This type of aesthetics involves overcoming adversity by turning pre-deportation into a narrative trope. The *mojarra*'s tragedy pivots on the stake of a joke. The lyrics of the above song make adversity funny. This is *Mojarra Aesthetics*: the ability to laugh in the face of adversity; a strategy that, along with their human experience, helps Latina students to persevere. Many of them suffer from *mojarra linguistic syndrome*, the ability to evade linguistic capture because of the way one speaks, either in English and/or Spanish. Latina students, when feeling uncomfortable, prefer to be unnoticed culturally and linguistically, a situation that often makes them the target of multiple forms of xenophobia, discrimination, and micro and macro aggressions. The condition of wanting to be unnoticed is portrayed in the following excerpt of one of my students' assignments:

> Mi cultura es algo que siento en el corazón y la defiendo por sobre todas las cosas. Soy como el pirata que esconde su tesoro para que nadie lo vea, no por miedo a que me lo roben, pero por miedo a sentirme humillada por otra cultura diferente. A pesar de que la esconda, nunca cambio su valor. (Xochitl)

Xochitl explains that she feels like a pirate who hides the treasure of her culture in her heart. She does it so that no one sees it; this is not out of fear of losing it, but out of fear of feeling humiliated by someone from another culture. The fact of hiding her culture, Xochitl affirms, does not diminish its value. This concept of hiding one's culture shows the stigmatized condition of Latinas/os in the United States. This is theory in the flesh. Cherrie Moraga (1983) argued: "A theory in the flesh means one where the physical realities of our skin color, the land or concrete we grew up on, [our language] our sexual longings—all fuse to create a politic born out of necessity" (p. 23). Xochitl presents a problematic situation that many Latina/o students experience in school: to prevent humiliation because of the way they speak, they prefer to hide their language—an unsuccessful attempt, because sooner or later students get caught by the "tongue," either by teachers or by classmates. To counteract this type of aggression, Latina students manage to retain and sustain the beauty of their language and culture by creating their own space. Emma Pérez, in *The Decolonial Imaginary* (1999) recognized the multiple meanings of language and the importance of creating *un sitio y lengua*, a space and language that allows Third World feminism to flourish where Chicanas/Latinas reclaim their place and language in society. In the case of Xochitl, xenophobia and intolerance push her to find alternatives in order to preserve and value the beauty of her culture and language.

Farzad Sharifian and Gary B. Palmer (2007) argued that language is rooted in culture and affirmed that "Cultural linguistics draws on, but is not limited to, the theoretical notions and analytical tools of cognitive anthropology and cognitive linguistics. Through these, it explores the relationship between language, culture, and conceptualization" (p. 15). These authors drew their work from cognitive linguists such as Ronald Langacker, George Lakoff, and Mark Johnson, who saw language as an instrumental element of culture; these authors argued that "cultural knowledge in the form of conventional images feeds into idioms based on metaphors. Moreover, complex categories are structured by experiential domains, which may be culture-specific" (Sharifian & Palmer, 2007, p. 15). In other words, culture, language, and thought are interrelated, interdependent elements that influence our conception of the world. Cultural linguistics derives from the complex lens that sees language as culture and as governed by culture. Norma González (2001) affirmed that "To speak of language is to speak of our 'Selves'" (p. xix), an assertive point that takes into account the multiplicity of "selves" and language variants of Latinas.

By exploring spaces to reclaim the place of their language, culture, and knowledge, Chicana/o theorists contend that teaching through oral language has big implications for Latina/o families. In "Learning and Living Pedagogies of the Home," Dolores Delgado Bernal (2006) wrote:

> The term 'Chicana feminist pedagogies' refers to culturally specific ways of organizing teaching and learning in informal sites such as the home—ways that embrace Chicana and Mexicana ways of knowing and extend beyond formal schooling...These pedagogies of the home extend the existing discourse on critical pedagogies by putting cultural knowledge and language at the forefront to better understand lessons from the home space and local communities. (p. 114)

That is, pedagogies of the home challenge traditional conceptions of teaching, learning, and knowledge, and recognize the legitimacy and value of culture and language in the unconventional forms of education that Chicanas/Mexicanas practice.

In the case of Latina students, the knowledge they obtain at home in their respective communities is an essential part of their life. However, this knowledge is often underestimated and undervalued by educational institutions that teach through remedial and deficiency approaches. Some scholars, trying to improve heritage-language abilities, find deficiencies in the way students of Hispanic heritage communicate. For instance, linguists find mistakes and language patterns that heritage speakers of Spanish constantly make while speaking and writing. Their purpose is to find ways to improve heritage-language abilities. In "Morphological Errors in Spanish Second Language Learners and Heritage Speakers," Silvia Montrul (2011) argued that heritage speakers of Spanish experience a type of morphological variation and contended that errors in heritage speakers are more recurrent in written than in oral practice. Montrul concluded that second-language learners and heritage speakers make their mistakes due to the type of experience they have with written and spoken language. Although linguistic improvement is necessary in the personal and academic development of students, it is also important to have an understanding of the value and cultural connection that language has for Latina/o students. Gloria Anzaldúa (1987) wrote:

> So, if you want to really hurt me, talk bad about my language. Ethnic identity is twin skin to linguistic identity—I am my language. Until I can take pride in my language, I cannot take pride in myself. Until I can accept as legitimate Chicano Texas Spanish, Tex-Mex, and all the other languages I speak, I cannot accept the legitimacy of myself. Until I am free to write bilingually and to switch without having always to translate, while I still have to speak English or Spanish when I would rather speak Spanglish, and as long as I have to accommodate the English [or Spanish] speaker rather than having them accommodate me, my tongue will be illegitimate. (p. 81)

Anzaldúa explained her discomfort when others see her language as illegitimate. Following Anzaldúa's frustration on language, I argue that Spanish classes targeted to heritage speakers of Spanish need a specific approach where teachers understand the cultural and linguistic experience of students. These teachers should make clear that the way that US Latinas/os speak is a legitimate and valid way of communication among themselves in their communities, and that when entering school, the standardized, normative culture in Spanish and English wants them to speak in a certain way. In other words, educators should move from a deficit approach, where they see students as lacking linguistic knowledge, to a new perspective, where they communicate to students that they are the product of cultural symbiosis.

The process of deliberately helping Latina/o students understand the importance of recognizing their linguistic and cultural value is highly empowering. This cultural and linguistic reflection must incorporate techniques that inform students about their position within the normative educational system in English and Spanish that often treats Latina/o students as lacking linguistic knowledge. In other words, teachers in Spanish-for-heritage-speakers classes should empower students by letting them know that they have the ability to focus their attention on diverse linguistic and cultural levels, and that even if they face a normative educational system that underestimates them, they have the capacity to overcome barriers because of their rich, multidimensional background. Talking *Mojarra* language is, I argue, a strategy that US Latinas/os use to evade capture and/or deportation.

Mojarra Language

Talking *Mojarra* language goes beyond linguistic abilities. It includes gestures, body language, clothing, cultural cues, and even silence to evade capture. This capture includes, but is not limited to, jail; it refers to any individual imprisonment. In the film *El Norte* (Black, Navarro, Thomas, & Nava, 1983), Central American immigrants avoid being deported to Central America by mentioning the word *chingado* which is a Mexican expression that means *fuck*. Immigration officers see them as Mexican because of the use of that particular word connected to Mexican idiom. Another example of talking *Mojarra* language is when in the film *Born in East LA* (MacGregor-Scott, Coleman, & Marin, 1987), some Chinese immigrants get dressed as Chicano gangsters, and when confronted by the police, they respond with gangster body language and exaggerated utterances of "Whaz up and orale!!!" This approach saves them from jail and deportation to China, because the authorities assume they are Mexican American gangsters. This same situation happens to U.S. Latinas/os. In this era of Latina/o persecution in the United States, talking *Mojarra* is the ability to manipulate language and/or the body to evade capture and/or deportation; people implement this strategy of survival in times of danger. For instance, when looks denounce you, and your tongue betrays you, talking *Mojarra* language can save your life. In other words, when indigenous appearance, color of skin, and language are motives of racial profiling, *mojarras* often prefer to go unnoticed. They often, as in the case of Xochitl, find ways that "seem" to honor the dominant culture either by "shutting their mouth," dressing in particular ways, and/or adopting certain behaviors in order to prevent humiliation. At times, to make life more bearable, *mojarras* pretend not to exist when their freedom is threatened. Such is the case of students whose family members are undocumented immigrants. They prefer to camouflage with whatever is available: people, things, animals, nature. In other cases, *mojarras* make public their condition of undocumented immigrant when it helps them to prevent deportation. Such is the case of many Dreamers, "Undocumented and Unafraid," who challenged immigration authorities by letting themselves be captured. Allowing themselves to get caught in order to not get deported is by itself an example of talking *Mojarra* language.

Linguistic Difrasismo: From Thinking to Feeling Language

Many heritage speakers of Spanish in the United States have a direct or indirect connection with non-Western views of the world and the many cross-pollinations between their cultures of origin and the Anglo culture. For instance, my first- or second-generation Latina students who still travel between Latin America and the US because of family and cultural ties, have a direct and personal experience with indigenous perceptions of the world, while Latinas who live in the Southwest of the US experience non-Western views of the world through their Hispanic and/or indigenous parents, relatives, and community members. This connection with indigenous views of the world can be conscious or unconscious; that is, heritage speakers of Spanish may be aware or unaware of this connection. This happens because indigenous views have been oppressed by the imperialist and capitalist uses of Spanish and English in the US and Latin America. I argue that educators need to make an effort to understand the student's perception of the world. Laura I. Rendón (2009) rescued a pre-Columbian perspective of seeing the world and explained that *difrasismo* is an Aztec notion that puts together two concepts or ideas that are in tension with one another. This juxtaposition of terms is used to refer to a third conception that gives birth to a new perspective where "a larger truth emerges from illuminating the hidden mysteries of the paired realities, which dance interdependently and in grand cooperation with each other. In essence, the *difrasismo* represents the resolution of dualities, the reconciliation of paradox" (p. 134). Along the same lines, trying to define the rupture of binary thinking, Antonio Valeriano and Guillermo Ortiz de Montellano (1990) argued in *Nicān mopouha* that a *difrasismo* in Nahuatl has a figurative meaning that is taken from two words or even phrases. These two words or phrases do not have to be binaries; for example, "flor y canto = poesía [flower and song = poetry] or agua, cerro = población, pueblo, ciudad [water, hill = community, town, city]" (p. 34). That is, *difrasismo* breaks the binaries and invites us to think in new ways that give birth to new forms of understanding the world. Eduardo Galeano (1991), in the poem "Celebration of the Marriage of Heart and Mind," wrote:

> Why does one write, if not to put one's pieces together? The moment we enter school or church, education chops us into pieces: it teaches us to divorce soul from body and mind from heart. The fishermen of the Colombian coast must be learned doctors of ethics and morality, for they invented the word *sentipensante*, feelingthinking, to define language that speaks the truth. (p. 121)

Indeed, *feelingthinking* is a necessary practice in order to understand the terms I attempt to describe in this section. I argue that culture, language, and thought are interrelated and interdependent elements that influence the particular conception of the world that peoples of Hispanic and/or indigenous backgrounds have. These peoples' ideas about the world differ from the Western conception of life. In the following section, I compare and contrast the cultural meaning of certain words and phrases that I came across in the assignments of my students. My hope is that by explaining the cultural meaning of these words and phrases, I will raise awareness about the direct or indirect relation that heritage speakers of Spanish have when interacting with family and community members. The following words and phrases are: *antepasado* versus "ancestor"; *estar grande* versus "being old"; *tener escuela* versus "to be educated"; *ser educado* or *mal educado* (*malcriada/o*) versus "having an education"; *sabiduría* versus "knowledge," and the concept of service. My hope is that the explanation of these concepts helps teachers and educators to have a better understanding of heritage-language students.

Sentipensando Palabras: Feelingthinking Words

The first concept that I want to explain is the word, *antepasado*. This is a compound word that uses the prefix *ante* which means "before," and the word *pasado* which means "past." In Mexican and Mexican American Spanish it is a noun and also an adjective. For instance: (a) "Este antepasado (noun) es mi tataruelo," which means, "This 'person from before the past' is my great grandfather"; and (b) "El año antepasado (adj.) llovió mucho," which means, "The year before last it rained a lot." The word *antepasada/o* in an English-Spanish dictionary is often translated as "ancestor." However, there is a hidden cultural meaning that the dictionary does not recognize when defining the concept; this meaning is felt and not reasoned. For instance, when my grandmother and people from previous generations talk about long time ago, they often say, *más antes*, which means "more before," implying that they are talking about "before the time that has passed." When using this particular idea, numbers and dates are irrelevant, because the purpose is to communicate the "feeling" of time passing. "Educated" people or people with too much schooling would consider this terminology as improperly stated, poorly said, or as a sign that the speaker is uneducated.

The second cultural difference that I want to analyze and which I came across in my students' assignments is the concept of age. For instance, when people of Mexican origins refer to their grandmothers, they often would say, "ella está grande." If we translate this concept literally into English, that means, "she's big." However, people of Mexican origins see grandma as "big in time." She has experienced much time; therefore, she's *grande* (in time). Telling someone that he or she is big in time does not imply that people see them as old; on the contrary, the phrase communicates admiration and respect because of the experience accumulated in the person's body. People of Mexican and indigenous roots see *la gente grande* or "the elderly" as having *sabiduría*, which is "knowledge"; but this concept of knowing is not what people get from going to school or the university. It is something profound that humans obtain from life itself. It is accumulated experience that allows them to be teachers with only their presence. Their experienced body teaches about the power of time to new generations; their body has wisdom at the human level, and deserves admiration and respect. My *abuela* and *tatarabuela* are *grandes*; they are big in time, and represent the union of time and space in a present moment. That is, my grandma's body has the experience of the past, and it gives me present awareness that I, in the future, can become "big in time," as well. In other words, the person who respects grandma's experienced body is able to feel the past, present, and future coming together in a vortex of presence. When asked to reflect on the elderly, one of my students wrote:

> Yo pienso que los latinos cuidamos mucho a nuestros ancianos porque nuestra cultura nos ha enseñado a cuidar a la gente. No solamente a la gente grande sino a todos. Los mayores nos cuidan cuando somos pequeños, después cuando crecemos, queremos hacer lo mismo por los que envejecen; es una forma de apreciar la vida. (Agustina)

> I believe that we, Latinas/os take care of our elderly because our culture has taught us to take care of people. Not only the elderly but all. Our elders take care of us when we are children, later when we grow up, we want to do the same for those who get older; it's a way of appreciating life. (Agustina)

The third concept that I came across in my class of heritage speakers of Spanish was the notion of education. "Being educated," in the communities my students come from differs greatly from the notion of education as understood in the United States. People of Mexican-indigenous origins would often say that a person *tiene escuela* or "has schooling," to indicate what people in the United States would understand as "having an education." A person of Mexican origins understands that *tener escuela* or "to have schooling" is not the same as "having an education." This can be observed in the adjective, *maleducada/o*, which literally translates as "badly educated." But there is a cultural and linguistic difference between these concepts. For instance, a person of Mexican origins is *maleducada/o* when she/he does not say "thank you," and/or when the person has no consideration of others [in Anglo English this would be more like "ill-mannered" or "inconsiderate"]. In other words, education and *educación* transmit inequivalent meanings. *Educación* in Spanish can also be understood as *formación*, something close to human integrity, and nothing to do with education as understood in the United States. "Being educated" or *ser educada/o* for people of Mexican origins, would mean to be considerate of others.

The fourth concept that I came across in everyday interaction with my students was the concept of service. Here, I want to reflect on the Spanish-language interrogative, *¿qué?*—the English equivalent of which is "what?"— and the nonequivalent, *mande*, which some of my students use instead. The uses of the interrogative *qué* and "what" have equivalent meanings in both languages. For example, María asks José, "where did you put the car keys?" José does not hear well, and he replies, "what?"—*¿qué?* However, heritage speakers of Spanish with Mexican and Mexican American backgrounds would answer, *mande*. The infinitive is the verb, *mandar*, which means, "to command or to order." The dictionary translates it as "yes?" or "pardon?" Nonetheless, *mande* has cultural implications. Superficially, it could communicate beliefs of inferiority or superiority, implying that the interlocutors expect commands or service from someone in a superior-inferior position. But through deeper examination, this expression, as used by my students, communicates the sense of "how can I be of service to you?"— not in a position of inferiority or superiority, but in a position of sensible awareness about the value of providing humane service to others.

The previous description of words was the product of the project based on oral histories and pedagogies of the home that I present in this chapter. My students provided information relevant to their cultural and linguistic abilities. I, as the professor, shared with them my findings, which included conceptualization of time, space, age, education, and service. I highlighted their capacity to focus their attention onto different levels of linguistic experience, and their ability to cultivate awareness of how they use language in the different environments where they interact.

Description of Project

This project was developed in class during the second half of the semester. It was inspired by a model of a dual-immersion program developed by Professor Judith Flores Carmona at Jackson Elementary School in Salt Lake City, Utah (see Flores Carmona & Delgado Bernal, 2012). The response to this project was very positive in my class; students learned about themselves and from one another. The project connects, as in a *cadena* or chain, students with their families, as well as with community members. Teachers can adjust the questions accordingly in order to fulfill the needs of students and the particular focus of the class.

Trabajo final

Instrucciones: Van a contestar las siguientes preguntas en forma de ensayo (por lo menos una página). Pueden responder tres de estas preguntas en la forma que se sientan más cómodas: inglés, spanglish, o español. El resto de las preguntas, por favor, respóndanlas en español. Al final del semestre escogerán una de estas preguntas para presentarla en clase. Vamos a trabajar en estas preguntas a lo largo de la segunda mitad del semestre; les daré comentarios, y ustedes re-escribirán sus composiciones siguiendo mis indicaciones. Al final del semestre pondrán todo el material en un folder que colectaré. Engraparán el primer borrador, con mis comentarios, y la versión final.

Final project

Instructions: Please answer the following questions in essay form (at least a page). Answer three of these questions in the form you feel most comfortable: English, Spanglish, or Spanish. The rest of the questions, please, answer them in Spanish. At the end of the semester you will choose one of these questions and will present on it for the class. We will work on these questions during the second half of the semester; I will give you feedback, and you will re-write your composition following my observations. At the end of the semester you will organize these compositions in a folder that I will collect. You will staple the first draft, with my feedback, to the final draft.

1. *¿Te identificas como latina, hispana, mexicana-chicana, tejana, anglo con raíces hispanas? Explica. ¿Cuál es la diferencia entre estas definiciones? Pregunta, investiga y explica lo que encontraste. Si te identificas de otra forma, explica.*
   Do you identify yourself as Latina, Hispanic, Mexicana-Chicana, Tejana, or Anglo with Hispanic roots? What is the difference between these definitions? Ask, investigate and explain what you found. If you identify yourself differently, explain.
2. *¿Cuál es la historia de tu nombre? Haz un estudio etimológico de tu nombre. Fíjate en el diccionario y/o el internet. ¿Qué significa? ¿Tiene un significado especial? Pregúntale a tus padres por qué te pusieron así. ¿Te sientes identificada con tu nombre o prefieres elaborar una definición más apropiada? Si prefieres extender o modificar la definición de tu nombre, explícala; elabora una definición de tu nombre que realmente te defina.*

What's the story of your name? Do an etymological study of your name. Research it in a dictionary and/or the Internet. What does it mean? Does it have a special meaning? Ask your parents why they named you as they did. Do you feel identified with your name or would you like to make a new one with a more appropriate definition? If this is the case, please elaborate a definition of a name that really defines you.

3. *¿Cuándo naciste? Dile a tu madre que te cuente la historia de tu nacimiento. ¿Dónde naciste? ¿Cómo fue el acontecimiento? Busca personalidades que tengan tu misma fecha de nacimiento y menciona por lo menos a tres personas famosas; ¿por qué son importantes? Relaciona la historia de tu nacimiento con la historia de tu país de origen. ¿Qué pasó en Saint Mary's College y en South Bend, IN cuando naciste? Para esta actividad les recomiendo que vayan al museo y/o los archivos de Saint Mary's College.*

When were you born? Ask your parents to tell you the story of your birthday. Where were you born? How was the occasion? Look for famous personalities that share your same birthday and mention at least three of them; why are they important? Relate the story of your birthday with the history of your country of origin. What happened in Saint Mary's College and in South Bend, IN when you were born? For this activity, I recommend that you visit the museum and/or archives at Saint Mary's College.

4. *Las familias latinas tenemos una historia de tradición oral muy fuerte. Aprendemos de las historias orales que nuestros antepasados nos relatan de generación en generación. Relata un cuento, historia, leyenda, canción, o chiste que te haya contado algún miembro de tu familia. ¿Tiene alguna moraleja? ¿Cuál? ¿Qué aprendiste de la relación?*

Our Latina/o families have a very strong tradition of oral history. We learn from the oral (hi)stories that our elders tell us generation after generation. Tell a short story, (hi)story, legend, song, or joke that a member of your family and/or community has told you. What's the moral of the story? What did you learn from the storytelling?

5. *¿Tienes algún modelo a seguir en tu familia? Un modelo a seguir es un "role model" en inglés. ¿Quién es y por qué te interesa seguir su ejemplo? Da una descripción de esta persona y explica por qué la admiras.*

Do you have any role model in your family? Who is that person and why are you interested in following his/her example? Please, give a description of this person and explain why you admire him/her.

6. *Nuestra cultura latina tiende mucho a respetar y apreciar a los ancianos. ¿Por qué piensas que hacemos esto? ¿Quién es la persona más anciana de tu familia? ¿De dónde es? ¿Vive en Estados Unidos? ¿Cuándo llegó aquí y cómo? Investiga la historia de esta persona. Si no tienes contacto con él o ella, pídele a tus padres que te relaten por qué es importante en sus vidas. La persona puede estar viva o muerta.*
Our Latina/o culture tends to show great respect and appreciation for our elders. Why do you think we do that? Who is the oldest member of your family? Where is he/she from? Does he/she live in the United States? When did he/she arrive in the United States and how? Investigate the (hi)story of this person. If you do not have contact with him/her, ask your parents or someone to tell you why this person is important in their lives. The person can be alive or dead.

7. *¿Crees que es importante valorar nuestra cultura latina? ¿Por qué es importante valorar nuestras raíces?*
Do you think it is important to value our Latina/o culture? Why is it important to value our roots?

8. *Si eres hablante nativa del inglés ¿qué te conecta con la cultura latina? ¿Por qué te consideras "hablante de herencia"? ¿Quién es la persona o personas que te conectan con tus raíces hispanas o latinas? Explica.*
If you are a native speaker of English, what connects you with the Latina/o culture? Why do you consider yourself a heritage speaker? Who is (are) the person(s) that connect(s) you with your Hispanic or Latina/o roots? Explain.

9. *Si eres hablante nativa del español ¿cómo te ayudará tu experiencia cultural latina o hispana en tu desarrollo académico, profesional y personal dentro de la sociedad anglo? ¿Hay algún aspecto de tu identidad con el cual tengas que batallar para desarrollarte en el mundo anglo? ¿Tienes alguna experiencia personal en la que te hayas sentido alienada en la escuela? ¿Te has sentido diferente al resto del grupo por tu forma de ser, hablar o actuar? ¿Qué has aprendido de esta experiencia? Explica. ¿Cómo nos reponemos al sentirnos alienados en un medio ambiente que nos recuerda que somos diferentes o que no pertenecemos?*

If you are a Spanish native speaker, how do you think that your Hispanic or Latina/o culture will help you in your academic, professional and personal development within the Anglo society? Is there any aspect of your identity that you struggle with in order to develop yourself in the Anglo world? Do you have any personal experience where you have felt alienated in school? Have you felt different from the rest of the group because of your way of being, speaking or behaving? What have you learned from this experience? Explain. How do we recover from experiences that make us feel alienated in an environment that reminds us that we are different or that we do not belong?

10. *¿Qué papel juega el humor en tu familia? ¿Tú o algún miembro de tu familia ha tenido alguna experiencia adversa en la que el humor les haya ayudado a salir adelante? ¿Puedes relatar una anécdota en la que se pueda percibir un problema de sobrevivencia familiar o personal donde el problema se transforme en risa? Si no tienes alguna vivencia, pídele a tus padres o abuelos que te cuenten un chiste, cuento o experiencia, referente a este tema.*

What role does humor play in your family? Have you, or any member in your family, had an adverse experience where humor helped you get ahead? Could you relate a personal or family anecdote where you perceived a problem and humor transformed the problem into laughter? If you do not have an anecdote, please ask your parents or grandparents to tell you a joke, story or experience related to this topic.

Conclusion

In this chapter, I argued that cultural linguistics, pedagogies of the home, and oral histories are potent tools to develop assignments in Spanish classes targeted to heritage speakers. The results of my students' projects revealed particular views of the world as mediated by language. One of my students explains it well:

> As Latina, I have problems in multiple-choice exams because I am used to seeing life different. I don't see things as whoever made the test wants me to. I see and analyze life with different lenses. I'm aware of that. This doesn't mean that I'm stupid; it only means that the way in which I perceive and understand reality doesn't match with the way others want me to see and understand. (Panchita)

In my analysis, I also argued that heritage speakers of Spanish suffer *Mojarra* linguistic syndrome, which is the feeling that some type of freedom depends on the ability to evade linguistic capture; in other words, getting caught in English and/or Spanish because of the way one speaks. This includes the prevention of micro and macro aggressions, such as being pointed out because of accent, looks, behavior, and/or reminded that they do not belong. Latina/o students, when feeling threatened, speak *Mojarra* language—the ability to manipulate language, the body, and/ or behavior to evade capture and/or deportation. This study proposed some strategies to empower Latina/o students through language and cultural practices. Educators will continue to discover and develop ways to legitimate home knowledges and the art of orality; these important sources of knowledge and pedagogical practices challenge traditional standard- and deficit-based approaches. Standard-based or deficit-oriented pedagogy keeps Latina/o students from seeing their already accrued cultural capital, and thus prevents them from reaching their potential. Further, these approaches ask students to reinvent the wheel, when they are already skilled drivers of their education. Emphasis on home knowledges and orality brings out otherwise hidden cultural and linguistic richnesses. Through such emphasis, students become more capable of discovering and rediscovering, inventing and reinventing, defining and redefining, and constructing and deconstructing their many "selves" in contemporary US society.[2]

Notes

1. I will use the terms Hispanic and Latina/o interchangeably to refer to people with Latin American roots.
2. Many thanks to John Emil Vincent for our many conversations on the topic.

Bibliography

Anzaldúa, G. (1987). *Borderlands: The new mestiza = la frontera*. San Francisco, CA: Spinsters/Aunt Lute.

Black, T., Navarro, B., Thomas, A. (Producers), & Nava, G. (Director). (1983). *El Norte* [Motion picture]. USA: Cinecom Pictures.

Delgado, R., & Stefancic, J. (2012). *Critical race theory: An introduction*. New York, NY: New York University Press.

Delgado Bernal, D. (2006). Learning and living pedagogies of the home: The Mestiza consciousness of Chicana students. In D. Delgado Bernal, C. A. Elenes, F. E. Godinez, & S. Villenas (Eds.), *Chicana/Latina education in everyday life: Feminista perspectives on pedagogy and epistemology* (pp. 113–132). Albany, NY: State University of New York Press.

Downs, L. (2001). El bracero fracasado. On *Border: La linea* [CD]. Milwaukee, WI: Narada World.

Flores Carmona, J., & Delgado Bernal, D. (2012). Oral histories in the classroom: Home and community pedagogies. In C. E. Sleeter & E. Soriano (Eds.), Creating solidarity across

diverse communities: International perspectives in education (pp. 114–130). New York, NY: Teachers College Press.
Galeano, E. H. (1991). *The book of embraces*. New York, NY: W.W. Norton.
González, N. (2001). *I am my language: Discourses of women and children in the borderlands*. Tucson, AZ: University of Arizona Press.
Lewelling, V. W., & Peyton, J. K. (1999). "Spanish for native speakers developing dual language proficiency." Washington, DC: ERIC Clearinghouse on Languages and Linguistics, Center for Applied Linguistics.
Loya-García, J. L. (2011). *Mojarra* a*esthetics in 'Piolin por la mañana': A time and space for the dislocated* (Doctoral dissertation). University of Massachusetts Amherst. Retrieved from ProQuest Dissertations and Theses, http://search.proquest.com/docview/882903255?accountid=14572
MacGregor-Scott, P., Coleman, S. (Producers), & Marin, C. (Director). (1987). *Born in East L.A.* [Motion picture]. USA: Universal Studios.
Montrul, S. (2009). Knowledge of tense-aspect and mood in Spanish heritage speakers. *International Journal of Bilingualism, 13*(2), 239–269.
———. (2011). Morphological errors in Spanish second language learners and heritage speakers. *Studies in Second Language Acquisition, 33*(2), 163–192.
Moraga, C. (1983). Entering the lives of others: Theory in the flesh. In C. Moraga & G. Anzaldúa (Eds.), *This bridge called my back: Writings by radical women of color* (2nd ed., p. 23). New York, NY: Kitchen Table, Women of Color Press.
Pérez, E. (1999). *The decolonial imaginary: Writing Chicanas into history*. Bloomington, IN: Indiana University Press.
Rendón, L. I. (2009). *Sentipensante (sensing/thinking) pedagogy: Educating for wholeness, social justice and liberation*. Sterling, VA: Stylus.
Sharifian, F., & Palmer, G. B. (2007). *Applied cultural linguistics: Implications for second language learning and intercultural communication*. Philadelphia, PA: John Benjamins.
Valeriano, A., & Ortiz de Montellano, G. (1990). *Nicān mopouha*. Ciudad de México, Mexico: Universidad Iberoamericana, Departamento de Ciencias Religiosas, Departamento de Historia.

INDEX

A

accommodation, 156
achievement gap, lack of student perspective on, 136
Adair, V., 45
Adam, 51, 53
Adamson, R., 13–14
adaptation, 156
affect, 28
African Americans
    use of term, 103
    See also Blacks
age, concept of, 211–212
Albemarle area (North Carolina), 96, 97–107, 108, 109, 110
Alexander, B. K., 96
Alexander v. Holmes, 190
Alicia, 46–47, 48, 50, 51–52
American Dream, 41–54
American Indians
    deficit view of, 158, 159
    education of, 155
    educational marginalization of, 153
    effects of colonization on, 153
    need for culturally relevant curricula, 156
    power of, 154, 156, 166
    recentering of in education, 157, 163
    shared interests with non-Indians, 160
    sovereignty, rhetorical, 155–158, 160, 164–165
    survivance, 156–158, 160, 161–164
    See also Indigenous peoples
Anderson, James, 183
Angelou, Maya, 97
Anna, 51
antepasado, 211
Anzaldúa, G., 78, 208
archives, 175

Archuleta, E., 153
Asians, median wealth of, 13
assignments, resistance to, 70, 162–163
autobiographies, educational, 61–62, 64–67, 138–139
autoethnography, 28, 37–38
autohistorias, 78–79

B

Baseball Saved Us (Mochizuki), 122
Bass, R., 44
Battiste, Marie, 117
Beauboeuf-Lafontant, T., 176
Bell, D., 189
Bell, L., 3, 201
Benmayor, R., 45, 79, 132, 147
Bertsch, T., 89
"Beyond Bean Counting" (Lee), 62–63
Biggs, Larry, 107
birthday, 215
Black Hands in the Biscuits Not in the Classroom (Hughes), 99
Black High School and Its Community, The (Rodgers), 177, 178, 182, 183–184
Blacks
    attitudes of toward race, 11–14
    considered inferior, 193, 194
    love for UNC, 108
    median wealth of, 13
    relationship with Whites during desegregation, 178–179
    and role of pedagogy at home, 99–100
    use of term, 103
    See also desegregation; segregation
Bobbitt, Alton, 182
Bonilla-Silva, E., 12
border crossers, 111
borderlands, 87

Borderlands/La Frontera (Anzaldúa), 78
Born in East LA (film), 209
Bourdieu, P., 42, 46
"boy," use of term, 108
Bracelet, The (Uchida), 122
"Bracero Fracasado, El" (Downs), 205
Brayboy, B. M., 153
Breese, J. R., 99
Brewer, R., 13–14
Bringing Desegregation Home (Willink), 110
Britzman, D., 59, 61, 63
Brown, Maureen, 177, 178
Brown v. Board of Education, 101, 174
    enforcement of, 190, 194–195
    failure of, 189, 192, 193, 194
    as remedy for image problem, 189
    success of, 195
    views of success *vs.* failure of, 197–198
    See also desegregation
Burciaga, R., 77
Burks, Gloria, 179
Busman, Debra, 81–82

C

capture, evading, 208, 209, 218
Castillo-Speed, L., 78
"Celebration of the Marriage of Heart and Mind" (Galeano), 210
Center for Women's Intercultural Leadership (CWIL), 203
Chabram-Dernersesian, A., 78, 80
Cherokee
    attempts to protect selves, 18
    Trail of Tears, 19
Chicana/Latina Feminist Theory, 76, 77, 87
children, maintaining innocence of, 116, 118, 124, 127, 128
Children of Topaz, The (Tunnell and Chilcoat), 122
CIRM (Critical Indigenous Research Methodologies), 159–160, 161
civil rights, in Rose Creek project, 118–121
class
    in critical pedagogies, 44
    effects of, 42–43, 53
    invisibility of, 41–42
    and school success, 43
    seeing, 51–53
    and shame, 48–49
class mobility. *See* mobility
classrooms, queering of, 59–60, 71
co-learning relationships, 139, 143–147, 148
co-reflexive critical dialogue, 95, 96, 97–112
collaborative methodologies, 95, 111–112
college access, 135
Coltelli, L., 154
communication, in ethnography, 109
conflict, confronting, 165–166
Connie, 164–165
Conquergood, D., 96, 101
conscientização
    concept of, 75
    development of, 88
    need to push toward, 79
    self-reflexivity and, 90
conscientization. *See conscientização*
consciousness, critical, 75, 79, 88, 90
continuity, 163–164
control, 49
Cooks, L., 38
counternarratives
    to dominant discourses, 173, 177–178
    in interpretation of Civil Rights Movement, 121
    making visible, 115 (*See also* oral history)
    to "Negro Problem," 176
    in Rose Creek project, 116
Covey, Mr., 135, 143, 144
"Cowboys and Indians," 164–165
Critical Indigenous Research Methodologies (CIRM), 159–160, 161
Critical Race Theory (CRT), 14, 100, 134, 189–190, 199–201
critical thinking skills, 116, 122–123
Cruz, N., 146
Cuban, Larry, 181, 183
culture, 216
Cummings, Elmer, 182
curricula
    community in, 115

elimination of family and community knowledge from, 141
integrating experience into, 140
curricula, culturally relevant, 156
curricula, standardized, 141
cushions
 access to, 25
 concept of, 23
 defined, 11
 family financial aid, 13–14, 19, 20
 interaction with work, 23, 24
 lack of, 42
 and legal favor for Whites, 15

D

Dahlberg, S., 45
Dahlin, M., 13
Daily Advance (Elizabeth City, N.C.), 110
Dana, 164–165, 167
Davies, B., 27, 28, 29–31, 32, 34, 197, 198
Davis, Lilly, 190, 191–192, 199, 201
de la Torre, A., 78, 80
Decolonial Imaginary, The (Pérez), 206
deeds records, 14, 15, 20, 23
deficit approach, 158, 159, 208, 218
Delgado Bernal, D., 77, 203, 207
Deloria, V., 153, 155, 160
Delta, Utah, 125
deportation, evading, 208, 209, 218
desegregation, school
 in Albemarle area, 96, 98, 99, 100, 101, 102, 105, 108, 110
 Black-White relationships during, 178–179
 Bringing Desegregation Home, 110
 interrogating oral histories of, 199–201
 in Mississippi, 190, 191–198
 outsiders during, 196, 197
 violence during, 179, 196, 197
 voluntary, 197
dialogue, critical, 95, 96, 97–112
dialogue, intersecting, 160, 161
 See also rivaling
difference, educational
 and American Indian students, 153
 and confronting conflict, 165–166
difrasismo, 210

discourse
 power of, 61
 products of, 32–34
Diversi, M., 37–38
Dixson, A., 201
Dovring, F., 19
Downs, Lila, 205
Dulin, Tom, 190, 191, 196–197, 198, 199–200, 201
Durham (N.C.) *Morning Herald*, 184
Dyson, A. H., 2–3

E

education
 equity in, 65, 67, 68
 Euro-Western influence in, 158
 expectations of, 68
 and Gender Studies, 61
 inequity in, 132, 136
 marginalization in, 68
 in non-Western worldview, 212
 and opportunity, 45–46
 and personal family histories, 66
 power relations in, 58, 60, 63, 66–67, 75
 queering of, 57–58, 66, 67, 71–72
 recentering American Indian rhetoric in, 157, 163
 resisting norms in, 59, 60
 unconventional forms of, 207 (*See also* pedagogies of the home)
education, Black. *See* desegregation; segregation; teachers, Black
education, rural, 101, 110
 See also Albemarle area (North Carolina)
Education and the American Dream (course), 41–54
education narratives. *See* narratives, critical education
Educational Histories/Educational Hopes (EHEH), 131–148
educational history, 61, 62, 64–67, 138–139
elders, 211–212, 216
Elizabeth, 49
Emory, Athalene, 177–178

Epstein, T., 12
equity, in education, 65, 67, 68
Erskin, Dora, 99
Erskin (family), 98
essentialism, 69
ethnographers
　emissarial approach, 99–100
　entering "field," 97–107
　leaving "field," 107–110
ethnographers, native, 97, 99, 107
ethnographers, non-native, 100
ethnography, critical, 158–159
exclusion, 200
experience
　and age, 211–212
　complexity of, 147
　and encouraging engagement with
　　　Social Studies, 144
　integrated into curriculum, 140
　interpretation of, 176
　as resource, 141
　sharing of, 137–140, 142–143, 147–148
　See also oral history; stories/story;
　　　stories/storytelling, digital
Eynon, B., 44

F

faculty
　at all-Black public schools, 172–173
　　(*See also* teachers, Black)
　at historically Black colleges, 172
"failure," 158, 166
Fair Housing Act, 22
faith communities, and race, 106
family financial aid, 13–14, 19, 20
family history, critical, 11, 22–23, 57, 66
Federal Housing Administration (FHA), 22
feelingthinking (sentipensante), 86, 89, 90, 210–213
feminism, Chicana/Latina, 77, 87
feminism, Lee's experiences with, 62–63
feminism, Third World, 206
"field," entering, 97–107
"field," leaving, 107–110
Fisk University, 172
Flores Carmona, J., 77, 79–82, 203, 213
Flower, L., 160, 166

footholds
　access to, 25
　concept of, 23
　defined, 11
　family financial aid, 13–14, 19, 20
　interaction with work, 23, 24
　lack of, 42
　and legal favor for Whites, 15
footing, 31
Fox, M., 3
Franklin, John Hope, 95
Freeman, M., 160
Freire, Paulo, 75
French, S., 190
Frisch, M., 118, 120

G

Gadamer, H.-G., 158
Galeano, Eduardo, 210
Gender Studies
　and education, 61
　Here I Stand: An Introduction to
　　　Gender Studies (course), 57–72
　interrogation of, 63
Genishi, C., 3
Giles, D., 146
Gilligan, C., 89
Giovanni, Nikki, 171–173, 175, 176, 180, 184, 186
Goffman, Erving, 31
González, Norma, 207
Grant, G. K., 99
grants
　for desegregation study, 95, 97, 100, 101
　for Rose Creek project, 116
Green, Maxine, 106
guilt, and White privilege, 24

H

Hall, Jacquelyn, 102
Halmo, D. B., 156
Hampshire College, 76–77, 83–84, 131–148

Harré, R., 27, 28, 29–31, 32, 34
Harris, Cheryl, 14
Hatley, M. T., 16
Here I Stand: An Introduction to Gender Studies (course), 57–72
Higgins, L., 160
Hijas de Juan, Las (Mendez-Negrete), 78
Hines, Mildred, 178, 179
Hispanics. *See* Latino/as
history
    critical interrogation of, 116
    kept at safe distance, 118, 120
    need for multiple perspectives in, 117
    persistence of narratives in, 126–127
    shaping of, 126
    shielding students from, 118, 128
history, educational, 61, 62, 64–67, 138–139
history, oral
    and allowing students to ask questions, 127–128
    and changes in perception, 126
    and critical thinking skills, 116, 122–123
    criticisms of, 185
    definition of, 176
    of desegregation in Mississippi, 190, 191–198
    interrogating, 198
    interviews on school desegregation, 101–110
    in language class assignments, 216
    in Latino/a families, 215
    and maintenance of childhood innocence, 116, 128
    in pedagogical practices, 122
    poetics of in qualitative research, 180–184
    politics of in qualitative research, 176–180
    in qualitative research, 173, 174–176, 185–186
    resources for, 3–4
    Rose Creek project, 115–128
    value in gathering, 127
home, 98, 108
home, pedagogies of, 99, 203, 204, 207, 216, 218
Homestead Act, 18
Hughes, Maise, 111
Hughes, Sherick, 95, 102–103, 104, 105, 106
    on entering "field," 97–101
    on leaving "field," 107–109
Hull, G. A., 45
humor, 216

I

identity
    claiming, 95, 214
    pedagogical implications of, 37
    and shame, 38–39
identity, ethnic
    claiming, 29–30, 214
    performance of, 28, 38–39 (*See also* positioning)
    and performance of shame, 35–37
    stereotypes of in media, 29, 30
identity, intersectional, 61, 62
identity, racial, 103
identity categories, 68–70
Illinois, 19–20
imagination, sociological, 180, 182
immigrants, German, 19–20
inclusion, 199
Indian-controlled organizations, 24–25
Indian Land Tenure Foundation, 24
Indigenous peoples
    attempts to protect selves, 18
    land reclamation efforts, 24–25
    seizure and sale of land, 16–19, 23
    See also American Indians
Indigo Girls, 97, 98
inequality, educational, 132, 136
inheritance
    and seizure of Indigenous peoples' land, 23
    and White economic supremacy, 14
    See also wealth
Inheritance in America (Shammas, Salmon, Dahlin), 13–14
innocence, childhood, 116, 118, 124, 127, 128
insiders, 105–106
integration. *See* desegregation

interest-convergence theory, 189
interpretation, storied, 160–161
intervention, critical, 179–180, 185
investment activity, racial discrimination in, 22
Iowa, 20
Irani, K., 3
isolation, in mobility, 49–51

J

Jackson, Michael, 2
Japanese Americans, 116, 122–128
Jessica, 47, 48, 50–51, 52
Jim Crow. *See* segregation
Johnson, Mark, 206
Journey to Topaz (Uchida), 122

K

kairos, 96
Kelly, Hilton, 174–186
King, T., 153
knowledge, 117, 184
knowledge, community, 141, 203
 See also oral history
knowledge, family, 141, 147
 See also pedagogies of the home
knowledge, subjugated, 176, 179–180, 185
"Knowledge of Tense-Aspect and Mood in Spanish Heritage Speakers" (Montrul), 204
Kohl, Herbert, 33, 34
Ku Klux Klan, 120–121

L

Ladson-Billing, G., 156
Lakoff, George, 206
Lakota Lands Recovery Project, 25
land
 in Illinois, 19–20
 in Iowa, 20
 See also property
land, Indigenous peoples'
 attempts to protect/reclaim, 18, 24–25
 seizure and sale of, 16–19
 See also property
Langacker, Ronald, 206
language
 in co-learning relationships, 145
 and cultural meaning of words, 211–213
 in EHEH project, 133
 as element of culture, 206–207
 hiding, 206
 legitimacy of, 208
 positioning and, 31
 value of, 208
 and view of the world, 216
 See also Spanish, heritage speakers of
Lanman, B. A., 3–4
Latina (Castillo-Speed), 78
Latina Feminist Group, 78
Latinidades, 87
Latino/as
 Alicia, 46–47, 48, 50, 51–52
 attitudes of toward race, 11–14
 experiences of, 78 (*See also testimonio*)
 legitimacy of language of, 208
 at Liston Middle School, 133
 median wealth of, 13
 perseverance of, 205
 portrayal of in media, 30
 See also Puerto Ricans; Spanish, heritage speakers of; *testimonio*
Laubscher, L., 97
Lawrence-Lightfoot, Sarah, 179
learning, community-engaged, 131–148
learning, distancing students from, 141
learning, transformative, 137, 143–147, 148
"Learning and Living Pedagogies of the Home" (Delgado Bernal), 207
Leary, Alex, 104, 105, 106
Lee, J.-Y., 62–63, 69
Leloudis, Jim, 100, 101
Leondar-Wright, B., 13–14
Lewelling, V. W., 204
Lewis, Fannie, 104, 105
LGBTQ studies, 76
 See also Gender Studies
life stories, 77, 78–79
 See also autobiographies; *testimonio*

Lindquist, Julie, 44, 51
linguistics, cultural, 204, 206, 216
Lisa, 47, 48, 50, 52, 161, 162–163
listening, costs of, 110
listening, deep, 88–89, 104, 159
Liston Middle School, 131–148
Lomawaima, K. T., 153, 155
Long, E., 160
loyalty, 125
Lucey, H., 43, 49
Luciano, Aymee Malena, 82–86
Lui, M., 13–14
Lyons, Scott, 155, 157, 159

M

"man," use of term, 108
Manifest Manners (Vizenor), 157
marginality/marginalization
    in institutions of education, 66, 68
    and knowledge, 147
    and outreach services, 69
    understanding of, 137
    See also exclusion; inclusion
Martin, Judith, 37
Matthews, Mr., 135, 143, 144
media, digital, 5
    See also stories/storytelling, digital
media, stereotypes in, 29, 30
media literacy, 28–29
media production
    and examination of narratives, 134
    goals of, 132–133
    support for, 139
Media Watchdog Project, 28–29
Medicine, B., 156
Melody, J., 43, 49
memory, collective, 174
Mendez-Negrete, J., 78
Miller, J. L., 61
Mills, C. Wright, 180
Milner, H. R. III, 97
Mississippi, desegregation in, 190, 191–198
mobility, social
    costs of, 43
    digital stories of, 46–53
    isolation in, 49–51
    as narrative of moral progress, 45
    opportunity for, 43
    and seeing class, 51–53
Mojarra aesthetics, 205
Mojarra language, talking, 208, 209
Mojarra linguistic syndrome, 205–208, 217–218
Montecinos, Carmen, 37
Montrul, Silvia, 204, 207
Moraga, C., 78, 206
Moreira, C., 38
Morgan, B., 33, 37
"Morphological Errors in Spanish Second Language Learners and Heritage Speakers" (Montrul), 207
mortgage discrimination, 22, 23–24
Muse, Clyde, 190, 191, 194–196, 197–198, 199–200, 201

N

Nakayama, Thomas, 37
name, 214–215
narratives
    persistence of, 126–127
    See also counternarratives
narratives, critical education
    examining discourses in, 70–71
    queering of, 57, 72
    reimagining of, 66
    tensions in production of, 68–70
    as texts, 61, 64–67, 72
    texts for, 62–63, 66
narratives, personal
    as academic writing, 67
    tensions in production of, 68–70
Nash, R., 67
Native Americans. *See* American Indians; Indigenous peoples
Need for Story, The (Dyson and Genishi), 3
neglect, benign, 177–178
Nelson, M. E., 45
Nicān mopouha (Valeriano and Ortiz de Montellano), 210
"Nikki Rosa" (Giovanni), 171–172, 184
Noblit, George, 100, 101, 111, 184–185
Nora, 48–49, 52

norms
  critical engagement of, 63–64
  and deficit approach, 208
  queering of, 59–60
  resisting, 59, 60
Norte, El (film), 209
North Carolina
  Albemarle region, 96, 97–107, 108, 109, 110
  qualifications of Black teachers in, 181–184
  teachers in segregated schools in, 173–184
North Carolina Department of Public Instruction (NCDPI), 177, 182, 183

O

Obama, Barack, 12
Obon, 123
O'Gorman, R., 28, 36–37
Ohler, Jason, 134, 146
opportunity
  American Dream, 41–54
  for mobility, 43
  through school success, 45–46
oral history. *See* history, oral
Oral History Association, 3
Ortiz de Montellano, Guillermo, 210
outreach services, 69
outsiders, 104, 105–106, 109, 196, 197

P

Palmer, Gary B., 206
papelitos guardados, 88, 89
Parkinson, Rob, 2
pedagogies of the home, 99, 203, 204, 207, 216, 218
pedagogy, critical, 89, 134, 137
  reactions to, 44
  stories as, 53–54
pedagogy, culturally relevant, 156
pedagogy, deficit-oriented, 158, 159, 208, 218
pedagogy, feminist, 77, 87

pedagogy, *sentipensante,* 86–90
pedagogy of possibility, 88
Pendergraft, Don, 105
Pérez, Emma, 206
performance, 35–37, 155, 158, 159, 161, 166
Peters, Fenton, 190–191, 192–193, 197, 198, 199, 201
Peyton, J. K., 204
Phelan, J., 16
Pollock, Dana, 101, 110
positionality, 140
  See also positioning
positioning, 27–28, 31, 32–34, 37
  See also positionality
possibility, pedagogy of, 88
poststructural feminist theory, 57, 71
poverty, and race, 12
Powell, Malea, 156–157
Powell, S., 97
power, Native, 154, 156, 166
  See also sovereignty, rhetorical; survivance
power, relations of
  breaking down, 71
  in education, 58, 60, 63, 66–67, 75
  limitations created by, 66
  understanding of, 137
praxis, 157–158, 161
predominantly White institutions
  American Indian students in, 155 (*See also* sovereignty, rhetorical; survivance)
  Hampshire College as, 77
Preparing the Next Generation of Oral Historians (Lanman and Wendling), 3–4
presence, 155, 156, 158, 159, 163, 166
principals, Black, 175, 177
privilege
  assumptions of, 81
  and exclusion, 200
  guilt about, 24
  and inclusion, 199
  in institutions of education, 66
  and marginalized identities, 86
  power of, 199–200
  and reflections on sharing, 142–143

Index

resistance to talking about, 41
and social justice, 200
understanding of, 137
used to support storytelling, 146
property
    as basis for Whiteness, 14
    and mortgage discrimination, 22, 23–24
    racial discrimination in acquisition of, 22
    seizure and sale of Indigenous peoples' land, 16–19, 23
    See also land
protection, discourses of, 127
    See also innocence, childhood
Puerto Ricans, 27–28, 29, 30, 31, 32, 33–35, 36, 37, 38, 39
    See also Latino/as

Q

queer
    meanings of, 60
    use of term, 58–59, 63
queer theory, 57

R

race
    attitudes toward, 11–14
    belief in U.S. as postracial, 13
    Black-White binary, 103
    Critical Race Theory, 14, 100, 189–190, 199–201
    and faith communities, 106
    mortgage discrimination, 22, 23–24
    and opportunity, 12
    positioning, 27–28 (*See also* positioning)
    and poverty, 12
    and shame, 35–37
    as social contraction, 27
    stereotypes of, 29, 30, 165
    and wealth, 13–14
    Winant on, 103
Race, Remembering, and Jim Crow's Teachers (Kelly), 174–184
racial profiling, 209
racism
    costs of, 104
    denial of, 103
    endemic nature of, 14, 199
    regional views of, 102, 119, 120–121
    role of in wealth, 23–24
    in Rose Creek project, 119–121
    in South, 179
    in South *vs.* North, 104
    stereotypes, 29, 30, 165
    views of, 12
    See also segregation
racism, institutional, 189, 200
    See also segregation
Rao, K., 147
Reay, D., 43, 45
reflexivity
    in digital storytelling, 147
    in media production, 134
    See also self-reflexivity
remembering, collective, 174, 176, 180
Rendón, Laura I., 86, 210
research, qualitative
    on desegregation in Albemarle, 98
    oral history in, 173, 174–176, 185–186
    poetics of oral history in, 180–184
    politics of oral history in, 176–180
research design, 98
Revelle, Billy, 105, 106
review, article, 162–163
Rhonda, 49, 52
Richardson, Laurel, 66
Ritchie, Donald, 185
rivaling
    rhetorical sovereignty, 164–165
    survivance, 161–164
"Roads Not Taken" (project), 101
Robillard, A., 49
Robles, B., 13–14
Rodgers, Frederick A., 175, 177, 178, 182, 183–184
role models, 215–216
Rose Creek oral history project, 115–128
Ross, S. L., 23–24
Rousseau, C., 201

S

Saint Mary's College, 203
salaries, teacher, 184
Salmon, M., 13
Sayer, A., 42
Schick, C., 12
school success
   and class, 43
   isolation in, 49–51
   and opportunity, 45–46
schooling. *See* education
Schooling in a Multicultural Society (SMS) (course), 131–148
Schuman, H., 174
Schwartz, B., 174
Scott, James, 173, 174
segregation
   challenges to narrative of, 175, 180
   counternarratives to, 177–178, 181–182
   See also desegregation; teachers, Black
Segrest, Mab, 103, 104
self-determination, 155, 156
   See also sovereignty, rhetorical
self-portraits, 62
self-reflexivity
   and *conscientização*, 90
   and digital storytelling, 136–137
   in pedagogy, 81
   on performance of identity, 37–39
   in *testimonios*, 75, 77
   See also reflexivity
sentipensante, 86, 89, 90, 210–213
service, concept of, 213
shame
   and class, 48–49
   performance of, 35–37
   in performance of identity, 38–39
"Shamefaced" (Werry and O'Gorman), 28
Shammas, C., 13
Sharifian, Farzad, 206
Simpson, Bland, 104–105
Síndrome de la Mojarra, 205–208, 217–218
Skouge, J. R., 147
Sleeter, Christine, 37, 42, 57, 66
SMS (Schooling in a Multicultural Society) (course), 131–148

So Far From the Sea (Bunting), 122
social change, progressive, 173, 176, 179, 185
social justice, 200
Social Studies
   EHEH project, 131–148
   encouraging engagement with, 144
   need for multiple perspectives in, 116–118
   Rose Creek project, 115–128
socioacupuncture, 161, 165, 166
sociology, 184
Solinger, R., 3
South (region)
   racism in, 104, 179
   residential segregation in, 179
   values of, 195, 198
   views of, 102
sovereignty, rhetorical, 155–158, 160, 164–165
Spanish, heritage speakers of
   defined, 204
   in EHEH project, 145
   errors of, 207
   final project for, 213–217
   identifying as, 216
   legitimacy of language of, 208
   linguistic dislocation of, 204
   and non-Western views of world, 209–213
   and pedagogies of the home, 203
   See also Mojarra language, talking; *Mojarra* linguistic syndrome
Speaking From the Body (Chabram-Dernersesian and de la Torre), 78, 80
Spencer, R., 89
St. Denis, V., 12
stereotypes, 29, 30, 165
Stoffle, R. W., 156
stories, critical
   approaches to, 4 (*See also* family history, critical; history, oral; stories/storytelling, digital; *testimonio*)
   defined, 1–2

stories/story
  as constructed and partial narratives, 134
  critical interrogation of, 190
  as critical pedagogy, 53–54
  power of, 1
  as theory, 153–154
  types of, 3
  and understanding of world, 87
  websites for, 138–139
stories/storytelling, digital
  Educational Histories/Educational Hopes (EHEH), 131–148
  importance of, 132
  linked with community-engaged learning, 136–137
  meaning made by, 44–45
  of mobility, 46–53
  potential of, 132, 137, 142
  production of, 45
  reflexivity in, 147
  resources for, 3
  screening of, 140
  and self-reflexivity, 136–137
  sharing experiences by, 137–140
  students' reflections on, 141–143
  technology in, 145–146
  websites for, 139
  work-shopping in, 139
  writing in, 146
  See also media production
story production, methodology and pedagogy of, 3
storying, critical. *See* sovereignty, rhetorical; survivance
storytelling
  lack of interdisciplinary texts on, 4
  scholarship on, 2–4
  and social transformation, 2
Storytelling for Social Justice (Bell), 3
"Storytelling Project Model," 3
strangers, intimate, 97–98, 99, 109
struggle, in educational histories, 139
students, first-generation, 44, 49
suffering, understanding of, 89
superintendents, White, 177
  See also Dulin, Tom; Muse, Clyde
survivance, 156–158, 160, 161–164

Suzette, J., 96
Swain, J., 190

T

Taliaferro-Baszile, D., 97
teacher education students, 41
teachers, Black
  cooperation of during desegregation, 191, 193–194
  in North Carolina during segregation, 173–184
  position of, 193
  qualifications of, 180, 181–184
  salaries of, 184
  training programs for, 175, 183
  See also Davis, Lilly; Peters, Fenton
technology
  in digital storytelling, 145–146
  and sharing of critical stories, 5
  See also media production; stories/storytelling, digital
Telling Stories to Change the World (Solinger, Fox, and Irani), 3
Telling to Live (Latina Feminist Group), 3, 78
Tennessee
  acquisition of land in, 20–21
  seizure and sale of land in, 16–19
testimonio
  concept of, 77–78
  and development of critical consciousness, 90
  goals of, 79
  legitimization of, 89
  as pedagogy of possibility, 88
  self-reflexivity in, 75, 77
  as *sentipensante* pedagogy, 86–90
  sharing of, 80–81, 82–86
  and social change, 3
  as teaching tool, 78–79
  and understanding of *Latinidades*, 87
  used to contest power relations in education, 75
  validation of lived experience by, 90
  writing of, 83

Testimonios: Chicana and Latina Epistemology and Pedagogy (course), 75–90
texts, critical education narratives as, 61, 72
theory
    negation of work by, 189–190
    story as, 153–154
theory in the flesh, 76, 80, 88, 90, 206
This Bridge Called My Back (Moraga and Anzaldúa), 78
tokenism, 62, 69
Topaz, Utah, 123–128
Trail of Tears, 19
transcripts, hidden, 173, 174, 175, 184
transcripts, public, 174
Transforming Tales (Parkinson), 2
Tribal Critical Theory, 153
Tyack, David, 181, 182–183
Tyeeme Clark, D. A., 153

U

UNC (University of North Carolina), 95, 108
United States
    control of resources, 11 (*See also* property)
    image of, 189
    loyalty to, 125, 126
    obligations to American Indian nations, 155
    as postracial, 13
    seizure of Indigenous people's land, 18
United States Land Office, 19
University of North Carolina (UNC), 95, 108

V

Valeriano, Antonio, 210
violence, during desegregation, 179, 196, 197
Vizenor, G., 87, 154, 157, 159, 161

W

Walkerdine, V., 43, 44, 49
Warren, J. T., 96
Warrior, R. A., 153
wealth
    closing racial gap in, 24–25
    family financial aid, 13–14
    in institutions of education, 66
    and race, 13–14
    and racial discrimination in property acquisition, 22
    racial disparities in, 13, 14 (*See also* inheritance)
    role of institutional racism in, 23–24
    and seizure of Indigenous peoples' land, 23
Weaver, J., 153, 155–156
Weinberg, M. K., 89
Wendling, L. M., 3–4
Werry, M., 28, 36–37
White Earth Recovery Project, 24
Whiteness
    as property, 199
    property as basis for, 14
    psychological presence of, 180
Whites
    attitudes of toward race, 11–14
    control of resources by, 11 (*See also* property)
    median wealth of, 13
    trust of, 191, 193–194
    use of term, 103
Whitmore (family), 98
Willink, K. G., 95, 96, 100–107, 109–110
Winant, Howard, 103
witnessing, co-performative, 110
Wolfe, Thomas, 98
Womack, C. S., 153
words, queering of, 59
work, 23, 24
working class, 41, 42, 43, 46, 48, 49, 52, 53
    See also class
world, conception of, 210–213
World War II, 116, 122–128

X

Xochitl, 206, 209

Y

Yinger, J., 23–24
"You gotta be ready for some serious truth to be spoken" (Busman), 81–82

Z

Zedeño, M. W., 156

Studies in the Postmodern Theory of Education

General Editor
Shirley R. Steinberg

Counterpoints publishes the most compelling and imaginative books being written in education today. Grounded on the theoretical advances in criticalism, feminism, and postmodernism in the last two decades of the twentieth century, Counterpoints engages the meaning of these innovations in various forms of educational expression. Committed to the proposition that theoretical literature should be accessible to a variety of audiences, the series insists that its authors avoid esoteric and jargonistic languages that transform educational scholarship into an elite discourse for the initiated. Scholarly work matters only to the degree it affects consciousness and practice at multiple sites. Counterpoints' editorial policy is based on these principles and the ability of scholars to break new ground, to open new conversations, to go where educators have never gone before.

For additional information about this series or for the submission of manuscripts, please contact:

> Shirley R. Steinberg
> c/o Peter Lang Publishing, Inc.
> 29 Broadway, 18th floor
> New York, New York 10006

To order other books in this series, please contact our Customer Service Department:
> (800) 770-LANG (within the U.S.)
> (212) 647-7706 (outside the U.S.)
> (212) 647-7707 FAX

Or browse online by series:
> www.peterlang.com

www.ingramcontent.com/pod-product-compliance
Ingram Content Group UK Ltd.
Pitfield, Milton Keynes, MK11 3LW, UK
UKHW022238230426
12048UKWH00018BA/1339